EXCLUSIVE!

EXCLUSIVE!

MAURICE CHITTENDEN

THE LAST DAYS OF FLEET STREET

MY PART IN ITS DOWNFALL

Biteback Publishing

First published in Great Britain in 2017 by
Biteback Publishing Ltd
Westminster Tower
3 Albert Embankment
London SE1 7SP
Copyright © Maurice Chittenden 2017

ISBN 978-1-78590-282-6

10 9 8 7 6 5 4 3 2 1

A CIP catalogue record for this book is available from the British Library.

Set in Minion Pro

Printed and bound in Great Britain by
CPI Group (UK) Ltd, Croydon CR0 4YY

MIX
Paper from
responsible sources
FSC
www.fsc.org
FSC® C020471

To the long-suffering Mrs C, as she is known throughout journalism, for her love and support.

CONTENTS

LAST OF THE HOT METAL BOYS

On a hot sunny day in August 2016, the last newspaper still working from an office on London's Fleet Street called 'stop the press' and closed its doors for the final time.

It was rather ironic, in such a cutthroat business, that the Dundee-based *Sunday Post* had kept a London office open for so long in a building that also served as the fictional address of Sweeney Todd, the demon barber.

Thirteen days later, it was my turn to make my excuses and leave. I was fired after almost forty years' working for national newspapers and taking Rupert Murdoch's shilling for my labours at *The Sun*, the *News of the World* and the *Sunday Times*.

It was the end of an era. The papers, the giant publishing houses, the pubs – they've all gone. And so has the fun. I should know, because I had most of it. My career took me to two Olympics and two World Cups, the opening night of a Rolling Stones world tour, the Spanish Grand Prix, lunch at the Commons with John Prescott and with others at the Dorchester in London and the Ritz in Paris, afternoon tea with Richard Branson at his Holland Park home, cocktails at Raffles Hotel in Singapore, drinks with the Queen at Windsor Castle and dinner at the Savoy.

Along the way I wrote splashes for three Murdoch titles (*The Sun*, *The Times* and the *Sunday Times*) and the Insight team I created and headed at the latter title won the Grand Slam of journalist awards.

When I left *The Sun* for the *Sunday Times*, Kelvin MacKenzie, the tabloid's editor, addressed the news desk and said: 'Thank you, Maurice. You have done for *The Sun* what the M1 has done for the hedgehog.'

Andrew Neil called for me as his 'dog of war' whenever he wanted to take action against some 'loony left' council or upstart in a rival newspaper's editorial chair. I served the *Sunday Times* in a variety of roles, including Insight editor, chief reporter and night editor, and became the most bylined reporter in the paper's history.

That's not to say I didn't occasionally end up in some hot water... I once sparked a diplomatic incident when I was thrown into jail in Borneo over a lobster and triggered a terrorist alert at the *Sunday Times* when 'armed' lesbians invaded the office eager to extract revenge on me for some imagined slight.

Now I have finally been 'let go', the Fleet Street I remember no longer exists. What was once the throbbing heart of London's last manufacturing industry has been reduced to a strip of banks and sandwich bars. The heavy beat of the newspaper press and the smell of the black ink and the booze on the reporters' breath are now a distant memory. Walk along Fleet Street today and you could be on any other boring London thoroughfare.

The culture I knew and loved has vanished like some long-lost civilisation. Fleet Street lives on only as a byword for national newspapers, now scattered across London. Its reputation as the 'Street of Shame' survives in the name of the column in *Private Eye*, which afforded me the plaudit of 'the legendary Maurice Chittenden' in its report of my professional demise.

I had a good run. Raised in the Cotswold town of Chipping Norton (before anyone had arrived to form a 'set'), I started in the days of hot metal, when printers, or 'inkies' as we called them, kept such a guard on their craft and own racketeering that not even an editor was allowed to enter their workspace without their permission.

It was Rupert Murdoch's move to Wapping to escape the stranglehold of the unions and the switch to computer typesetting that signalled the start of the end of Fleet Street.

Before I was sacked I was one of the last surviving combatants from the so-called Battle of Wapping. An attack on my car led to a police cavalry charge to sweep the pickets from the streets outside the News International plant and sparked a bloody riot.

When victory was finally won, Bruce Matthews, Murdoch's managing director, allowed a handful of reporters working at *The Sun* to walk on the once-hallowed ground of the printers and help themselves to slugs of print from the composing cases.

Some searched for their own bylines. I picked up ones that spelled 'Sun World Exclusive' and 'News of the World Scoop', as befitted one of the last of the hot metal boys.

My career, which had started on a local newspaper covering fetes and flower shows, was now to take me on a new course at the *Sunday Times* in which we tried to bring down governments, explain disasters, expose wrongdoing, solve murders and live up to our reputation as the world's greatest newspaper.

Maurice Chittenden
June 2017
teston@aol.com

CHAPTER ONE

MY FIRST SCOOP

I must have looked a sad sight standing at the bar of the Bull, a timber-framed old pub at the top of the high street and an oasis of sanity amid the regeneration of Bracknell in Berkshire.

A kind regular with a London accent asked me what I was doing here. I told him I had come for an interview that afternoon with the editor of the *Bracknell News,* one of two weeklies fighting a circulation war in the new town.

I was only nineteen, but I already thought my dreams of finding a job as a reporter were destined for failure. I had written letters to eighty editors – some in response to adverts, some just on the off chance – and had been to interviews all over southern England.

My new friend in the Bull bought me a brandy and port. Then another. By the time I reached Roy Bustin's office at the newspaper above a bookmaker's shop, I was rather drunk.

It is strange how a bit of Dutch courage can sometimes do wonders. I had written off my chances before I arrived, so I was able to shoot the breeze with Roy in a very relaxed manner and show him some book reviews I had written for the English Westerners' Society magazine.

For some reason, he took to me and I got a job as a trainee journalist at £11 a week. Perhaps he had a talent for spotting promising youngsters. When I turned up to work seventeen days later, there were already two other juniors in the office: Bob Strange, who was to become deputy news editor at the *News of the World*, and Chris Stevens, future features editor of *The Sun* and whose wife was to later edit the *Bracknell News*.

I had wanted to be a journalist since, as a little boy, I had seen news of the Great Train Robbery break in news bulletins on my grandmother's television. The only other thing I can remember wanting to be was a customs officer. I guess a psychiatrist would spot a link in that both involve going through people's dirty laundry in public.

When not doing my homework I would write my own crime stories, based on cases like the train robbery and the rivalry between the Kray and Richardson gangs, and then design pages to display them.

I was born in Melton Mowbray, Leicestershire, which explains my lifelong love of pork pies, Stilton cheese and Leicester City Football Club. Both my parents were from large, poor families. My mother, Betty, was one of seven children. Her maternal grandmother had been killed, scalded by boiling water when a pan overturned, while she was making beer at home. Her father was a groom at various country estates where the family lived in tied accommodation. As a teenager, my mother had been in service as a housemaid in the Oxford home of Howard Florey, the professor who won the Nobel Prize for his role in the development of penicillin. Sadly she died a year before Dominic West played Florey in a docudrama on television.

Charlie, my father, was one of eight children and had driven a fire brigade lorry during the German bombing attacks on Coventry during World War Two. His father, James, had been a chauffeur and gardener to titled families but lost his job so often that by the time he retired he had had no less than fifty-seven places of employment. One lady sacked him with the words: 'Chittenden, you were looking at my ankles as I got out of the car.'

My mother and my father had been married and had had children before they met each other (mum's first husband was a glider pilot who was killed during the Sicily landings), so I grew up in a rather dysfunctional family in which I had a nephew six months older than me.

When my father died when I was eight, we were plunged into dire straits. We were evicted from three tied homes over the next five years until we were finally given a council flat in Chipping Norton in Oxfordshire in 1963. (So I preceded David Cameron, Jeremy Clarkson, Rebekah Brooks and the rest of the Chipping Norton set by almost thirty years.)

I remember my education at the local comprehensive mostly for the embarrassment of the free school meals and the second-hand uniforms. I once got a ticking off from my history teacher for writing an essay entitled 'the Black Hole of Calcutta' as if it was a journalist's eyewitness account. My A level results

3

were pretty poor: two Es and a D thanks largely to mixing in bad company and going to the Blue Lion pub to work behind the bar at lunchtime, and as a result I failed to get a place at university. At first I went to work as a porter in a mental hospital (to wash all that education out of my head) but I still harboured dreams of making it as a journalist, so I started to look at ways I could do it.

At this time I had some success as a disc jockey at the Langston Arms, a local nightclub in nearby Kingham, run by a Londoner called Jack Bond who was connected enough to attract big bands and bring in heavies from the capital when the locals acted up.

I won a 'Britain's best new DJ' contest at the club after it was advertised in *Melody Maker*, then a popular music weekly, for which the prize was a regular weekly spot behind the turntables. Amongst the bands I introduced were Earth, who later became Black Sabbath, and The Gift, who had a hit when they changed their name to Blackfoot Sue.

I tried to use the experience to get a job as a presenter at the launch of BBC Radio Oxford, but flunked my audition. (This is despite being told by Nick Ferrari years later, when I tried to get a TV job on Sky News, that I had the perfect face for radio!)

In those days, newspapers were so union-controlled that you couldn't get a job in the industry unless you were a member of the National Union of Journalists (NUJ). Unfortunately you couldn't join the NUJ unless you were a journalist.

My way around this conundrum was to get a job as a production controller at Pergamon Press, Robert Maxwell's publishing house in the grounds of his home at Headington Hall, Oxford. At the age of eighteen, I was in charge of the print runs for ten trade and educational journals, reading and subbing copy, liaising with the scholarly editors and going to the printers with the final versions. It was enough to get me an NUJ card and bring me, a year later, to the *Bracknell News*.

The *News* was the upstart compared with the more established *Bracknell Times* owned by Thomson, the Canadian publishing empire. It had been founded in 1959 by Bert Melhuish, a former car mechanic, in a flat above his father-in-law's newsagent's shop. That same year, he hired Roy Bustin, who at twenty-nine was then the youngest editor in the country. My first story was about a rent rise for the tenants of the Bracknell Development Corporation and within six months I had my picture on the front page, inspecting the damage at a house hit by an arson attack.

It was not always so exciting. As juniors, Bob, Chris and I had to do the weekly chemists' rota (telling sick people where they could get the medicine to fill their prescriptions outside of normal shop hours) and cinema times. Later I would taunt graduate trainees by telling them: 'You can't be a real journalist if you've never done the chemists' rota.' (It was nonsense of course.)

One of the memorial moments was an interview I conducted with a real-life Corporal Jones: Ted Sykes, the last survivor of the Battle of Omdurman in 1898. The day after his twenty-first birthday he found himself amongst the Grenadier Guards under General Kitchener who stood their ground in the scorching heat of the Sudan desert, shooting the Dervishes who had earlier hacked General Gordon to pieces. I described him as the 'last of the thin red line'. My journalistic licence should have been suspended right there and then. For a while, Victorian propaganda prints had shown the Guards in red tunics, but they had long since switched to khaki. The last thin red line had in fact been at the Battle of Ginnis in the Sudan in 1885. Luckily, none of the older journalists in the office picked me up on my mistake.

One such veteran in the *News* office, Chris Ward (for some reason a common name in journalism), claimed to have Fleet Street experience and boasted he was once one of the top four gossip columnists in the country. But when he showed us juniors his cuttings we were never quite sure which Chris Ward had written them. A heavy drinker, his party piece when interviewing the council leader or some other worthy dignitary was to break off briefly from the conversation and rub the hearing piece of the phone against his crotch. He once produced a doctor's note that claimed he was suffering from 'overwhelming lethargy'. But, despite all his faults, he could produce a splash as if from nowhere when it was needed.

Another of the 'oldies' was Dorothy Cannell, the women's editor who went to great pains to tell me that I was a *reporter* and needed far more experience before I could call myself a *journalist*. Then there was Horace Cheney, the ageing sports editor who used to love to wind Dorothy up and who would regularly fall asleep over his typewriter after a night in his village social club.

Working there was great fun as we chipped away at the

circulation lead held by the *Bracknell Times*, which at first had a monopoly on all the display advertising in the town. One of its reporters, Alec Reid, was a Scotsman with a hearing aid. He once came back from the local magistrates with a story about the driver of a horse and cart caught speeding at 45 miles per hour. When his news editor queried this, Alec was forced to ring the court and ask for a transcript of the evidence. It turned out that the errant driver was at the wheel of an 'Austin car'.

There were a few characters in Bracknell to give us good copy. One, Joe Brant, was an ex-army man who hated the rules and regulations imposed on the town. One day, for his idea of a joke, he went into the offices of the Bracknell Development Corporation and covered the receptionist's legs with mud. Another time he snatched the minute book from the offices of Bracknell Council and did a runner. He dashed into our office and shouted: 'Come on, lads! They're all after me! Let's have some mischief!'

Today he would probably be arrested, but I have fond memories of him standing up in a council meeting to deflate plans for some official pomp and circumstance to mark a royal visit by declaring: 'Why don't we just run a kipper up the flagpole?'

There were some hiccups. During one Christmas I spent in Bracknell, I lost my annual bonus playing cards and, after one boozy lunch, Bob Strange and I got into a fight over the editor's daughter, another trainee journalist, and all three of us were suspended for a week without pay. I probably didn't eat that week. My £11 a week was £3 less than I earned at Pergamon Press and I had to pay for a room out of it. I would go home to Chipping Norton at weekends, often hitchhiking, and would return with a batch of my mother's cheese scones which I would try to make last until press day on Thursday. (Thanks, Mum, but I have hated cheese scones ever since.)

Part of my daily routine was to go to the police, fire and ambulance stations each morning to find out what had happened in the past twenty-four hours. The subsequent stories were the bread and butter of a local newspaper, along with council meetings, fetes and flower shows.

As a result of these visits, I became friendly with various members of the emergency services. The head of the ambulance station was also the head of the local St John Ambulance brigade, so a few write-ups about his volunteer work turned him into a valuable contact.

I also became drinking buddies with a Liverpudlian fireman named Brian Windle. He was a handsome, charismatic chap who was also a pal of John Maus, co-founder of the singing Walker Brothers with Scott Engel. One of our drinking bouts went on too long and when I went to retrieve my car the next day I could not find it and reported it stolen. I was the butt of the jokes at the following morning's press conference at the police station. The boys in blue had had no trouble finding my car – exactly where I had parked it.

Through Brian I met the other firefighters, including 29-year-old Joe Benney, the station officer, who had started in the service in London at the age of eighteen.

One morning in October 1970 I went to the fire station as usual and found everything had changed. Benney had been replaced with an officer installed from the county brigade headquarters and the usual warm greeting from the boys was replaced with depressed-looking faces. Something was wrong, and so naturally I began to investigate. I knew where some of the boys lived so I started there.

It turned out that most of them only earned about £14 a week and they had been recruited two years earlier to act as firemen in feature films and television programmes when they were not on duty.

Peter Purdue, who ran a company called Studio and Location Fire Services, supplied fire appliances of all ages ('manned by fully trained crews') to the studios. Directors who paid to use his vintage fire engines did not want to spoil the effect by having actors pointing the fire hose the wrong way. What better solution than to use real firemen? They could wear period costumes and work the antique apparatus convincingly.

Purdue had approached members of the Bracknell brigade, asking them if they wanted to earn an extra pound or two in their spare time. A recent work-to-rule had emphasised firemen's demands for a better deal and the men at Bracknell realised they could get one by working with Purdue.

'The Berkshire fire service is the one brigade in the country who treat their men so badly that they have to seek part-time employment,' Purdue told me when I tracked him to his home in Burnham, Buckinghamshire.

The Bracknell men had only ever played firemen on screen and in most cases had been involved in fighting real fires started by stage hands. I discovered that they had handled all the fire sequences in the movie *The Battle of Britain*, had featured in a film with Suzy Kendall entitled *Assault*, had dressed up as German firemen in a war thriller called *Manhunt*, had filmed a *Z-Cars* story at Holyport and had soaked Roger Moore with water for a rain sequence in *The Man Who Haunted Himself*.

Unfortunately, it was a strict condition of service that men did not engage in outside employment unless they had permission from the Fire Brigade Authority.

Someone, perhaps overlooked for the part-time work, had written to the county's chief fire officer to inform him of the men's extra-curricular activities, and he had launched an investigation. During the inquiry into the running of the station and the allegations of unauthorised employment, Benney had offered his resignation. It was accepted 'with considerable regret' by the chief fire officer.

We splashed on the story in that Thursday's *Bracknell News*. I realised I had my first scoop on my hands and that morning I was up early to 'file' it around the nationals before it was picked up by the freelance news agency in Reading.

In those days, filing copy meant occupying a phone box for anything up to two hours while making reverse charge calls to each newspaper office in turn and reading the story out loud over the phone to copytakers. They were all members of a print union and notoriously took no prisoners. Hearing 'Is there much more of this?' at the other end of the line was a regular occurrence. Some were rude enough to pull the plug after four paragraphs. It was a thankless task. Years later, I was a full-time freelance and, heeding the need to earn money even as my wife was in labour with our daughter Holly in 1984, I fought off nurses and visitors to occupy a phone box under the stairs at St Albans Hospital and file an 'all-rounder' (a story that went to every paper) about a row at a car park run by the Royal British Legion. It made one paper, the *Daily Star*, and I earned a measly £25.

Luckily, the novelty of my story about firemen working in film studios kept the copytakers entertained. The next day it had 'shows' in all the tabloids. It was a page lead in the *Daily Mail* under the headline: 'Damper on the telly firemen'.

I felt sorry for Benney. Married with three young boys, he was very popular locally. He insisted that he had never appeared in any of the films or TV work, but had acted as an 'unpaid adviser'. Nevertheless, he knew it was breaking the rules. Not only did he have to sever links with the industry he knew best, he had to leave his fire brigade-owned house. He was even banished from the brigade's football team, of which he was the secretary, as a result.

I ended my piece in the *News*: 'While Joe Benney looks for a new home, Peter Purdue will have to look to other sources to man his celluloid fire appliances'.

Bert Melhuish, the paper's owner, was so pleased that I had put one over on the *Bracknell Times* (and then rubbed their noses in it by giving it to the nationals) that he gave me the chrome tax-disc holder from his Rolls-Royce, complete with its 'RR' badge. 'I have a feeling you're going to need it one day,' he said.

In those days most people did not enter the newspaper business straight from university. Instead, you signed up for a three-year apprenticeship while studying for your exams with the National Council for the Training of Journalists (NCTJ) with block release, two months at a time, at a higher educational college.

I duly attended Highbury College at Cosham in Hampshire, where my fellow students included Ian Markham-Smith, who would go on to become a star freelance in Los Angeles (where he was once famously punched in the face by Sean Penn), and Duncan Marsh, a future editor of weekly titles in Kent.

Cars were banned from the campus but Ian insisted I accompany him as he drove his Mini around the grounds for a wheeze. Not just drive, mind you, but reverse all the way. It was this sort of prank that made us natural suspects when some nutty kid with Angry Brigade ambitions exploded a fertiliser bomb in one of the college lifts.

Ian always looked after his mates and I remember, years later, when I was penniless as a result of a journalists' strike, he gave me freelance work and shifts on the *Miami National Enquirer* while he was its London editor.

College was a boozy time. I had digs in the George pub in Cosham and celebrated my twenty-first birthday there by trying to drink twenty-one Scotches in one lunchtime session. Duncan and I would go to Nero's night club in Southsea (I was there the opening night when they thought it would be fine to ride a horse-drawn chariot into the club) and we posed as talent scouts from *Top of the Pops* to chat up the prettiest girl dancers.

When I was locked out of the pub one night, he took me back to his student digs to sleep on the floor. The next morning I tried to hide from his landlady in the wardrobe. She discovered me and thought it was such a hoot that I ended up staying in another room at her house.

We were at college to learn such things as newspaper law and Teeline, an alphabet-based form of shorthand most journalists use because it is supposed to be easier to get to the 100 words a minute required by examiners than by doing Pitman's shorthand. Not that we needed to worry. After reading a passage to us while we tried to keep up in Teeline, our examiner kindly left the room for ten minutes so we could fill in any missing words by comparing notes.

One day I was in class when the head of the course came into the lecture room and asked me to follow him to his office. Whoops, I thought. What have I done now? It turned out, nothing bad, actually. I had sold a first-person piece by one of the Bracknell firemen (basically this means writing in someone else's words and putting their name on it) to *Weekend* magazine and a sub had tracked me down with a query. The feature told how he had been run over and crushed by a fifty-ton tank yet survived while doing his National Service as an infantryman in Germany.

I do not know if this raised my kudos with the college authorities, but six months later I was named the NCTJ's Young Journalist of the Year and had to drive back to the college to collect my award in front of that term's intake of journalists. It was a cash prize presented to me by John Arlott, the cricket commentator, who had decided to give it annually in memory of his eldest son who had been killed in a car accident driving home late one night in his sports car from Southampton.

My old Ford Anglia overheated and broke down en route and I had to hitchhike. I made the award ceremony by the skin of my teeth. I could tell all my lecturers were nervous when I arrived. I didn't improve their temperament by saying in my acceptance speech that the last time I had won anything it had been at school twelve years earlier. The prize was *The Observer's Book of Automobiles* and I informed the audience that young journalists were paid so badly that I still took it with me as a guide when I went to buy a car. Given the circumstances in which the prize was given, it was not the most diplomatic thing to say in front of Arlott and his wife.

Armed with my new award and looking to progress, I left the *Bracknell News*, by now the town's leading paper with a healthy 30,000 circulation, and joined Southern News Service, a freelance agency run from Guildford by Denis Cassidy and Don Leigh, two Fleet Street veterans.

Denis, with his neat moustache, clipped Mancunian voice and lively eyes that could charm the angriest of people, who died in April 2017 at the age of eighty-one, had a great doorstep manner, and kept at it well into his seventies. Ringing the bell of someone already not best pleased at being disturbed by the press, he would disarm them immediately by saying how wonderful the roses in their garden looked. He loved 'doorstepping', and we had that in common; I always liked to do my own when I could. I'll always remember what Jimmy Nicholson, the crime reporter known as 'the Prince of Darkness' on account of his black cloak, used to say about himself: 'I've been on more doorsteps than a milk bottle and I've covered every siege since Troy.'

I was only ever hit once while on the job, and that was a punch in the back as I was leaving a doorstep, although Adam Faith, a pocket-sized 1960s pop singer turned financial columnist who operated from his own permanent table at the Savoy, once set his dogs on me. I had refused to be outdone by a locked electronic gate and crossed a cornfield to get to his house to ask him about his relationship with Roger Levitt, a financial adviser who had duped him into persuading his show business friends to join an investment firm that had collapsed with £34 million worth of debts. I did not mention my discomfort, running back through the corn, when I came to write his obituary in 2003.

My predecessor in the job at Cassidy and Leigh, as it was known in Fleet Street, was one Greg Dyke, later director-general of the BBC. This was only the first of several occasions when I would take over from soon-to-be famous faces. Later I succeeded Diane Abbott, now a leading Labour politician, as a freelance researcher at *Thames News*, the London news programme. At both the *Evening Post-Echo* and the *Sunday Times*, I followed in the footsteps of Anthony Holden, the royal biographer. I had a fleeting presence at the *Sunday Mirror* where I failed my audition to replace Wensley Clarkson, the true crime writer.

I learned a lot at the agency, especially about how freelances make money from doorsteps (knocking on somebody's door), stakeouts (staying outside an address until something happens) and such tricks as 'clearing the mantelpiece' (borrowing a family's prized photographs of a loved one).

Much was made at Lord Leveson's inquiry into the press

about allegations that reporters sometimes stole photographs. I do not think this ever really happened but the idea that it did may have come from the practice of asking a family for every photograph they had of a murder or disaster victim. No one would want to publish all of them, of course, but it prevented the next reporter to call upon the family from getting a picture for his agency or newspaper.

Stakeouts could be very lucrative if they went on for a long time, such as the siege of the Libyan Embassy after the murder of WPC Yvonne Fletcher. Some were awful. I once spent a freezing night in my car, with just a Mars bar to eat, outside an address linked to Bernard Matthews, the purveyor of 'bootiful' turkeys, in case he turned up with his alleged girlfriend. He didn't, but I learned the trick of tying a single strand of cotton around the gate when I went to telephone the office or use a lavatory. If the cotton was broken when I returned, he would be none the wiser, but I would know he was home.

Much better was the stakeout of Cecil Parkinson's Hertfordshire home after it was revealed he had had an affair with Sara Keays, his personal secretary, and she was expecting his baby. Parkinson was forced to resign from his job as Trade and Industry Secretary. He did not want to talk but he was perfectly civil. The first night, one of the photographers produced a small portable television and, after plugging it into the cigarette lighter of my Vauxhall Cavalier, we watched *Gone with the Wind* while drinking gin and tonics that another snapper had fetched on a silver tray from a nearby pub. Of course, it drained the battery and if Parkinson had looked out of his window late at night he would have seen some of Fleet Street's finest pushing my car for a jump start.

I was still there a few days later, this time on an order from the *News of the World*. As gales sent rain lashing into our faces, Parkinson sent a message inviting the reporters into his double garage, where they squeezed between the red Daimler and the deep freeze. 'I'm sorry, it's not the best place for a party, but it's better than getting wet,' he shouted from a side door. Later a secretary arrived at the garage with a bottle of Scotch whisky, with Parkinson's compliments.

Much of my time in my days at the agency was spent waiting around police stations for news snippets on the latest murder. In the days before relations between police and press were so tightly controlled for fear of cross-contamination, you waited in a police station until the lead detective was ready to go to the pub. There you bought him a pint and he might give you a new angle. It was often beneficial to both sides. In one case, the detective leading the hunt for the killer of Barrie Page, a car dealer found shot dead at the wheel of his car on the A4 near Slough, gave out enough information for us to find his chief suspect.

The interview with this man gave us a page lead in most of the nationals and what he said contradicted what he had told the police and gave them new reason to lean on him. Nevertheless, it is quite chilling to look back and realise that you have talked to a killer even if you did not know he was one at the time.

After eighteen months cutting my teeth with Cassidy and Leigh, I moved to the security of a staff job at the *Hemel*

Hempstead Evening Echo, where I replaced Anthony Holden. The *Echo* was one of several satellite evening papers around London (there were others in Reading, Slough, Chatham and Southend) that tried to compete with the nationals by taking wire copy and alternating their splashes between international despatches and local crime stories.

We looked to London as well as covering the events in Watford, St Albans and Hemel Hempstead. If there was a train crash in Harrow, we would go. London also looked to us. The national dailies copied the *Echo*'s design tricks and feature ideas. In return, many of us in the newsroom looked to the money and fame of Fleet Street.

There were many days when I and John Chapman, later a reporter at the *News of the World* and *Daily Express* and still a close pal, would try to look busy while constantly ringing the Scotland Yard automated press line for the latest news stories. We would then compete to be the first to rush out and file them to the nationals from a payphone in the corridor.

I would finish work at the *Echo* at 4.30 p.m. and drive to London (in the office car of course) to do an evening shift at a national ending at 2 or 3 a.m. *The Sun*, the *Sunday Mirror*, the *Daily Express*, the *News of the World*, the *Daily Star* – I shifted at all of them at various times in my career. Then it was back home to grab a few hours' sleep before an 8.30 a.m. start at the *Echo*, which did not know about my nocturnal activities until someone spotted my byline in *The Sun*.

One night, the tiredness caught up with me and, turning right from Fleet Street into Bouverie Street, where *The Sun* was based, I did not notice the motorcycle messenger until he rammed into the side of the office car. Luckily, Ralph Slater, the news editor at the *Echo*, was a great guy who covered up for me, saying I had gone to review a concert in London for the paper.

It could have been true. As well as becoming chief reporter and deputy news editor, I had snaffled up the job of music reviewer, which, as well as providing me with free vinyl, meant I got to go to all the best shows.

I saw Elton John play two intimate gigs as benefit concerts for Watford football players and was able to watch my favourite acts like Dr Feelgood and Frankie Miller whenever they performed within a thirty-mile radius. I went to see the Rolling Stones, Genesis and Led Zeppelin headline in different years at Knebworth, and was there when Queen and The Police topped the bill at the Milton Keynes Bowl. I came back from the Stones gig with another wrecked office car after trying to drive to the exit through a sea of 250,000 departing fans. Some of them kicked the door in.

I was one of the first outside the music press to interview punk rock singer Dave Vanian of The Damned, in the Hemel Hempstead cemetery where he used to work as a gravedigger, and watched from the side of the stage as The Clash played St Albans City Hall before learning from my police contacts next morning that they had been arrested for allegedly stealing bed linen from their hotel. I put the story 'all round'.

My interest in music came in particularly handy during one horrendous period in 1978 when the NUJ was on strike, nationally and locally, for a total of eleven weeks. I had to sell the record collection I had lovingly put together from the freebies I received as record reviewer to pay the mortgage. I even managed to persuade the editor's secretary, who had been collecting the albums that had arrived in my absence, to cross the picket line to deliver them to me.

Long before the dispute I had arranged annual leave so that my wife and I could go on holiday to America. While we were there, the Thomson management sent me a letter, along with everyone else on the picket line, threatening us with the sack if we did not report for work on the following Monday. The letter went unheeded of course, and, in any case, that Monday was booked off as annual leave.

When I returned to work, the management refused to pay me my holiday wages. Even though I was still employed by them, I took them to an industrial tribunal and represented myself. I must have done a good job because by lunchtime the management had caved in and met all my demands, including compensation, in an out-of-court settlement. It taught me that it pays to stand up for yourself.

Of course, these strikes had a disastrous effect on circulation. The paper merged with the *Luton Evening Post*, its sister title, to become the *Evening Post-Echo* and went from broadsheet to tabloid, all to no avail. The increasing cost of newsprint (that is, the paper the news is printed on, not the ink) and the drop-off in advertising revenues meant it was unsustainable for any of the satellite evenings to keep going.

When the end finally came, we all got a handsome pay-off, in my case more than I had paid for my first house. Some of the now-former staff went to an oak-beamed pub called the Olde Leather Bottle to commiserate. Chapman and I turned up to celebrate, which didn't go down too well. For us, however, it meant only one thing: Fleet Street was beckoning.

CHAPTER TWO

THE SUN INVADES FRANCE

O ne night I was doing a shift on *The Sun* news desk when one of Radio 4's flagship shows (*Any Questions?*, I think) was disrupted by protestors. As soon as we heard what was going on, I grabbed a radio from an office drawer, tuned in to the programme and turned up the volume.

Just then, a well-dressed man walked through the newsroom, saw what I was doing and grabbed the radio. Annoyed that I was missing what was happening, I grabbed it back. He then walked up the steps to the editor's office.

'What did you say to him?' demanded Roger Ward, one of the night desk regulators.

'I told him I was listening to the broadcast,' I replied.

He stared at me. 'Don't you know who that was?' he asked, incredulously.

'No.' I responded, bemused.

'That's Larry Lamb, the editor,' he said, giving me the sort of pained expression that was meant to suggest I was for the high jump.

Somehow, despite the faux pas, I survived and a few months later it was Sir Larry, not me, who left *The Sun*. It was he who had introduced the Page Three girl and sent *The Sun's* circulation soaring.

Working at *The Sun* was great fun and when I was not on duty in the office as a casual reporter contracted to work three nights a week, it was easy to sell them stories as a freelance. One night I went to see David Bowie's Serious Moonlight tour, which had sold out several nights at Wembley Arena, with Stuart Morrison, an old colleague from the *Evening Post-Echo* who had gone into public relations. Outside, some spivs were selling bootleg tapes of the previous night's opening show. I 'did it up' (the *Sun* parlance for writing a story) and sold it to the paper. It was on page one and the subsequent cheque for my services more than covered the tickets.

There was only one time I had to deny working for the tabloid. In the early 1980s, London was hit by street riots in Brixton, Notting Hill and Tottenham in which gangs of youths set fire to cars, ransacked shops and fought running battles with the police. One night I was out reporting the trouble with the tallest photographer I have ever seen. His name was Don and he always used to go on about his own glory days at the *Daily Sketch*. We suddenly found ourselves cornered by a knife-wielding youth, who demanded to know which newspaper we were from. '*The Guardian*,' said Don. 'Yes,' I said, going along with the ruse, 'we are here to find out what social injustices are causing you to rebel against the Thatcher regime.' We got away with it but, a few nights later, Don, out with another reporter, had all his camera equipment stolen.

Kelvin MacKenzie had become the new editor in 1981. In more recent years Kelvin had a regular column in *The Sun* until he was sacked in 2017 over a piece about Ross Barkley, the Everton footballer, which really should have been better fact-checked. He had realised early in his career, however, that his real talents lay in writing headlines and designing pages.

Before *The Sun*, he had been working at Murdoch's *New York Post*, which was pioneering in its use of clever, sometimes provocative, headlines. Indeed, one of its most famous heads – 'Headless Body in Topless Bar' – was coined two years after MacKenzie's departure but such is his reputation that many Fleet Street veterans still believe it was one of his.

Headlines have long been *The Sun*'s forte, sometimes more than stories. Indeed, my first ever bylined story for the paper was tweaked to fit the headline. It was a page-three lead about a learner driver who had failed his test because he had been coughing so much from a cold that he kept taking one hand off the steering wheel to cover his mouth. The sub-editor who wrote the headline thought it would be better if he had a runny nose instead. He had already come up with the headline: 'Blow me! Peter fails his L-test by a nose.'

MacKenzie was responsible for some of the most famous headlines in *The Sun*: 'Gotcha', when the Argentinian cruiser *General Belgrano* was sunk during the Falklands War; 'Freddie Starr Ate My Hamster', above a story cooked up by Max Clifford that ranks as an early example of fake news; and, on the day of the 1992 general election, 'If Kinnock wins today will the last person to leave Britain please turn out the lights'. Kinnock's face was shown inside a light bulb, a trick re-employed a decade later when the head of Graham Taylor, the unfortunate England football manager, was traduced into a turnip.

My personal favourite was the headline to a story about Princess Diana supposedly being bitten in the nether regions by a mosquito while on a royal tour of Australia with Prince Charles: 'Aussie Mozzie Bites Di Down Under'. *The Sun*'s sub-editors could turn almost any story into a one-paragraph Sun Spot aimed at tickling readers' ribs as much as educating their brains. When Emperor Haile Selassie was spared from a death sentence after a military coup in Ethiopia, 'Haile delighted' was the headline on the briefest of stories.

I have always thought that the best editors are those you fear and love in equal proportion. Kelvin MacKenzie fell into this category. I once saw him tear into Walter Terry, a journalist twice his age who had fathered the two sons of Marcia Falkender, Harold Wilson's private secretary, for missing a political story, basically humiliating him on the newsroom floor.

But, however much you hated his nasty side, everyone knew he had a natural instinct for news. One Friday night in August 1985, I was working at *The Sun* and he was unhappy with the first-edition splash. He suddenly came down the steps from his office into the newsroom brandishing a copy of the forthcoming weekend's *Sunday Times Magazine*. Supplements like these are printed several days ahead of the newspaper and Kelvin had simply picked up a copy from the circulation department. They are only kept under wraps if the editor of the magazine thinks they have a good exclusive.

''Ere, 'ere, take a look at this,' Kelvin said to those of us sitting on the news desk, and opened the magazine to an interview with Viscount Althorp, Princess Diana's brother and the future Earl Spencer. It had an innocuous headline, 'You can get very lonely at Oxford', and was full of mundane stuff – until you got to the penultimate paragraph. This is what Kelvin had spotted:

'I find it quite frightening in London by myself too … I keep a gun under my bed which I know how to use,' said Althorp.

I spent an hour getting reactions from what we called 'rent-a-quote MPs' (because they could always be counted on to say something to get their name into the paper). By 10 p.m., I had written a new splash. I christened the technique 'block and tackle', a phrase that was still being used at *The Sun* to describe lifting a rival's story a decade after I left. Nobody said a word when I turned up for a shift at the *Sunday Times* the following day

As well as having an undeniable eye for a splash, MacKenzie could also be funny and entertaining. One night, a reader rang in to the news desk to complain about *The Sun*'s coverage of a story. If he was passing the news desk and heard such a commotion, Kelvin would say, 'Let me talk to him' and seize the phone. On this occasion, he had soon had enough of the man's effing and blinding and told him: 'Right, you are banned from reading *The Sun* for the rest of your life.' Perhaps it is indicative of *The Sun*'s readership that a few minutes later the man's wife rang in and asked if she was banned too.

Kelvin's prickly nature was mirrored on the news desk by Ken Donlan, the news editor – a northerner who could turn on you in seconds. For some reason he took a shine to me, twice defusing a one-to-one meeting over my exaggerated expenses with questions about my young family. Others were not so lucky. One day Keith Deves, a shambling Australian reporter, greeted him with 'Good morning, Ken', to which Donlan replied: 'If I want a weather forecast, I will ring the Met Office.'

Such a tough management style helped produce a great camaraderie amongst the reporters as a sort of cumulative defence strategy: each had his story of being monstered by Kelvin and Ken.

One of the staff guys was Harry Arnold, a dapper dresser never without a handkerchief in his top pocket, who competed with James Whittaker of the *Daily Mirror* for the best royal stories. One day, I heard him tell Hilary Bonner, one of the few female reporters in the newsroom (and now married to the actress Amanda Barrie): 'Hilary, I am going to make mad, passionate love to you.' In a shot, Hilary fired back with this superb put-down: 'If you do, Harry, and I find out about it, I shall be very cross.'

Then there was Vic Chapple, who was a guest at all four of Arnold's weddings and best man at the fourth, when Harry's exasperated brother declined. Vic had enough gravitas to moonlight as Saturday night news editor at the *Sunday Times*. Another of the big hitters was John Kay, the most charming of colleagues, but one who suffered from inner demons. He once succumbed to the pressures of the job to be convicted of the manslaughter (by diminished responsibility) of his first wife by drowning her in the bath in a murder/suicide bid. He bounced back to become the first journalist to twice win Reporter of the Year at the British Press Awards but despair again got the better of him when he was arrested as part of the Operation Elveden investigation into alleged bribes to police and civil servants. He was cleared at the Old Bailey but not before again reportedly attempting to take his own life, this time by jumping off a bridge.

There was Ian Hepburn, who specialised in crime backgrounders and was a stoic member of the newsroom. He, too, loved working there. 'I have had a ball,' he said when he filled his boots with voluntary redundancy money at the same time I left the staff at the *Sunday Times*. 'It is a job I would have done almost for nothing.'

Barrie Mattei, who alternated between reporting and helming the night news desk, was a great operator on the phone. I worked with him on the night Grace Kelly, Princess Grace of Monaco, was killed in a car crash. While I was telephoning Monte Carlo, Bazza rang the British Embassy in Paris and used the magical phrase 'London calling', which while technically true might have led those on the other end of the line to think it was the Foreign Office in London and divulge all they knew. A clever trick.

Given Kelvin's right-wing, pro-British views, it was only natural that he would take exception to France's boycott of our lamb exports. Lamb chops should have been 30 per cent cheaper in Paris than they were, but the French agricultural ministry stubbornly refused to let British lamb be unloaded in its country's ports because it wanted to protect its own inefficient sheep farmers. It was a flagrant violation of the European Economic Community's free trade principles and, even when the European Court of Justice condemned the lamb ban as illegal, France's answer was to accept some British lamb and then offload it to the Soviet Union at a loss.

Of course, the lamb war was to get a lot worse over the years, with French farmers armed with pitchforks barricading roads, hijacking British lorries and burning their cargoes of meat.

Kelvin's plan was to send a warning shot over French bows by launching *The Sun*'s very own invasion. Forget the real D-Day of 1944. This was to be the D (for Doubled-up with laughter) Day of 1984, the day Rupert Murdoch's *Sun* newspaper invaded France on a pathfinding mission that was to help ignite the flame of Brexit amongst a generation of its readers.

The cause of the conflict was a French attempt to block imports of British lamb, in defiance of the 'common market' of what was then the supposedly free trading, made up of nine nations, including the UK.

Britain had fought various cod wars with Iceland over the preceding quarter of a century, often sending gunboats to protect our trawlers. So what better way to hit back at the French than launch an invasion of Calais, their biggest trading port with Britain?

The idea was that we would storm Calais wielding legs of lamb and claim it back for the English crown for the first time since Mary Tudor lost it to the French in 1558. I was teamed up with Nick Ferrari, then a hotshot show business reporter still a few days short of his twenty-fifth birthday, and George Lynn, a strait-laced journalist approaching retirement who was far too serious for such japes.

Nick was the son of Lino (better known as Dan) Ferrari, who had started the Ferrari Press Agency covering south London and Kent after World War Two. Kelvin and Richard Stott, a future *Daily Mirror* editor, both worked there as youngsters. So did Nick, answering the phone and filing copy from the age of six (his voice was so high some copytakers thought he was a girl). Dan was known for his inventiveness and it probably rubbed off on them all: if a murder story needed selling he would say that the body had been found 'in an attitude of prayer', so intriguing the national news desks that they would order copy from him. This was an important lesson for a freelance: ordered copy had to be paid for whether it was used or not.

Our first job was to round up some celebrities to join us on the adventure. Kelvin would have liked the whole cast of *Dad's Army* but both Arthur Lowe (Captain Mainwaring) and John Le Mesurier (Sergeant Wilson) had died in recent months. Instead we got Ed 'Stewpot' Stewart, the disc jockey newly dropped from Radio 2, *Carry On* star Jack Douglas, whose party piece was a nervous character called Alf Ippititimus, actor Derek Deadman, who had just appeared in the James Bond film *Never Say Never Again*, singer Maggie Moone and Julie Wooldridge, a 23-year-old Princess Diana lookalike.

To add to the glamour, we took three Page Three girls – Helle Kjaer, Caroline Christensen and Karen Kelly. I had got to know some of the Page Three girls from the simple expedience of sometimes being called on to write the pun-laden two-par caption that accompanied their topless photograph. Naturally this took me to photographer Beverley Goodway's studio and I somehow managed to time it to arrive while he was shooting one girl so I could ask him about the girl whose picture was going in the paper the next day. I also covered the Page Three Girl Party at Stringfellows night club for *The Sun*. Caroline Christensen was a blonde, girl-next-door type from Jersey who to this day still recalls her role in the expedition as part of 'a vortex of adventure'.

Karen was naughtier, and on our coach trip down to Dover she would tease me by peeling and eating a banana in an erotic way.

For my part, I was tasked with getting some stellar backing for the invasion. I telephoned the 8th Duke of Wellington at his Stratfield Saye home in Hampshire. The Duke, referring to the latest outrage across the Channel, told me: 'I wish *The Sun* invaders luck. It was stupid of the French students to take over our consulate in Bordeaux. As a nation of claret drinkers we must be Bordeaux's best customers.'

Next on my list was the 9th Lord Nelson, who had succeeded to the earldom on the death of his uncle three years earlier. The fact that he was a police sergeant at the time must have been the source of some interesting banter down at the station. Luckily, he was up for it too and ready to remind the French of their debt to Britain in two world wars. 'We've bailed the French out twice in the past sixty years,' he said. 'They are supposed to be our friends, but judging by their attitude over the past fifteen years we'd be better off allied to the Mongolians.'

Unfortunately Winston Churchill, the MP grandson of our wartime Prime Minister, did not join in the spirit of things. 'I've never heard a more juvenile proposition in all my life,' he told me. Hardly what the invasion fleet wanted to hear as it prepared to set sail…

On the coach with us for what Kelvin back in London had already dubbed the 'Ooh La Laugh Invasion' were a town crier to announce our arrival, a butcher with his stock of lamb and a milkman ready to hand out British pints of milk from his crate.

We travelled to Calais by hovercraft. When we emerged down the gangplank, Derek Deadman was in full Coldstream Guard uniform. Nick Ferrari was dressed as a British bobby (he was briefly detained by the gendarmerie who thought he was for real). The Page Three girls and I wore Union Jack T-shirts, tin helmets and 'Hop Off You Frogs' badges. Poor George Lynn looked uncomfortable in his suit, refusing to surrender his dignity at MacKenzie's whim.

Heading into town, the butcher handed out chops and legs of British lamb to bemused French shoppers while the milkman provided pints of fresh silver top.

French farmer Gaston Mattheu, thirty-seven, told us: 'We don't like your lamb. It will put us farmers out of work. Most French people would rather eat horse than your lamb.' But he took a free leg anyway.

Gaston Le Begue, a retired Parisian, insisted: 'Our French lamb is the best. However, I am prepared to accept this free gift.' He ambled off with half a dozen prime chops.

By the time we got to the Town Hall, with its Rodin statue

outside of the six burghers symbolising French resistance to the English in medieval times, the mayor and his deputies had fled. Instead we found some receptionists and, in a brief but dignified ceremony, our 'Princess Diana' handed in a letter condemning the hijacking of British lamb.

The wartime spirit shone through as we sang 'It's A Long Way to Tipperary' while pushing on to the Place d'Angleterre. There we planted a Union Jack flag while Maggie Moone led us in 'God Save the Queen'.

Resplendent in his tricorn hat and official gown, Ray Goode, the town crier of Hastings (admittedly the scene of one slight reversal against the enemy), rang his bell and read out the proclamation I had written earlier:

All French subjects of Her Majesty Queen Elizabeth II draw near and pay heed. We have come in the name of Her Majesty, Mrs Margaret Thatcher and *The Sun*, Britain's biggest selling newspaper, to undo the wrongs of 1558 and restore Calais to England, her rightful owners. In that the gallant force of 800 English soldiers only surrendered after a siege by 30,000 Frenchmen, we declare that the city was unlawfully seized and that we now want it back.

And, further to our declaration, we must insist that no more British lamb is hijacked by French farmers and that no more utterly horrid UHT milk is forced on British housewives. We have come fully armed with an arsenal of jokes provided by loyal readers of *The Sun* in defiance of the French outrages.

Then he fired off a volley of French jokes…

What is the difference between a £5 note and a box of French Golden Delicious apples? You can give the money away.

Heard about the anti-British farmer? He swallowed an Oxo cube and made a laughing stock of himself.

What happened to the French onion-seller? He cried so much he went in-Seine.

Our celebrities were soon ready for lunch after all this exertion, so we retired to a restaurant. I kept popping to the phone to file copy and by the time I returned for a final time most of them were fortified on French wine. The hovercraft crossing back was very rough and I remember seeing my Scotch leap out of my glass at the crest of a wave and then fall back in again without a drop being lost.

Next day the story of our jolly little jaunt made the splash and a spread across two pages inside. Kelvin came up with the headline: 'We raise Union Jacques' – a precursor of his famous 'Up Yours Delors' insult to the French premier a decade later.

The front-page story read: 'Calais was captured without a shot yesterday … by *The Sun's* laugh-a-minute invasion. And the French had to admit: "You're all right, Jacques".'

Of course, they admitted nothing of the sort. Our invasion did nothing to appease Anglo-French relations and the lamb war escalated in future years with French farmers setting fire to British trucks, slitting the throats of British sheep, poisoning them or burning them alive, while rioting against their own government and police. *The Sun* urged a boycott of French goods but when mad cow disease broke out in Britain, the

French imposed a new blockade on British beef. Finally, the European Court of Justice in Luxembourg found France guilty of breaching European law and the attacks ended.

Roll forward to the autumn of 2016 and French consumers voted British quality standard mark lamb as the best butchery product of the year in the Europe-wide *Meilleur Produit de l'Annee* competition. *Merci!*

CHAPTER THREE

THE FIRST TIME WE HACKED
THE ROYAL FAMILY

By 1981 I had managed to wangle a regular Saturday shift at the *News of the World* on the strength of a page lead I had sold the paper about 'a king-size swindler who called himself God'.

The *News of the World* had its own offices in Bouverie Street, but on Saturdays everyone decamped downstairs to the *Sun* offices. We needed the extra room to accommodate all the sports subs who came in for one day to ensure the paper's unrivalled football coverage got off on time.

I remember one quiet Saturday in the newsroom when I happened to be wearing a white jacket. Bob Strange, the deputy news editor, whom I'd worked with as a junior reporter on the *Bracknell News* a decade before, took a phone call. The man on the other end told him he had the ability to listen in to calls to Buckingham Palace, and he was willing to meet. Looking over at me in my jacket, Bob said a man in white would meet him at the location of his choice. He nominated the Thomas a Becket, a pub on the Old Kent Road known for its boxing champion patrons, such as Henry Cooper, who used to train in the gym upstairs.

Within the hour, common sense had prevailed. Eddie Jones, the news editor, had returned from lunch and decided it was potentially too important a story to leave to a Saturday casual rather than a full-time staff man. He despatched Andrew Drummond, the paper's best reporter, to go with me to meet the mystery caller.

Andrew, who later became the go-to freelance in Bangkok for any story involving Britons in Thailand, was another former colleague and rival. The son of an RAF squadron leader, he was on the *Reading Chronicle* when I started on the *Bracknell News*, its sister paper in the Berkshire new town. Later he had worked for the Thames Valley News Service based in Reading, while I had signed up with Cassidy and Leigh's Southern News Service, an agency operating from offices in Guildford and Amersham.

We had been on opposite sides years earlier, when we were both sent to doorstep the Buckinghamshire home of Jonathan Snasdell, a BBC editor whose ten-week-old son had been snatched and murdered by a wicked woman called Genevieve Parslow. Both of our agencies had orders to cover the story from various national newspapers.

We waited outside all morning until Mrs Snasdell came out of the house to fetch in the milk. Andrew went off to file this minor piece of information while I stayed put, only to be bollocked by Don Leigh, my boss, when newspapers who had put us on order demanded to know why the Reading agency had filed copy all round and I had not.

Andrew was rather pleased by this and soon called it a day. I decided to try a different tack and telephoned the local vicar, telling him about the murder, inviting him to visit the family and entrusting him with my business card to pass on to them. It was pretty shameless on my part, but, as Jimmy London, the newspaper reporter hero of John Rowland's British Library crime classic *Calamity In Kent*, puts it: 'A journalist, unless he is doing something really flagrantly illegal, will always let his news sense get the upper hand.' My persistence paid off. I waited outside all day and well into the evening until the Snasdells took pity on me, invited me into their home and allowed me to have a photograph of their son.

I drove into London and took the picture to all the newspaper offices in Fleet Street and waited while they copied it for use in next morning's editions. The bolshie union members at the *Daily Telegraph* held me up for ages, insisting on finishing a game of cards for half an hour before even looking at the photo. Nevertheless, the photo gave the agency a scoop over its opposition and it was something Andrew had not forgotten.

In the car to the pub he told me he would do all the talking. The man we were meeting said he worked at a GPO telephone exchange around the corner. Surprisingly, he also told us he was a special in the Metropolitan Police.

He claimed to have listened in to a romantic conversation between 22-year-old Prince Andrew, the Queen's second son, who was fresh home from flying helicopter missions during the Falklands War, and Koo Stark, a 26-year-old actress turned photographer.

The romance between the two was already front-page news – they had been on holiday together on the Caribbean island of Mustique, famous as Princess Margaret's hideaway – and it had cemented Andrew's tabloid nickname of 'Randy Andy'.

In the past fortnight, the *News of the World* had run two front-page stories on Koo in which they insisted on labelling the poor girl a 'soft porn star' ever since she'd played the lead role in a film called *The Awakening of Emily*, which told the story of a young woman discovering her sensual side.

One of the stories was a splash about Koo taking part in 'a wild five-day romp fuelled by coconut cocktails and pot'. The other was about a friend of hers 'touting the whole inside story of love under the palms for up to £100,000'. The rumpus this created supposedly caused a royally enforced separation between the couple.

What was missing in this story from a journalistic standpoint was any real interaction with the royal family as an institution. Our contact promised to give us this missing piece of the jigsaw. Now, at this point in time, no one had hacked the royals before. This was a quarter of a century before the actions of one supposed 'rogue reporter', Clive Goodman, whose hacking of the mobile phones of Princes William and Harry triggered a multi-million-pound police investigation that led to jail sentences for those involved and the eventual closure of the *News of the World*.

Even the revelation of the existence of the 'Camillagate' tapes of conversations between Prince Charles and Camilla Parker Bowles and the 'Squidgygate' tapes of conversations between Diana, Princess of Wales, and a close friend, James Gilbey, which were to fuel the so-called Wars of the Waleses, were ten years in the future.

Nevertheless, the *News of the World* was very interested in the whole idea of bugging. The previous year, eleven weeks before the marriage of Charles and Diana, it had splashed on 'Lady Di in New Bugging Shock'. The story claimed police and telephone chiefs were investigating a tip that calls between the couple were intercepted while Diana was in Australia earlier in the year staying on a farm owned by her mother.

We had a perfectly good splash ('The Spy Who Fell in Love: British Girl Agent Wins Over KGB General') lined up for the next day when we received the phone call from the GPO telephone exchange contact, and Andrew had written a good exclusive about the stormy love life of Nicholas Fairbairn MP as the second lead, so we did not need to rush into print with this story. It was also very important to check our contact out and make sure his story stood up to scrutiny. Over the next week, other reporters took over while I was busy working at my day job at an evening newspaper.

Koo Stark has always maintained her phone calls were hacked during her romance with Andrew. She probably thought it was the phone at the Kensington flat where she was staying that was bugged, not that her phone calls to Buckingham Palace were intercepted.

When I went into work the following Saturday, I was told someone had listened in as she telephoned the palace, using the pseudonym 'Fiona Campbell', and asked to be put through to Andrew.

The call was dynamite. She mentioned 'the green thing', perhaps a wash bag or make-up case, that she had left on a bedside table in his room and asked for its return. She was clutching a wrapped present when she was photographed returning to her flat that Saturday morning in a smart Burberry jacket.

A team of reporters went to work on the following day's splash. At one stage I saw the news editor go over to Derek Jameson, the editor famed in *Private Eye* as 'Sid Yobbo', but, in truth, a quiet presence on the news floor compared with some editors I have worked under. Jameson wanted to know the provenance of the story. He heard enough not to want to know any more and waved the news editor away.

Next day's story covered half of the front page. 'Koo's Night at the Palace' ran the headline. A heart-shaped graphic declared: 'They're still in love'. 'The great romance is on again,' ran the story. 'Despite all the fuss Koo Stark and Prince Andrew have just spent the night at Buckingham Palace.' It added that the tryst at the palace, at that time uninhabited by the Queen and Prince Philip, who were on a Pacific tour, was proof that the romance was over.

The story went to great lengths to explain how Koo had dodged waiting reporters and taken a circuitous route to avoid discovery and enter the palace through a side entrance, as if the *Screws*, as the paper was known amongst press and public alike from its staple diet of stories about sex, had followed her every step.

A few paragraphs of the story came dangerously close to revealing how the paper really got its information:

A close friend said that within minutes Koo and Andy were talking together on the phone.

Andrew wanted to know whether she had got home safely, despite the waiting pressmen.

They arranged another meeting later this weekend – before the 22-year-old Prince returns to duty to the Royal Navy air base at Culdrose, Cornwall.

Of course, this close friend was actually *our* close friend, and all the information was gleaned from listening in to Koo's call to the palace.

Another 'friend' was quoted as saying: 'They call each other "Darling" all the time and are still very much in love.'

The story was huge for the whole of the next week and one night I found myself on assignment for *The Sun* staking out the flat where Koo was staying.

This was before the days of digital photography, when snappers needed messengers to transport their rolls of film to the Fleet Street dark rooms while they stayed on watch. We were used to greasy-haired motorcyclists turning up and disappearing again. Suddenly this girl in a figure-hugging leather outfit, her hair concealed under a helmet with a blacked-out visor, walked through the melee. To this day I am convinced it was

Koo and that she had conceived a brilliant guise to get back into the flat undisturbed and, more to the point, without being photographed.

With such pressure on her it is no surprise that the romance fizzled out after eighteen months. A year later, when I was writing a page-three lead in *The Sun* about Koo having her bag stolen, I referred to her as 'Prince Andrew's old flame'.

'Police were called and security officials alerted in case the bag contained any of the tapes Prince Andrew sent Koo while he was fighting in the Falklands,' I wrote. 'Unscrupulous foreign magazines would pay a fortune for such tapes.'

Not to mention the *News of the World*! But by then Prince Andrew had new fish to fry. Three months after the bag snatch I was writing a spread in *The Sun* about his new love, actress Katie Rabett. Then there was another showgirl, Vicki Macdonald, a dancer at the Royal Variety Show and co-owner of a new discotheque in Piccadilly. We had a tip that Andrew was due to meet her there at a film promotion. He failed to show but, bizarrely, Koo arrived at the shindig, fleeing after just thirty minutes when she was questioned about the prince.

All this was forgotten a year or so later when I wrote a splash in *The Sun* predicting that Andrew was to marry Sarah Ferguson, the daughter of Prince Charles's polo manager. The big clue was that Andrew had been photographed showing her around his ship, HMS *Brazen*, with Diana and a little Prince William.

'This is the picture that means it's wedding bells ahoy for Prince Andrew and his flame-haired girlfriend,' I wrote.

I could be so certain because Sarah would never have been

allowed to step into the public spotlight with the royal family unless the romance was the real thing. Poor Koo, who had become an acclaimed photographer in her own right, never had such a photo opportunity.

CHAPTER FOUR

A SHAMEFUL EPISODE

The one episode of my journalistic career of which I am most ashamed ended up with me lurking in the bushes on an embankment in my raincoat like some horrible flasher.

It was April 1985. I had had a call an hour or so earlier at my home in St Albans from Jeremy Selwyn, a photographer friend who lived in Berkhamsted, fifteen miles away. He had himself been tipped off that Norman Tebbit, Trade and Industry Secretary in Margaret Thatcher's government, and his wife Margaret were having lunch at the home of some friends in Jeremy's home town.

It was Margaret Tebbit he was interested in. She had not been seen in public since being permanently disabled as a result of the IRA bombing of the Grand Hotel in Brighton the previous year. If he could get a photograph, it would make the front page. Would I come along and do the words?

I should never have agreed, but at the time I was a freelance, running my own agency, Chittenden of St Albans, and shifting on every Fleet Street paper I could get work with, from the *Daily Star* to the *Sunday Times*. I had a mortgage to pay and a wife and three young children to feed.

I should have been more grateful to the Tories. When the *Evening Post-Echo* closed with the loss of 470 jobs, I took advantage of the enterprise allowance scheme introduced by Thatcher while Tebbit was Employment Secretary. At the time there was mass unemployment in Britain but, if you signed on the dole for two weeks, you could apply for the scheme to set up your own business. This is what I did. It was very entrepreneurial. You had to produce a basic business plan and put up the first £1,000 out of your own funds. It only paid £40 a week but that was better than the £25 you got on the dole and it had the added bonus that you regained your self-esteem. I had spent most of my redundancy money on a new car and an extension to our home, so I was ready to go, working from a spare bedroom turned into an office. I would start work at 8.30 a.m., ringing police, fire and ambulance services across four counties. I got the first ever mention of *EastEnders* into the press as a paragraph in *The Sun* after picking up a report of a small fire at its Borehamwood studio set in 1984, a year before it started broadcasting. I would try to sell stories to news desks in the morning, grab two hours' sleep in the afternoon and, four days a week, leave at 5 p.m. for a night shift in London, getting home again at 3 a.m.

The enterprise allowance scheme funded 325,000 people in all. They included, amongst others, the artist Tracey Emin; Alan McGee, the head of Creation Records, Oasis's record label; and Julian Dunkerton, the founder of Superdry. Strangely, when

Iain Duncan Smith announced plans to revive the scheme in 2010, it was still only going to pay £40 a week.

Tebbit had also been good to me as a journalist. He had once worked at the *Financial Times* before going off to fly Vampire jets in the RAF and becoming an airline pilot prior to his parliamentary career. So he knew what journalists wanted.

I telephoned him once when he was Employment Secretary after his ministerial car had been clamped in Westminster (his chauffeur had parked it on a single yellow line). Tebbit strode out of his office to find the vehicle immobilised, did a swift about-turn and was whisked off minutes later in another car. The clamp was released soon afterwards after a £29.50 fine was paid. 'I suppose it's one way of internal government financing,' he told me. 'Transferring money from the Employment Ministry to Home Office accounts.' It made a nice basement (that's a story at the bottom) for page one of *The Sun* next day. A week later, Tebbit was off to Trade and Industry following the resignation of Cecil Parkinson.

It was at 2.54 a.m. on Friday 12 October 1984 that a long-delay time bomb planted a month earlier in the bathroom wall of Room 629 by the Provisional IRA exploded at the Grand Hotel in Brighton during the Tory Party conference. It missed Thatcher, who was still up writing her conference speech for later that day, but five people, including an MP, Sir Anthony Berry, were killed, and thirty-four, including Margaret Tebbit, were injured. Norman Tebbit escaped serious injury because a mattress landed on top of him. The cameras caught him, ghostly pale, being stretchered from the rubble. When he arrived at hospital, he was asked by a nurse if he was allergic to anything. 'Bombs,' he is said to have replied.

Margaret Tebbit, a nurse at St Bartholomew's Hospital in London, fell four floors and was crushed by the weight of the falling rubble. She was left permanently disabled with spinal injuries that confined her to a wheelchair. She spent two years in the Stoke Mandeville and Royal National Orthopaedic Hospitals, during which time she recovered limited use of her hands and arms.

In March 1985, I reported in the *News of the World* that Margaret was going to have some days out before moving back home permanently. Her husband was having a new house designed to help his wife lead as normal a life as possible. The home, at a secret London address, would be fitted with widened doors, ramps and a lift.

Six weeks later, here I was, lurking in the bushes, spying on her day out visiting former neighbours in Berkhamsted, where Norman Tebbit had started his political career.

At about 4 p.m., we saw them preparing to leave and Jeremy began taking pictures. I was convinced they would hear the clicks of his camera below or the spring sunshine would betray a glint of the lens, but no, we got away with it.

I watched as a smiling Tebbit insisted on manoeuvring his wife's wheelchair out of the house, refusing offers of help from an accompanying detective. I could see that Margaret had a new hair-do and was wearing a pink trouser suit.

As they got to their car, a specially adapted Austin Maestro, Tebbit showed their hosts how the front passenger seat revolved outwards when the door opened to allow his wife to move easily from her chair.

The picture and my story were the splash in the *Daily Star* the next day under the headline: 'The Tender Touch'. I had shifted at the *Star* and knew it was run on a shoestring so would not pay that much, but Jeremy had a good relationship with the paper. To this day I still feel guilty about my part in the whole incident.

A few years later I laughed and joked with Tebbit when he came to one of the *Sunday Times*'s parties but I did not mention my betrayal.

(As an aside, these social functions at summer and Christmas were always quite a draw. Andrew Neil took us down the Thames in a pleasure cruiser for one, and John Witherow even managed to draw Diana, Princess of Wales, to a Christmas event (although I suspect it was the royal connections of Geordie Greig, the future *Mail on Sunday* editor, that swayed her). 'What brings you here, ma'am,' I asked as I sidled up to her, a re-stocked wine glass in my hand 'An invitation,' she shot back, at which point I retired, hurt. Next Christmas, staff will be lucky to get a sandwich and a soft drink on the canteen floor of News UK's London Bridge headquarters.)

The IRA was, of course, a constant feature through the early part of my journalistic career, no matter where I was working.

In my days with Cassidy and Leigh at their Amersham office, I was one of the first on the scene after a 50lb bomb exploded nearby at the National Defence College, on a wooded hill above the picture-postcard village of Latimer. I watched as young female army drivers, still in their nightdresses, were evacuated, grabbed the usual quote from a builder working in the village ('I thought it was an earthquake at first') and filed copy in time to make the lunchtime splashes of both the *Evening Standard* and the *Evening News* in London.

I revealed the discovery of an IRA plot to bomb other seaside hotels in *The Sun* and I was so quick to arrive at a 1992 blast at the Baltic Exchange building, which killed three people in the City of London less than a mile from the *Sunday Times* office, that my car was taped off as part of the crime scene and I was unable to recover it for twenty-four hours.

I reported the arrest of Patrick Magee for the Brighton bombing in a hamper (that's the story on the top of the page) on page one of the *Sunday Times*. He subsequently received eight life sentences but was released from prison in 1999, having served fourteen years, under the terms of the Good Friday Agreement.

CHAPTER FIVE

ELTON JOHN MARRIES ... A LADY

Both the news and the incredulity went around the world. So did my story. Except this time there was a strange boomerang effect.

I had first seen Elton John in the 1970s, when he had played a couple of testimonial concerts at Baileys nightclub in Watford for the local team's footballers. I reviewed the first of these ('Suddenly he was before them, bedecked in a sequined red jumpsuit with Marilyn Monroe on the back, seated at a bejewelled piano rolling out his greatest hits') for what was then the *Watford Evening Echo*. I also produced a twelve-page supplement for sale to fans at Elton's sell-out Wembley Stadium concert when his support bands included the Beach Boys and the Eagles.

Born Reginald Dwight in Pinner, not a million miles from Watford, the son of an RAF trumpeter, he had become easily the biggest pop star of the early 1970s. I read somewhere that two out of every 100 records sold in the United States during this period had his name on them. It may not sound that high, but if you think how many thousands of musicians were competing for the other 98 per cent of sales, he should have got the Queen's Award for Industry as well as his well-deserved knighthood in 1998.

I first met him when I was working at the *News of the World* and he was chairman of Watford Football Club. It was a Saturday and 6,000 Manchester United fans were due to descend on the Hertfordshire town that afternoon for a match. This was in the bad days of football hooliganism and on their last visit to Watford the previous season for an FA Cup match a policewoman had been attacked and a fan stabbed.

Elton's solution was to open his club's own railway station to keep the visiting fans away from the town centre. The £160,000 stop (naturally dubbed 'Hooligan Halt' by us hacks) was part-funded by the Football Trust, which was itself funded by profits from football pools companies, and the local council.

The singer seemed rather shy and overwhelmed by our attention as he boarded a special train, which broke through a tape in his team's colours to declare the new platform open. Certainly there was no hint of the 'tantrums and tiaras' reputation that was to come in what became known as his 'cocaine years'. 'This is one way to combat hooliganism,' he told me. 'It's the end of a tremendous headache.'

Three months later I was to play Cupid and announce his forthcoming wedding to a female sound technician on the front page of *The Sun* and, if the bride had black circles under her eyes on her big day, it was all my fault.

Elton was on tour in Australia when Patti Mostyn, a show

business agent, stunned the world by announcing that Elton was to marry Renate Blauel, a German-born but London-based studio technician in four days' time ... on Valentine's Day.

It was a surprise because, eight years earlier, in an interview with *Rolling Stone* magazine, Elton had revealed that he was bisexual. He later said that it was a compromise; he was afraid to reveal that he was gay to the public even though everyone in the pop world and the media knew. Rod Stewart even called him 'Sharon'.

I was working a regular Friday night shift at *The Sun* when we received the agent's announcement. Like many young reporters I was a 'casual', paid every time I worked but with no permanent contract, which was a clever way of keeping us keen and desperate for a staff job. It's a system that still works today on many newspapers, with the crucial difference being that today's 'casuals' are usually unpaid interns.

It was 8 p.m. at *The Sun*'s office in Bouverie Street. I checked the wires, the show business magazines and the cuttings. Elton liked staying at the exclusive Sebel Townhouse hotel in Sydney, and it was probable that he and Renate were now in the same hotel. I figured she would not yet be used to her new celebrity status and wouldn't have thought to ask the hotel switchboard to block all calls.

Today there are rules and regulations about telephoning people at night, but this was then. Around the same period, I phoned a vicar at 1 a.m. to see if he knew anything about a brutal double murder on a rough south London housing estate that formed part of his parish. 'Do you know what time it is?'

he demanded indignantly. 'Well, I'm still working,' I replied, in a rather holier-than-thou voice. Years later, when I was at the *Sunday Times*, Paddy Ashdown thanked me profusely for raising his head from the pillow late on a Saturday night so he could put the Liberal Democrat spin on a story affecting the two main parties.

On this occasion, it was just after 5 a.m. Sydney time when I made the call. I decided to ask for Miss Blauel rather than Elton, thinking that the night staff at the hotel might not be aware of who she was. I told the hotel receptionist that I was calling from London and that it was urgent.

After a few moments, Renate answered. She was clearly taken aback at being woken but she was not cross in any way.

'Hello,' I said. 'I hope it's not too early but I am phoning to pass on the best wishes of 4 million readers of the *Sun* newspaper.' It was always a good line to defuse such situations.

'Thank you,' she said. She proceeded to tell me that it had been a 'whirlwind romance' and that she and Elton had adjoining suites in the hotel with 'Do not disturb' signs on the doors.

'Can you tell me where and when you met?' I asked. She normally worked at Air Studios in London's Oxford Street but she had flown to the Caribbean island of Montserrat eighteen months earlier to work on his last album, *Too Low For Zero*. The sessions had yielded Elton's 'comeback' single, 'I'm Still Standing', as well as a curiously prophetic track called 'Kiss the Bride'.

However, it was not until she flew out to Australia to help him record new material that, she said, the romance began. Elton was thirty-six. She was thirty.

'We hit it off immediately,' she told me. 'Elton's wonderful. He's the nicest guy I've ever met.'

She added that the singer had popped the question over a candlelit curry just a week ago but they were due to marry in a few days' time.

'He said, "Will you marry me?" I said, "Yes." It was as simple as that.'

I had to ask the obvious but I tried to distance myself from the question even as I said it: 'What about these curious stories in the past that he is supposed to have said he is homosexual?'

Renate had clearly prepared herself for such questions. 'I've heard all sorts of stories, but they don't worry me,' she said.

She said lots more but my second edition deadline was approaching and *The Sun* only had a limited amount of space.

The story was the splash the next day under the headline: 'I'm Going to Wed Elton!' and my byline.

After I had sent my story, I was approached by the man from the syndication department. At night, in many of the big papers, someone sits at a rear desk, somewhat apart from the action but close enough to know what's going on. It's their job to hoover up stories with international appeal and then try to market them abroad or pass them on to a foreign paper under the same ownership. He wanted the full transcript of my interview with Renate, and although it takes about ten times as long to transcribe a taped recording than the actual conversation lasts, I was happy to oblige.

When I picked up the *News of the World* that Sunday, I was surprised to see all the quotes I had not used in *The Sun* recycled in the *Screws* under an Australian reporter's byline. The *News of the World* had taken back my interview from the syndication department of the Murdoch-owned *Sunday Telegraph* in Sydney, which, because of the time difference, had already published it there.

I was peeved, and it was perhaps by compensation that I got two bylines in the following week's *News of the World*. But I still wanted my revenge. On Friday nights, a man from the *Screws* sat behind the *Sun* news desk in Bouverie Street to take calls for his paper, watch out for breaking news stories and generally keep an eye on what was going on. Knowing him, he had been at the pub the whole time I was filing the Elton story.

A few months later he was in the pub again when the phone on his desk was ringing. I was on the *Sun* news desk and picked it up. It was usual practice to take messages for our absent colleague, and this time it was a 'call in', somebody with a story. They did not want to give a name, but they said they knew all about a justice of the peace who had been interfering with handicapped children.

I took copious notes and, for the sake of appearances, pretended to leave a note for the *News of the World* man. Instead, on Sunday I telephoned it in as my story to the *Sun* news desk. Even better, they managed to pay me twice by mistake. £500 in all. It was a lot of money in the 1980s.

Three days after my Elton John story appeared, Renate wore a wedding dress studded with sixty-three diamonds, while Elton was sporting a white jacket, straw boater and mauve bow tie. To those who commented that there had never been a woman in his life before, Elton said: 'I've never met the right person and now I have.'

Nick Ferrari, *The Sun*'s pop correspondent, had flown to Sydney for the nuptials and was punched on the nose by John Reid, Elton's manager, after, unbeknown to him, the subs at *The Sun* had put the headline 'Good On Ya Poofter!' on his story. 'You've destroyed his wedding night!' shouted Reid. (Most doubt there ever was one.) After three years it was all over and Elton announced he was gay after all. Renate received £5 million and a cottage in Surrey as part of the divorce settlement. She has never spoken about their marriage.

Five years later, Elton began his relationship with David Furnish, the Canadian film producer. It has not always run smoothly. I was at the *Sunday Times* in 2001 when an executive on our magazine came up with a tip that the couple had split and Furnish was now in Hollywood.

These things are tricky. You don't want to leave yourself short-staffed in case a major story breaks, but a tip from an executive could not be ignored. I sent David Brown, our best casual, to Elton's home in Old Windsor to doorstep.

David, like me, had started out in local papers before trying his luck as a casual on the nationals. He is now one of the top reporters at *The Times*. Early on Saturday morning, he drove up the immaculate, tree-lined driveway of Elton's estate and nervously pushed the intercom at the final gate. It was answered by someone he took to be a housekeeper and he asked to speak to Mr John. A minute later, he was speaking to Mr Furnish instead. David Brown explained that he had it on good authority that he had separated from Elton (although he was actually less confident now because, according to the tip, Furnish was supposed to be in California). Furnish insisted it was untrue but David persisted and demanded to know where Elton was at that precise moment.

'Next to me in bed,' came the reply. 'I'll hand you over.'

David had a brief, rather awkward conversation with Elton before Furnish came back on the line. He said he had been in Hollywood to sign a deal to make a cartoon. David left and, professional that he is, filed copy about the cartoon rather than a memo for my scoop about a celebrity split. That's show business as they say.

CHAPTER SIX

AMBUSH ON THE HIGHWAY

I was the last man in the convoy as we headed out through the barbed wire fence to face 5,000 baying pickets. I had seen too many Westerns not to know that the last wagon was the likeliest to be picked off by the marauding Indians.

'Running the gauntlet' was what it had become known as. I was leaving the News International plant after a shift as night reporter at the *Sunday Times*. Riding shotgun in the front passenger seat of my Vauxhall Cavalier estate was Mike Burrows, the night reporter for the *News of the World*.

As I turned the corner from Pennington Street and the exit from Fortress Wapping onto The Highway, there was an almighty crash as a house brick smashed into the car, taking out the off-side rear window. It was hurled with such force that it rebounded off the roof of the vehicle and smashed the nearside panel as well before landing with a thud on the floor of my carpeted boot.

I slowed to a halt but a voice on the loudspeaker of our police escort screamed: 'Don't stop. Don't stop. Keep moving.'

It was 2.45 a.m. on Easter Sunday 1986 and the attack on my car triggered the worst night of violence yet in the so-called Battle of Wapping. There was a cavalry charge by mounted police. Batons rained down on the heads of striking printers. Missiles and fireworks were thrown in reply at some of the 1,400 police on duty.

With the early morning air blowing like a gale through the holes in my windows, I eventually managed to stop at King's Cross police station, where the incident was logged as criminal damage.

Behind I had left a pitched battle that saw police with riot shields and helmets fighting to clear the streets. There were dozens of arrests, dozens of injuries.

By then we had been working under siege conditions for two months. Of course, the Wapping dispute, along with the miners' strike two years earlier, was a turning point in breaking the stranglehold of trade union power in the UK.

Today it is difficult to believe the Mafia-like grip the print unions had on the British press. I had been introduced to it when I turned up for my first reporting shifts at *The Sun*. In those days you would get a docket signed for your pay and take it downstairs to a cashier's window. A printer was ahead of me in the queue.

'What's your name?' the cashier asked him. 'You haven't filled it in.'

'Mickey Mouse.'

'Address?'

'77 Sunset Strip.' The money was duly paid over, tax-free.

Upstairs, the company-subsidised canteen was like a thieves' kitchen, with a whole area set aside for stalls selling car parts and bootleg cassette tapes.

It was one of the few areas you could mix with the 'inkies' as we called them. Elsewhere there were so many demarcation lines that if you stepped in any part of the building deemed printer-controlled you risked a walkout.

In those days you typed your copy on a typewriter. A printer's assistant would take it to run off several copies on a Roneo machine, a stencil duplicator. When it was subbed it would go to the typesetters to make up the page, which would be printed using trays of 'hot metal'. Once printed, the papers would be loaded onto lorries for distribution. Each of these stages was controlled by a different union. Most of the printers made three times the national pay average. Many drew full pay without turning up for work. Many were well past retirement age. It was so tightly controlled that there was an understanding that son would replace father.

So bad were the industrial relations that *The Times* and the *Sunday Times* were closed for nearly a year under their previous owners, the Thomson Organization, in the late 1970s. When Rupert Murdoch bought the papers in 1981 to add to *The Sun* and the *News of the World*, it was understandable that he would want change.

I started working for the *Sunday Times* as a Saturday casual at its then offices in Gray's Inn Road in 1983, while Frank Giles was editor. I got my first shift through Robin Morgan. I had been Robin's chief reporter at the St Albans office of the Thomson-owned *Evening Post-Echo*. He had gone on to be a skilled feature writer for the paper and when the *Sunday Times* had re-opened after the year-long strike it had cherry-picked Robin to work there.

I have always been terrible at job interviews, and it was not the first or last time I got work because of the people I knew rather than *what* I knew. I had met Bill McLennan, an avuncular Scotsman who was a night editor at *The Sun*, on a press trip aboard the inaugural journey of Electric Scots, a train running from London to Glasgow in under five hours, and I used his name to get my first shift at *The Sun*. I had sold the *News of the World* a story but also used my friendship with Alex Marunchak, another from the St Albans office who had gone on to better things, to get in there.

The *Sunday Times* needed casuals on a Saturday because, believe it or not, some of the specialist journalists had clauses in their contracts that said they didn't have to come into the office at weekends. They weren't the only ones. One night, I got a tip from a freelance in Arizona who had heard that Truman Capote, author of *In Cold Blood*, had just been found dead in his Los Angeles home. I telephoned the police in LA and then started writing a page-one story. Needing some background, I went to our library only to find it in darkness, the door locked and the librarians long gone home. I had to break in and rifle through files of yellowing press cuttings, reading them on the floor by the light of a cigarette lighter, to get what I wanted.

Back at my desk, I rang the *LA Times* to see what they had. They did not even know he was dead. They had learned about it from a newspaper 6,000 miles away!

Murdoch wanted to break the stranglehold the unions had on his papers. Even when I started a Saturday night shift I did not know if the paper would come out the next day because the printers would down tools over some imagined slight. Frank Giles had stood down in the wake of the Hitler diaries fiasco of 1983. Murdoch had been keen to publish them after acquiring the British rights at a knockdown price from *Stern* magazine. When Hitler expert Hugh Trevor-Roper (Lord Dacre) finally expressed some doubt about their authenticity after first approving them, Murdoch responded: 'Fuck Dacre! Publish.' He knew it still made business sense. The paper put on an extra 60,000 in circulation. Rigorous forensic tests soon confirmed that the diaries were a modern forgery.

With the arrival of a young, new editor in Andrew Neil at the *Sunday Times*, Murdoch started negotiations to introduce technological innovations such as computerised typesetting, which meant most of the printers would be redundant. It was clear the unions would have nothing to do with it, so he quietly built a new plant at Wapping which would have no closed shop. The printers were offered redundancy payments of up to £30,000 each. When they rejected the offer and went on strike, Murdoch was ready to switch production to Wapping.

Some of the loftier journalists decided they would not cross the printers' picket line and became 'refuseniks'. This was a surprise to people like me who had cut their teeth in the provinces and had to watch helplessly as printers crossed our picket lines every day during an eight-week strike in 1978.

Still, it meant more work for freelances such as I. In those days I ran my own news agency from home, worked as a researcher at Thames Television, did three nights a week at *The Sun* and a 'double' on a Saturday, working for the *News of the World* during the day and the *Sunday Times* at night. Indeed, Nick Lloyd, editor of the *News of the World* and now Sir Nicholas Lloyd, recognised me at the Wapping gate on the day we moved operations and signed me safely into the building.

One day I walked through a large army of pickets camped at Tower Hill with Simon McCoy, then a fellow researcher at Thames and now a distinguished BBC newsreader. I was going for an evening shift at *The Sun*. Simon was going home to his luxury apartment on The Highway, which overlooked the plant. Suddenly I was recognised and a printer I had known from late-night poker sessions at *The Sun* gave chase. 'Thanks, Maurice,' said Simon. 'I'll have to move now!'

We were promised the earth for agreeing to man the fortress. There would be luxury restaurants, gyms and even a crèche for our children. Murdoch was gambling big time; there was a plan to buy the Fleet Street News Agency, then a lucrative operation, to man *The Sun* if not enough reporters turned up for work.

In the end, it was the free food that won us over. Wapping became like a cruise liner for a few months, where, at any time, night or day, you could go and eat your fill for free. Most of us journalists knew how to play the game but the strike-breaking electricians bussed in from Southampton to print the papers rather spoiled it for everyone. There were boxes of KitKats kept by the tills in the canteen. Most of us would take two or three bars. The electricians began to haul out whole boxes.

One of my jobs during the dispute, especially when shifting at the *Sunday Times*, was to sneak out to get copies of rival newspapers. There has always been an agency, still known throughout the industry as Dalton's, which has provided a service, picking up the first editions of each newspaper and delivering a set of papers to each news desk in turn.

This role was even more important before the advent of the internet and rolling news programmes so news editors could see what stories were breaking elsewhere and to react to them. But Dalton's could hardly cross the picket line for fear of being blacklisted by the printers at other newspapers.

So I had to slip out, meet Dalton's, get the other papers and read the headlines over the phone to the news desk back at the office. This soon became a nice earner because the *Sunday Mail*, then the biggest selling Sunday newspaper in Scotland, outselling the *News of the World* by two-to-one, latched on to what I was doing and got me to read the front pages of the London papers, especially the tabloids, to them. I could always blame the longer-than-usual time it took me to get back to the plant on having to elude the pickets.

The Sun sometimes wanted an early copy of the *Daily Mirror*, especially if they had wind of a big story. I would hang around outside the *Mirror*'s printing presses in New Fetter Lane until I saw a printer leaving on a break with a copy tucked under his arm. Usually they were happy to hand it over and go back for another. Of course, as far as the *Sun* news desk and its managing editor were concerned, I had to bribe him with a £10 note.

The oddest request I got for a newspaper was from Andrew Neil during his romance with Pamella Bordes, a former Miss India who used a separate flirtation with Donald Trelford, his rival editor at *The Observer*, whenever she wanted to wind him up.

I do not know what she said to Andrew but he was desperate to get hold of *The Observer* as soon as the first copy rolled off the presses. Perhaps he thought Bordes had spun some terrible line in the paper and he might need to take legal action. She had apparently removed cassette tapes on which he had kept an audio diary of his first months at the *Sunday Times* from beside his bed.

Anyway, I found myself outside *The Observer* press hall, then in the City near Blackfriars station. A door opened and as someone came out I slipped in, acting as if I owned the place. I walked into the press hall and picked up a copy of the paper from the conveyor belt. This is not as foolhardy as it sounds. During the start of the print run in the hot metal days, executives and print managers would regularly pluck a paper from the belt to check the ink wasn't smudging, the columns were not repeating on another page and the pages weren't creasing. I turned on my heels and walked to the exit. 'Excuse me,' said a voice from behind. Oh no, I had been caught. Terrible thoughts went through my head. What was the penalty for stealing a newspaper? Would I have a criminal record? Sheepishly, I turned around and went up to my tormentor. 'Your flies are undone, mate,' he said.

I took the paper back to Wapping and delivered it to Andrew. I don't think there was even anything in it in the end. The *News of the World* later exposed Pamella for moonlighting as a call girl while having a security pass as a researcher at the House of Commons. A week later, Peregrine Worsthorne, the editor of the *Sunday Telegraph*, published an editorial headlined 'Playboys as Editors', arguing that Neil was unfit to edit a quality newspaper. It was the old establishment snobbishness coming to the fore.

I had taken a phone call from Worsthorne asking if Andrew was in his office on a Saturday night. I suppose the inference was if he had not been in the office he was either at Tramp or Annabel's nightclubs. He may have had this 'playboy' reputation, but on Saturdays he was usually in his office until late and then ringing in from home to see what the latest news was. When Alex Butler was the night editor, he and I used to joke about the five editions of the paper: the first, the 2G, the third, the fourth and the Onslow Gardens edition. The latter was a reference to Andrew's then London address and had a print run of a few dozen copies just to show the editor we were on top of the latest news at 3 a.m. A copy would be 'biked' around to him by motorcycle messenger.

Andrew sued Worsthorne for libel as a result of the editorial, and, because of this telephone conversation, I was listed as a witness. I was not called to the stand, but after a High Court trial lasting six days Neil was awarded £1,000 damages. He probably blew that on the lunch he threw for his witnesses and his legal team at Quaglino's in St James's to celebrate. The *Sunday Telegraph* was left with a legal bill of about £200,000.

During the Wapping dispute, another of my jobs on a Saturday night was to stand on the patio outside Andrew Neil's office or climb on a ladder to the roof of the modern office block (it was supposed to be called La Lumiere but nobody used that) in the centre of the plant to observe the printers and measure their appetite for violence.

It was scary. We thought we might be killed if they broke into the plant. They would chant 'Burn it down' as they poured petrol over barriers before igniting them in a bid to block the newspaper lorries from leaving. Some had their windscreens smashed.

On the worst night, 9,000 demonstrators gathered outside. Smoke grenades, bottles, bricks, wooden staves and lumps of concrete were hurled at the police.

It went on for fifty-four weeks like this until the strike collapsed. Not a single day of production was lost during that period. It cost £4.7 million in policing and there were 1,471 arrests.

I was offered a staff job on the *Sunday Times* at £26,000 a year at the start of the dispute, but turned it down because I was earning £10,000 more as a freelance. Looking back, I must have been mad to refuse a job on what I consider the world's greatest newspaper. Most reporters would give their eye teeth for such an opportunity. Then, as the weeks passed, I was aware that other titles were less keen on taking my copy because I was so closely associated with the Murdoch stable.

Luckily, Tony Bambridge, then managing editor of news, came back after I had written separate splashes in three different

editions of *The Sun* on a Friday night about the tragic drugs
death of Olivia Channon, daughter of Paul Channon, the Tory
Trade Secretary, and then came up with a new line on the Saturday for a page lead in the *Sunday Times*. 'Andrew [Neil] insists
he has got to have you,' said Tony. This time I said yes.

It suited my style of journalism. Jonathan Holborow, the
news editor of the *Daily Mail*, once asked me at an interview (in
between bollocking a reporter for not getting carrion to entice
a runaway eagle down from a tree) whether I preferred gathering the material or writing the story. I stuttered that I enjoyed
both, but what I didn't say was that I hated having my copy
rewritten by the subs. The *Sunday Times* was a reporter's paper,
whereas *The Sun* and *News of the World* were subs' papers. In
other words, what you wrote at the *Sunday Times* usually went
into the paper more or less as you had filed it, apart from the
odd tweak from the news desk. Sub-editors, or subs, were not
supposed to change anything unless it was incorrect and they
had cleared it with the writer. Tabloids were different. The subs
were king and could change what they liked to get a better intro
or to fit a headline they had already written.

Sundays (or 'Bloody Sundays' as my pal, Ron Emler, a former
chief sub at the *Sunday Telegraph* calls them) are a different
animal entirely. Daily papers have the courts, Parliament, in-
quests and the press conferences of the previous day to report.
But nothing usually happens on a Saturday apart from sport,
which has its own section anyway. No, each week for a Sunday
paper starts on a Monday with a set of blank pages. The Sunday
journalist has to think ahead and second-guess the agenda for

the week ahead and even set that agenda with a good story. I once gave a lecture to journalism students on how to invent news, by which I did not mean making up stories, but creating page leads out of small nuggets of information, perhaps talking to people on opposing sides to manufacture a row. Matthew Norman once wrote in the *Guardian* diary that I was 'well loved for his craft in inflating small stories'. I took it as a compliment.

When 8,000 books go missing from the British Library, you forget the vanished Shakespeare and write that the first issue of the *Beano* to feature Dennis the Menace has disappeared and get yourself a page lead. Likewise, Amanda Foreman being accused of turning the genteel world of historic biography into a playground for glamorous young female writers to make a quick killing may not sound earth-shattering news. But once you build up the row, refer to the time she posed naked in *Tatler* magazine behind a pile of her books after finding success with her first book, *Georgiana: Duchess of Devonshire*, and print both that picture and one of Keira Knightley, who was to play Georgiana in the upcoming movie *The Duchess*, you have what we call a 'confection' and a guaranteed page-three lead.

Now I had a staff job and a brave new world awaited. By the end of the Wapping dispute, the fleet of coaches that had bussed staff into the plant, their windows meshed with armour, were fit only for scrap. Paul Larsmon and his camera crew from Thames Television were the first allowed inside Fortress Wapping and interviewed both Andrew Neil and me.

'Tell me, Maurice,' Paul asked me on camera. 'What difference will the end of the dispute make to your working life?'

'It means we can go out and come in as we wish,' I replied, a smile creasing my face. 'We can even perhaps get to the pub. Journalists occasionally like a drink as you probably know. We can just go out, perhaps to the bank, rather than coming in in armoured coaches and travelling out in convoys and having bricks thrown at our vehicles.'

Years later I was told by a reputable source in the security community that the brick that had hit my car had been thrown by a police agent provocateur. It made sense. Although the brick had missed my head by three feet, it had obviously been carefully thrown and it gave an excuse for the police commander to send in his cavalry.

With all the promises that had been made to us, I felt confident in presenting Peter Roberts, then managing editor of the *Sunday Times*, with the invoice for my two new car windows.

'Claim it on your car insurance,' was his response. Bang went my no-claims bonus.

CHAPTER SEVEN

DISASTER AT SEA!

It was a cold Friday evening in March 1987 and London was closing down for the weekend. Most people had deserted their offices and headed for home by Tube or car.

Not, however, in the newsroom of the *Sunday Times*. This was our busiest time, and reporters were still at their desks putting together the stories they had spent all week developing.

I was just back from Liverpool. The previous week, *The Sun* and the *Daily Star* had taken to fighting amongst themselves to save a Spanish donkey from what was alleged to be a ritual crushing to death at a fiesta. Seeking to create a mirror image, I had taken a Spanish woman journalist to the Waterloo Cup in Lancashire so that she could save a British hare from hare coursing in retaliation.

Blackie the Donkey is part of Fleet Street folklore. The *burro* was 'saved' from supposed Latin bloodlust *after* it took part in the Shrove Tuesday festival at Villanueva de la Vera, in which his predecessors were reputed to have been crushed to death under the fattest men in the village. Hugh Whittow, a suave Welshman from *The Sun* who today edits the *Daily Express*, was first to reach Blackie's owner and paid the Spaniard the equivalent of £250 to ensure the donkey lived happily ever after. But then along came Don Mackay, a tough Scot from the *Daily Star*. He paid the same Spaniard £225 to buy Blackie, obtained a receipt and put him in quarantine prior to shipping him to a donkey sanctuary in Devon. Both papers claimed to have saved the donkey from being sacrificed but the *Star* taunted *The Sun* with the same 'Gotcha!' banner headline the latter had used during the Falklands War.

My own efforts were not so heroic. I didn't realise that all the hares were wild. There was no Julio the hare locked in a cage that we could buy. In the end, we had to settle for a dead hare 'similar to Julio' that the Spanish reporter could hold for a photograph.

I was putting the finishing touches to this confection, a page lead on Sunday under the headline: 'Forget Blackie – save our Julio', when the first call came in just after 7 p.m. A British ferry, the *Herald of Free Enterprise*, had capsized after leaving the Belgian port of Zeebrugge and people were feared dead.

A shout went up in the newsroom. 'Does anybody have a passport?' Well, I still had my overnight bag from my trip to the north, and a weekend in Belgium sounded like fun. I would be home on Monday and there was always the duty free. My hand shot up.

The news desk had the brilliant idea of hiring a private jet. At such short notice, it must have cost about £5,000. In today's hard economic climate, nobody would dare suggest such a bold move. Nowadays it would be a question of rousing the staff reporter in Paris and ringing up Belgian stringers to see who was available.

I was teamed with Mazher Mahmood, the future 'Fake Sheikh', and Rowena Webster, a future BBC strategy director who clearly disapproved of our tabloid roots and methods. We piled into Mazher's Audi and hurtled down to Gatwick at speeds of up to 100 miles per hour to catch the plane.

Fortunately for us, Mazher had recently turned over a guy named Dave West, who ran the EastEnders pub and wine warehouse in Zeebrugge, for tobacco smuggling. Far from bearing a grudge, West recognised that there was no such thing as bad publicity in his line of work and welcomed us with open arms.

We were able to use his pub as our headquarters and I spent the next twenty-four hours on my feet, fuelled by lager, putting the story together.

Disasters can happen at the most inconvenient times if you are a journalist. I was called out of bed at my home in Kent at 6 a.m. after the Piper Alpha oil rig exploded in the North Sea in 1988, killing 167 workers – many of whom were watching a film in the platform's cinema at the time – in what is still regarded as the world's deadliest oil rig accident.

The Kegworth air disaster, in which a British Midland passenger plane crashed onto the embankment of the M1 motorway in Leicestershire while attempting an emergency landing, killing forty-seven passengers, happened on a Sunday evening in January 1989.

My wife and I were out at a belated New Year party and my mother had been left babysitting. When we got home at 11 p.m., she said the office had been calling me and, by the way, had I heard about this awful plane disaster on the M1? She had not put two and two together.

This time I was in less of a hurry. Well, I had had a few drinks after all. It was Sunday night so by the time the *Sunday Times* next came out the story would be a week old and there would be little left to say. I left it a good hour before calling the news editor back at his home. By that time, he had sent a colleague, Graham Brough, to the scene. Graham would spend the next week living in his car on the hard shoulder of the closed motorway.

By and large (unless it is something world-shattering like 9/11), disasters have a three-day shelf life on the front page. Day one is who, when, what, and where. For a Friday night ferry disaster, that was the easy bit, and that would fill Saturday's papers.

The Townsend-Thoresen-branded (but now P&O-owned) roll-on, roll-off car ferry *Herald of Free Enterprise* had left Zeebrugge harbour around 6.05 p.m. with eighty crew and 459 passengers. About twenty-five minutes later she had capsized. The first reports came from nearby ships, suggesting she had hit a sandbank. 193 people died as a result of the sinking.

Likewise the 2015 Shoreham air show disaster, which killed eleven people in West Sussex, happened on a Saturday afternoon and gave Richard Kerbaj and myself an easy splash in the *Sunday Times* the next day. Such a story usually fills page one, page two, page three and beyond. If you are working on it, you research past disasters and telephone experts, such as pilots and professors, and use conjecture, however inaccurate, to fill the pages.

Day two is how. In the first instance this is gleaned from survivors. By the time you have spoken to half a dozen you can put together a picture of what might have happened. That was our job once we had landed at Bruges, twelve miles from Zeebrugge.

The best place to go under such circumstances is the hospital. I am afraid there are few scruples amongst journalists when they want to get the story. A survivor lying on their back in a hospital bed makes a good photo and, filled with drugs or boredom or both, they are more likely to talk.

When we arrived at the hospital in Bruges by taxi at around 10 p.m., Kate Adie of the BBC was in full flow, leading the press pack around the wards as she followed the doctors, throwing questions at them.

Mazher and I sloped off and spent the next hour going to the bedsides of the injured. If the nurse asked, I was a relative and Maz was my driver. This way we got exclusive interviews with some of the survivors.

I knew the ship quite well. Two weeks earlier I had been on it, taking advantage of a sail-for-£1 offer in the *Sun* newspaper to buy duty-free goods. Many of those on board the night she capsized were on the same deal.

At the time of the sinking, families were settling down to meals at the fixed tables and chairs in the cafeterias, the bars were doing steady business and some passengers were still on deck watching the ferry clear the harbour walls.

Then the glasses on the tables started to tremble, and the

7,951-ton ferry began to list to port. There was, for a few moments, ribald cheering. Then pandemonium broke out as the lights went out.

As the eight-deck ferry continued to roll over, ending up at 90 degrees, three-quarters under water, the chairs and tables had suddenly become the only means of survival for the panic-stricken passengers as they were hurled up to 40ft across the decks. Anchored to the floors, they now became improvised ladders as people scrambled in the darkness to climb away from the water rushing into the vessel.

The only sounds were of screaming and the gushing noise of the water, rising first to the ankles and then to the armpits of men, women and children clinging at different heights to the tables and chairs. The only light came from the 6ft square windows, now acting as skylights above them, with those at the top trying to smash their way out.

One of those I interviewed was Stan Mason, a soldier from Wigan who was returning from a tour of duty in Germany with his wife Catherine and their four-month-old daughter Kerry.

Mason was in a wheelchair, suffering from spinal injuries he had received in the disaster. He told me: 'As the ship started to tilt, with one hand I grabbed my wife. I caught her arm but as it began rolling over I felt her slip away. I grabbed Kerry with my teeth to hold on to her as I desperately searched in the darkness for Catherine. I didn't see her.' Sadly, Catherine Mason, aged twenty-eight, was amongst those who died.

Over the course of an hour I had gleaned half a dozen interviews. When I got back to the EastEnders pub, I filed from my notebook, starting with the story of how a man in a wheel-chair had described saving his baby in his teeth. In those days, we shared the same copytakers with the other newspapers at Wapping.

Saturday was spent gathering more information and follow-ing Margaret Thatcher's heels as she cancelled plans to attend a Conservative conference on local government and flew to visit survivors in hospitals in Bruges and at hotels around Zee-brugge. I bumped into David Rigby, a reporter from the *News of the World*. He told me there was talk at Wapping of a man in a wheelchair telling how he had saved his child in his teeth. I was not surprised. The *News of the World* would have copytakers on their payroll to tip them off about any good stories being filed to other newspapers in the group that might interest them. Years later, they were reputed to have regularly hacked into the *Sunday Times* news list, which was presented to the editor at the Thursday morning editorial conference. Anyway, David asked me to file my copy to the *Screws*. He was a mate. It was our sister paper. I agreed.

There was an invitation to return to the hospital from the Belgian authorities. These sort of 'facility' trips to see survivors willing to talk are often offered in such circumstances, the idea being that it will slake the media's interest and leave other vic-tims to recover in peace.

Michael and Maureen Bennett from Crawley in Sussex were also travelling aboard the *Herald of Free Enterprise* on the *Sun* offer and they had reason to want publicity.

As they lay side by side in twin hospital beds, a priest giving them words of comfort, Maureen Bennett told me: 'I am desperate to find out what has happened to my daughter Theresa. She and her boyfriend were aboard and we haven't seen them.'

As we crowded around the bed for more details, a hospital orderly burst through the throng and told her: 'Your daughter is alive and well and upstairs in another ward.'

The Bennetts clutched hands across the gap between their beds and burst into tears. 'She's alive, she's alive,' said Maureen. 'Thank God.'

I still don't know if it was a carefully planned piece of news management by the hospital, but I don't mind admitting I had a tear in my eye too.

It was a lot more dignified than the scenes in the Aberdeen hospital after Piper Alpha a year or so later. I remember a Canadian journalist going from ward to ward shouting: 'Any Newfoundlanders killed or injured?' It brought to mind the hopefully apocryphal tale from the 1960s Belgian Congo, when journalists were reported to have run over to a party of nuns and yelled: 'Anyone here been raped and speak English?'

Half an hour later, Theresa Bennett, just twenty years old, suffering from a broken arm and unconscious, was wheeled to the Bennetts' bedside. They had been on a day trip to Belgium to celebrate their wedding anniversary.

Maureen Bennett said:

Michael and I had gone into the restaurant and were sitting with cups of coffee. We'd separated from Theresa and her boyfriend. We left them upstairs minding the luggage.

Suddenly everything was turning on its side. The windows cracked and water came rushing in. I just panicked. I can't swim. The boat just started to tilt and next minute it was gone onto its side. I was up to my armpits and trying to clamber and climb up to safety.

Everybody was trying to find things to hang on to but the flood of the water was breaking the tables up. The far end of the restaurant was completely under water. It was half an hour before the rescue teams broke in.

Day three of any disaster is usually when you as a journalist ask why it happened (or, more often than not, who is to blame). For Sunday newspapers, the days can seem to stretch far ahead if a disaster happens too early in the week. Piper Alpha happened on a Wednesday night, which meant we were always playing catch-up. I remember focusing on one good nugget: what film the men were watching in the rig's cinema when it exploded. After scouting for film schedules and interviewing workers who were on leave when it happened, I managed to come up with *Brewster's Millions*, the 1985 film starring Richard Pryor and John Candy in which a man has to spend a fortune to claim an inheritance. Such a good piece of colour can really lift a four-page 'focus' on a disaster days after it has happened. The *Sunday Times* will always print such long reads, complete with timelines, detailed graphics and huge photographs because the reader expects to see them, not necessarily because he or she intends to read them. Tony Bambridge, the paper's managing editor, coined the wonderful phrase 'the dignity of unread print' to describe them. He also had a poster on his office wall that said: 'You will not find yesterday's fish in the house of the otter'. The allegory was not lost on us reporters. Luckily, Paul 'Red' Adair, a 73-year-old Texan firefighting specialist, was lowered onto the platform on the Saturday to cap the fire and this gave us our page-one story.

The *Sunday Times* had run an article a year before under the headline: 'Safety Fear On "High Rise" Ferries'. The contacts we had made then gave us something of a head start in exploring the causes of the disaster. We sent reporters to Dover. One, Steve Ellis, was so conscientious photocopying the marine plans of P&O's fleet of ships and faxing them to London that investigators from the Department of Transport had to wait for him to finish.

We knew early on from talking to lorry drivers that, in the rush to leave port, the bow doors of the ferry were left open until she was at sea. The *Herald* was late leaving Zeebrugge. But the blame at Zeebrugge was always going to be about the company, not the man who left the doors open.

The page-one headline in the *Sunday Times* the next day was: 'Ferry Mystery: Were the Loading Doors Left Open?' They were indeed. The boatswain whose job it was to close them had been asleep. A coroner's inquest jury subsequently returned verdicts of unlawful killing. P&O European Ferries (Dover) Ltd was charged with corporate manslaughter and seven of its employees were accused of gross negligence. The case later collapsed after a judge ordered a jury to acquit the company and five of the defendants.

It was not this headline, but that of the *News of the World*, that drew my attention, however: 'Baby Saved in Dad's Teeth'. It told the gripping story of a man in a wheelchair who had rescued his daughter, apparently wheeling his chair uphill at a 90-degree angle away from the rising sea water. Was this, I ask myself, the first recorded example of fake news?

CHAPTER EIGHT

THE DEMON FIXER OF FLEET STREET

The pictures on the wall of Max Clifford's office two flights of stairs up above London's New Bond Street told their own story of success about Britain's self-proclaimed greatest publicity agent. There was the photograph of the Beatles, whose first single he claims he helped push into the charts. There was *The Sun*'s front-page headline: 'Freddie Starr Ate My Hamster', behind which was the motive of putting a fading comedian back in the spotlight.

I first met Max when I was working for the *News of the World* and was sent one hot summer's day to the home of the latest young showgirl linked to Prince Andrew at the time he was enjoying his 'Randy Andy' tabloid reputation.

But who should answer the door? As it turned out, it was not some bubbly blonde as I had been expecting, but a half-naked forty-something towelling his wet hair and upper torso.

'Excuse me, Maurice,' he said after I introduced myself. 'But it was so hot when I got here that I needed a shower.'

A likely story, but then Max Clifford made his living from fixing likely stories to sell to the media that were just on the right side of plausible. It was also perhaps strangely prophetic of the hot water (and prison cell) he was to land himself in later.

I did not tell anyone about Max's indiscretion. It was none of my business. But I think Max thought he owed me a favour. He seemed to take a shine to me immediately and would often call me 'Young Maurice'. Over the next few years I was invited to his home in Raynes Park, south-west London, to meet his wife and Louise, their disabled daughter to whom he was devoted, and was sometimes given lifts in his white Rolls-Royce (the models changed but the number plate was always 100 MAX).

Louise, a teenager when I first met her, suffers from the rheumatoid arthritis that attacks the joints. Her father had just set up his business, Max Clifford Associates, when she developed a swollen finger, the first symptom of a condition that has left her in terrible pain and limited her ability to walk or write. Nevertheless, she was to work for her father for fifteen years until his downfall.

His business involved 'packing the facts (or what he claimed were the facts) for the hacks'. He was at the early summit of what turned out to be a slippery slope – one that would end with the tabloid press in a quagmire of legal disputes at the start of this century.

Maybe one of the reasons Clifford took a shine to me was that we had followed a similar path into journalism from school. He liked it to be known that he went to school just 400 yards away from John Major and at the same time. According to Clifford, the sports editor of the local paper saw him box, play water polo and football, and paid him, while still a schoolboy, to write reports. On his own matches. Naturally, his performance always merited particular praise.

When he left school, his older brother Bernard used his print union connections to get him a job as an editorial assistant at the *Eagle* comic. There were similarities with my start at Pergamon Press. Armed with an NUJ card, he was able to get a job as a trainee reporter on his local paper. While there, he opened a discotheque and promoted it through the paper's columns. He too progressed to record reviews, selling the free records on through a friend who did haircuts at Chelsea barracks.

At the age of nineteen, he was offered a job in the EMI press office promoting records. His first assignment was the Beatles' 'Love Me Do'. Later came Tamla Motown, Jimi Hendrix, Cream and the Bee Gees.

Starting his own firm at the age of twenty-seven, Clifford went on to redefine the role of PR man. Instead of begging newspapers for a column inch, he had tabloids coming to him, competing with each other for the ready-made 'stories' he provided. The cast always included at least one person desperate for publicity.

The classic, of course, was 'Freddie Starr Ate My Hamster', which gave *The Sun* such a boost that a few weeks after it had moved its operation to Fortress Wapping in east London. It has since been nominated as one of the most familiar newspaper headlines of the past century.

Clifford always claimed that it was not him who started the

'story'. Starr had been staying at the home of Vince McCaffrey, a friend and writer, in Birchwood, Cheshire, because the two were supposed to be writing a book together. Starr's erratic behaviour soon got the better of Lea La Salle, McCaffrey's girl-friend. She claimed that Starr came home in the early hours after a nightclub performance and demanded that she make him a sandwich. She refused and Starr is supposed to have gone into the kitchen, put her pet hamster Supersonic between two slices of bread and eaten it. I suspect he merely threatened to eat the pet as a joke. Starr had at one time been a rock singer, and the story should have been familiar with anyone who had heard the tale about Ozzy Osbourne biting the head off a bat a few years earlier.

La Salle is supposed to have contacted *The Sun*'s Manchester office about the story. Kelvin MacKenzie, seeing the potential, was desperate to run it. Clifford had been Starr's publicity agent and he persuaded the comedian that the story would boost his career rather than damage his reputation. He told me later he had merely 'encouraged' a true story to be made public. He told Starr that any of his fans who could actually read would not be too upset to find he had 'eaten a hamster'.

The story ran under the byline of Dick Saxty, a hard-drinking cotsman who had originally joined *The Sun* when it was a harm-less broadsheet, before it was owned by Murdoch. Initially, as Clifford had predicted, the story gave Starr's career a boost. He was about to go on a tour that had until that day not been doing too well with its bookings. It sold out within hours of the sto-ry's publication and another twelve dates were added, earning him an estimated extra £1 million. Over the years, however, the comedian tired of being stopped in the street by people asking him if it was really true. In his 2001 autobiography, *Unwrapped*, Starr said the story was completely fabricated: 'I have never eaten or even nibbled a live hamster, gerbil, guinea pig, mouse, shrew, vole or any other small mammal,' he said.

●　●　●

'I *love* the telephone. I love talking to my friends.'

David Mellor, the Tory Cabinet minister, is speaking on *Desert Island Discs* in July 1992. His chosen luxury is 'a telephone (disconnected)'. One of his chosen pieces of music is Jussi Björling, the opera tenor, singing 'Sa Tag Mit Hjerte' ('Now Take My Heart'). A few weeks later Max Clifford was to take his reputation.

Eight months earlier, Mellor, who had become Chief Secretary to the Treasury in John Major's new Cabinet, had become a target for the tabloid press after he appeared on the Channel 4 magazine programme *Hard News* in the wake of the establishment of Sir David Calcutt's inquiry into press standards.

'The press – the popular press – is drinking in the Last Chance Saloon,' he said. It was a great quote. (At one time I thought of calling this book *Bartender in the Last Chance Saloon*.) But it infuriated newspaper proprietors and editors who claimed he was prejudging the findings of the inquiry.

Enter Antonia de Sancha, the 6ft, thirty-year-old star of a soft porn film in which she simulated sex with a pizza delivery man.

Mellor fell for her after they were introduced by Paul Halloran, the chief investigative reporter for *Private Eye*, and the pair would cavort at her Earl's Court flat.

The affair was exposed after Nick Philp, the owner of the flat, bugged his own phone and sold the tapes to the *People* newspaper. It was not illegal to bug a phone in those days but, to be on the safe side, a story was concocted that a microphone had been dangled from the flat above to catch their lovemaking through an open window.

When news of the affair broke, many of Clifford's contacts thought they detected his fingerprints on the story. In fact, he was not involved until de Sancha's theatrical agent called him more than a week later.

A deal was struck: Clifford would work with them on condition that de Sancha was prepared to do what she was told. The plan was simple: to make as much money as possible for both of them while her name still had cachet.

Within twenty-four hours, she made her first public appearance with Clifford at the premiere of the Tom Cruise film *Far and Away*. He claimed to be unaware that John and Norma Major would also be there, but the fact that they were guaranteed headlines the next morning. The following day was also to be de Sancha's television debut, for which Clifford schooled her to the last detail, even scripting an apparent ad lib that 'if all else fails I shall become a chiropodist'.

It was an odd choice of future profession, but Clifford was working on details of his masterstroke: the kiss and tell. Paparazzi pictures had emerged the previous month of John

Bryan, an American financial manager, apparently in the act of sucking on the toes of a topless Sarah Ferguson, the Duchess of York, in the south of France.

From the TV studio, he took de Sancha to Cheerleaders club in Manchester (by happy coincidence another of his clients). There had been a piece in the *Manchester Evening News* that said de Sancha would be there (Clifford had telephoned to tell them), so the venue was filled – to everybody's advantage.

Meanwhile, Clifford was offering de Sancha's story to various tabloids, including the *News of the World*, the *Daily Mirror* and *The Sun*. But there was a problem: de Sancha had vowed in an interview with *The Independent* before Clifford was involved never to 'kiss and tell' on her relationship with Mellor. A solution was devised that will be familiar to newsrooms around the world. De Sancha would not speak, but a 'friend' would tell her whole story instead.

Joanna Horaim Ashbourn, who had written and self-published her first novel and needed help to shift the stacks of unsold copies, duly obliged. Clifford, of course, added all the necessary saucy details.

'Mellor Made Love in Chelsea Strip' ran the headline of the *Sun* splash alongside a photograph of the politician mocked up in the kit of his favourite football team. There were tales of toe-sucking and spanking. *The Sun* paid £20,000 for it.

I smelled a rat. Two years earlier, I had been offered a job by Patsy Chapman, the editor of the *News of the World*, but had been 'bought' back by the *Sunday Times* for a £10,000 pay rise before I could leave. I had biked bottles of champagne around to each of the *News of the World* executives who had been involved in hiring me so I still had plenty of goodwill at the paper. I discovered that, five years before the Mellor story, Clifford had offered to sell a story involving Derek Hatton, the former deputy leader of Liverpool City Council, making love to a girl while dressed in an Everton kit.

Investigating further, I discovered that Ashbourn was also a client of Clifford's. She had claimed in one interview that her friendship with de Sancha had formed after she had nursed the actress's pet hedgehog, Bill, to health. Now she claimed she had approached *The Sun* without de Sancha's knowledge to 'set the record straight' after meeting a female journalist from *The Sun* at a sale in Marks & Spencer in Oxford Street.

'Our hands met over the jumpers,' she said. 'We both went for the same turquoise jumper. "Give it to me, I'm from *The Sun*," she said. I said, "Give it to me and I will tell you a story."'

What rubbish. I soon found out that the reporter who wrote the 'as told to' stories in *The Sun* had spent ten days interviewing de Sancha in a London hotel before whisking her away to the south of France, while Ashbourn stayed at home with her husband, two daughters and her own sick hedgehog called Gabby.

I went to see Clifford at his office. Just how did he manage to put both the discarded flower and the unknown author on the front pages? It was a testament to his skill in manipulating stories, or 'directing traffic' as he described it, that he not only succeeded but now refused to acknowledge his achievement. As if to write a hidden signature, he had sold a new story to *The Sun* about de Sancha having a new boyfriend, a French waiter who supported Arsenal. He suggested the paper bring an Arsenal football shirt for him to wear as they snapped them together. This time de Sancha was prepared to kiss and tell: 'He can make love all night. The first night was amazing. I was exhausted.'

De Sancha made about £35,000 in all from her moment in the spotlight – Clifford probably just as much. As for Ashbourn, whenever she was interviewed there would be a plug for her book.

'Max,' I said to him. 'Both of these women are your clients.'

'But people don't know that,' he said with a wide grin. 'There's nothing I can say, is there? You can't ask me to shoot myself in the foot.'

But had these women ever met? I asked him. He laughed.

My story was published on page one of the *Sunday Times* that weekend under the headline: 'Revealed: Chinks in Stories That Pilloried Mellor'. It ran next to a picture of a cheerful Mellor at a Chelsea home game the previous day, dressed in a suit rather than a Chelsea strip. He was cheered by home supporters who sang 'There's only one David Mellor' and 'Throw us your shirt, David.' His long-suffering wife Judith had confided that, while he owned a Chelsea tracksuit, he had never had a team shirt or shorts.

Mellor told me: 'The story about the Chelsea kit is pure fantasy. It's disgusting that such a man as Clifford can be accepted by newspapers as a witness of truth.'

Nine days after my story was published, Mellor was gone. While the grandees of the Tory Party had decided that the affair was not a resigning matter, his enemies used the scandal to drag up a story about a Mellor family holiday hosted by Sheikh Zayed, the ruler of the UAE.

A few days later, with Mozart on the CD player and his curtains drawn against prying photographers, he gave me his first full interview since resigning, at his London home. 'The press will use any stick to beat me and I came to question whether I could expect my colleagues to put up with it as well,' he said.

Mellor lost his Putney seat at the 1997 election. De Sancha went on to do a stint as the agony aunt of the magazine *Erotic Review*. 'The Chelsea strip was made up,' she said in a 2013 interview with *The Independent*. 'I went along with everything at the time. It was almost like I was having an out-of-body experience.' Asked to sum up the whole episode, she said: 'Screwed by Mellor, screwed by Max.'

Clifford, however, went on packaging his stories. He always told me that he was not just motivated by the money but also the hypocrisy he found in public life. It is why he enjoyed stories like David Mellor's.

We had many more dealings over the years, but in 2012 he was arrested by police as part of Operation Yewtree which had been set up in the wake of the Jimmy Savile scandal. In May 2014, he was sentenced to eight years in prison for a series of indecent assaults on children and young women. He is due for release in 2018.

CHAPTER NINE

DON'T BASH THE BISHOP!

When is it okay to halt a religious procession in its tracks? When you are desperate for a quote, of course.

It was Good Friday and I was in Lincoln, waiting in the shadows of its great cathedral, for 250 years in medieval times the tallest building in the world. I had soaked up the atmosphere and had a splendid lunch of Lincolnshire lamb and Jerusalem artichokes in the twelfth-century Jew's House, one of Europe's oldest remaining houses which was now a restaurant on the city's Steep Hill.

All that was missing was an interview with Brandon Jackson, the dean, who had caused a huge rift in the cloisters by questioning a controversial fund-raising visit to Australia. The Lincolnshire police had previously been called in to investigate but found no evidence of wrongdoing. Jackson had stonewalled me when I'd tried to speak to him.

Lincoln Cathedral houses a 1215 copy of Magna Carta, the first charter to document the freedom of the Church and the liberties of the people. It is the only original copy that is still in sufficiently good condition to travel.

Canon Rex Davis had taken the copy to his native Australia for a six-month exhibition, which cost £600,000, attracted a million visitors and yet returned with only £938 in donations. Davis took his wife and daughter with him on what Robert 'Bob' Hardy, the Bishop of Lincoln, had said 'looked to outsiders as a good excuse for a family outing'. The adventure left Lincoln with a £56,075 debt and a lorry-load of unwanted souvenir booklets.

When Jackson arrived from Bradford Cathedral, on the appointment of Prime Minister Margaret Thatcher no less, he launched an internal inquiry which signalled the start of hostilities between the new dean and the cathedral's canons.

A modern parallel to the parable of the widow's mite illustrated the divide. A former parishioner from Bradford came up to Jackson in Lincoln Cathedral and said: 'I've been collecting 20p pieces in a jar on the mantelpiece until I had £20. I've been thinking what charity to give it to and I thought of you, Brandon,' she said.

A few days after he gratefully took the money for the cathedral funds, Jackson was studying items of expenditure at a chapter meeting. He allegedly discovered that Davis had spent £48 from the funds on a dog gate for Rosie, his golden cocker spaniel, at the house where he lived rent-free in the cathedral yard.

Jackson objected to a life-sized golden statue of a naked man in the 919-year-old minster. He soon found it had been moved to the spot where he knelt in prayer before a service. Every time he gazed up, he found himself looking into the figure's genitals.

I had covered a previous clerical dispute over a historical document three years earlier, when the Dean of Hereford Cathedral determined to solve a £7 million financial crisis in the diocese by selling its Mappa Mundi, a map of the world showing Jerusalem at its centre and dating to 1300. The National Heritage Memorial Fund offered to give the cathedral up to £2 million if it withdrew the map from sale at Sotheby's. After much controversy, large donations from the fund, Paul Getty and the public kept the map in Hereford and paid for a new centre to house both the map and the cathedral's chained library.

However, as I delved into the Lincoln row, I realised this was more a dispute between personalities than it was a row over money. The more I dug into the affair, I discovered it had more twists than Anthony Trollope's *Barchester Chronicles*.

Davis and his fellow canons had invoked a bishop's statute of 1439 accusing Jackson of meddling in their affairs. They claimed that the dean, while espousing concern for starving people in Africa, had had two successive houses refurbished for his accommodation since he arrived.

Jackson was censured after Bishop Hardy conducted a visitation, an official inquiry without precedent for a century. 'It all seems a long way from Jesus of Nazareth,' the bishop concluded.

The dean was also charged with publicly slighting his fellow clerics. He had accused Canon David Rutter, the cathedral's blind precentor, of being too disabled for evensong, but able 'to see plenty well enough to trot off for lunch in the White Hart'.

Rutter, who insisted that he had not been to the hotel since

Boxing Day, said he would not give in. 'I will die in office. I spend my time praying, thinking, brooding,' he told me.

The strain was telling on Russell Pond, the chapter clerk, who kept a picture of a teddy bear on his office wall. 'Why?' I asked. 'After a chapter meeting, it is very calming to go to bed with a teddy,' he said.

The fraud squad had occupied his office to pore over the minutes of the chapter meeting, which are locked from public view for thirty years. Twice he and his wife had given up their home while the dean and canons sat in their front room to thrash out differences at six-hour psychotherapy sessions organised by Brian Thorne, head of counselling at the University of East Anglia.

Given the atmosphere, it was not surprising that the dean did not want to try to pour oil on troubled waters, but Davis and his family were on holiday in the United States and I needed words with at least one of the main combatants in the dispute to make my story work.

As he made a procession towards the cathedral in his cassock, buttoned at the collar, with some of his sub-deans in tow for the Good Friday service, I stepped from the pavement to ask him questions.

He still did not want to talk about the cathedral's affairs. Were the counselling sessions working? I asked in desperation.

'I know it's a waste of time,' he said. 'They know it's a waste of time. But if I was to say that, they would point a finger and say, "See, we mean to conciliate. You don't."'

It was enough. My last task was to pick up an order of service for Easter Sunday. The story about the feuding clerics was a page lead across eight columns in the *Sunday Times* that day.

'Riven Cathedral Brings in the Freud Squad' was the clever headline the subs put on it.

'When Lincoln Cathedral choir bursts into "The strife is o'er, the battle done" at Easter morning service today, the Bishop of Lincoln will pray for peace among his warring clergy,' I wrote.

It is a prayer that Robert Hardy has offered daily for two years. Until divine intervention comes, he is pinning his hopes on an unorthodox cure: psychotherapy.

Once a month as Great Tom, the cathedral bell, tolls 10 a.m. Brandon Jackson, his dean, and four resident canons meet to shout out their anger in front of a professional counsellor, whose task possibly requires greater familiarity with the works of Freud than those of the Almighty.

It was not the end of Lincoln's problems. The sniping between the dean and the canons went on for another six years. At one stage Jackson faced a consistory court (an ecclesiastical hearing established by a charter of William the Conqueror) on charges of sexual misconduct with a female verger but he was acquitted. Dr George Carey, the Archbishop of Canterbury, was eventually forced to intervene in 1997 and Jackson left Lincoln. There was a new rift, however, when an attempt was made to sack Colin Walsh, the cathedral's venerated organist. Eventually, though, the waters stilled, and the copy of Magna Carta even went back to Australia in 2014.

Until I went to Lincoln I had led a charmed life when it came to the Church. I was chief reporter of the *Evening Post-Echo* in St Albans in the 1970s. My family and I had moved to the city with its wonderful cathedral and even more wonderful bishop.

Robert Runcie was a lovely man who, unlike the Dean of Lincoln, was very press-friendly. He was not the sort to lead a cloistered life. P. G. Wodehouse would have loved him: tall and upright, he bred prize-winning Berkshire pigs and had been a tank commander in the Scots Guards during World War Two. He saw action across northern Europe following D-Day and won the Military Cross for rescuing another soldier from a blazing tank while under heavy fire. Years later he would say he was the first Archbishop of Canterbury since Thomas a Becket to have been into battle. Not your stereotype of an uptight clergyman. He would often invite me into his home to discuss his latest mission or give his, admittedly left-wing, view on the topics of the day.

What a gifted household it was. I would be shown in by Richard Chartres, his young chaplain who was to rise through the ranks to become Bishop of London. His wife Rosalind, 'Lindy' to her friends and a gifted pianist, might be seated at the piano rehearsing for a recital. The daughter, by bizarre coincidence, of a Military Cross holder, she was like a breath of fresh air. She, like Runcie, did not give a fig leaf for keeping up sanctimonious appearances. She hated the sound of church bells and once said that 'too much religion makes me go pop!' Peter Green, a rival on the *Herts Advertiser*, the local weekly, even managed to persuade her to pose, vamp-like in a black evening dress, atop her piano for a photoshoot, which even I felt a little risqué for a bishop's wife and which, needless to say, several years later was picked up by the *Daily Star*.

There would be their son James, the future author of the *Grantchester* books, and their daughter Rebecca, who went on to work for a top PR company. James had a pet nickname within the family: 'Seven Sherries Runcie'. It dated back to the time when he was seven years old and his father was running a theological college near Oxford. One Sunday after church, some of the students decided to let him join their post-church sherry party, with predictable results. The fact that his parents were able to laugh and joke about it is testament to the love and warmth in that family.

When Dr Donald Coggan announced his forthcoming retirement as Archbishop of Canterbury in 1979, it was inevitable that Runcie would be linked with the post. The official announcement came shortly before lunch and the *Evening Post-Echo* was first to press that afternoon with my splash, 'Runcie is Named as Archbishop'. (The 'Latest' section on the same page, a half-column left blank for breaking news from the wires, announced the closure of *Reveille*, a Mirror Group weekly that was one of the first print casualties, and a quote from Robert Mugabe, who had been vilified in the press as a savage rebel but who, on emerging from the bush, had all the eloquence and diction that was expected of an archbishop.)

Runcie told me he was genuinely astonished at the Church's choice. As he arrived at a press conference at Church House, Westminster, he told the assembled journalists: 'I hope you won't eat me up, I'm not used to press conferences of this size. When I was appointed Bishop of St Albans I remember reporters asking me everything from my promotion prospects to the promotion hopes of Luton Town Football Club.'

Runcie had a short honeymoon period as archbishop with the press. His words graced the wedding of Charles and Diana ('Here is the stuff of which fairy tales are made'), he greeted Pope John Paul II as the first pontiff ever to visit Canterbury Cathedral, and he deployed Terry Waite as his 'special envoy' to rescue hostages in the Middle East.

The relationship soured when he spoke critically of the Falklands War. He then became a target for the right-wing press, which tried to drag his marriage through the mud. The couple were forced to issue a formal statement to confirm they had been 'a happily married couple for nearly thirty years, and we both look forward to our rewarding partnership continuing for the rest of our lives'. Rosalind got her own revenge in literal terms. She was holding a press conference to publicise her campaign for funds to restock the gardens at Lambeth Palace, hardly a newsworthy event, when forty journalists turned up. She knew what their agenda would be. So, looking at their polished Oxford brogues and fancy high heels, she put on her Wellingtons and insisted on leading them through the mud and puddles of the garden.

Meanwhile, after refusing to support the Falklands War, her husband infuriated Margaret Thatcher further by speaking out about the emergence in Britain of a 'Pharisee society' of self-interest and intolerance.

When Runcie retired in 1991, a few months ahead of his seventieth birthday and deeply regretting that Waite was still being held hostage in Lebanon (he was eventually released that November after almost five years in captivity), he and his wife retired to a modest terraced home near St Albans city centre, where their rewarding partnership continued for another decade before he died.

I was never a religious affairs correspondent. If the newspaper reporter is a dying breed, then the religious affairs correspondent is the dodo. Fleet Street's last full-time religious affairs post was axed in 2014 when Ruth Gledhill left *The Times* after twenty-seven years. 'I'll admit it was a shock when I was told, but then again I am the last one left,' she said. 'So I did feel the post was probably vulnerable in the present climate.'

By then the last religious affairs correspondent on the *Sunday Times* had already departed. Chris Morgan should have had a head start in the role. A committed Anglo-Catholic, he had been best man at the wedding of his friend Rowan Williams in 1981. When Williams became Archbishop of Canterbury in 2002, Morgan had already been the *Sunday Times* religious affairs correspondent for five years.

It should have been a marriage made in heaven, but the relationship eventually deteriorated because of the pressure on Morgan to produce good stories. He always got very excited about any minor schism in the Church and probably took the need to get stories in the paper too seriously. If one was turned down, his face would redden as he charged up to any executive he could find in the office to argue the merit of his story, not realising that this was not how it was done. I christened him 'the Papal Bull' because of this and it was a nickname that both stuck and which he rather liked.

A bon viveur, he enjoyed his lunches at the Savoy and the Connaught. But, sadly, his own inner demons got the better of him. I do not know if it was the death of his mother, his closet homosexuality, the break-up of a relationship or financial pressures after he 'left' the *Sunday Times* to go freelance, but he suffered from clinical depression. On Friday 30 May 2008, he climbed off the platform at Kings Langley railway station and bowed his head one last time – into the path of a Manchester to Euston express. Charles Hymas, then news editor, rang me two days later to break the news after he had been formally identified.

'Christopher Morgan – The Loss of a Wonderfully Kind and Decent Man' ran the headline above Mick Smith's obituary in *The Times* the next day. I could not put it better myself. RIP Chris.

CHAPTER TEN

HOAXBUSTERS

Walk up to the True Crime section in any bookshop or library and you will find the shelves stacked with books written about Jack the Ripper, Britain's first and most infamous serial killer. Pick one out, take a peek at the index in the back and, chances are, you will find my name.

I am public enemy number one to many of these so-called Ripperologists. My crime? Revealing that a convenient and tidy solution to the case, that the Ripper was in fact a man named James Maybrick, who had been poisoned by his wife, was a hoax.

I may have arrived too late to save Rupert Murdoch from the Hitler diaries fiasco ten years earlier, but I did save him £25,000 and another red face by proving that the diary of Jack the Ripper was a forgery.

The case started for me in June 1993. A publisher named Robert Smith had approached the *Sunday Times* a few weeks earlier and claimed he had a 'sensational document'. At subsequent meetings with the paper's executives he revealed he had acquired the rights to the diary and knew exactly who the Ripper was.

The *Sunday Times* had done a tentative deal to serialise the document in its News Review section and had paid a non-returnable advance of £5,000. I was asked to do due diligence on the diary to make sure we weren't going to be left with egg on our face again.

I teamed up with a bright young reporter named Chris Lloyd, nephew of Christopher Lloyd, the gardener of Great Dixter fame. By chance I had visited Madame Tussauds' Chamber of Horrors with my family earlier that year so I was quite familiar with the legend. To immerse ourselves in all things Ripper, I took Chris with me on a guided tour around his haunts, visiting murder scenes and the Ten Bells pub, where his prostitute victims drank.

Next morning, we went to see Robert Smith, who was to publish the diary as part of a book on the Ripper. The first hour was taken up with signing stringent confidentiality statements before we were allowed a glimpse of the diary. The agreements barred us from divulging the contents of the book if we decided not to take up the option to serialise.

The black-and-gilt leather-bound book supposedly contained the confessions of Maybrick, a Liverpool cotton merchant, scrawled across yellowing pages. At first sight, it looked as if it might be genuine. Maybrick had been poisoned with arsenic in May 1889, six months after the last murder generally credited to the Ripper.

The murders had coincided with a new appetite for crime in Victorian Britain. Sherlock Holmes had made his first appearance the previous Christmas and newspapers like the *Pall Mall Gazette*, the *Illustrated Police News* and *The People* were ready to adopt a tabloid-like attitude in their coverage of the slayings.

The name Jack the Ripper was given to the killer after a letter signed with that name was sent to the Central News Agency in London. It is widely thought that it was written by a journalist with a creative imagination. As if the press would make things up! (I once covered the case of a sex offender with a strange fetish that led him to run up to women in the street and cut their hair off with scissors. Naturally I dubbed him 'Jack the Clipper'.)

The Metropolitan Police files for those ten weeks of terror in London's East End offer only three suspects by name: Montague Druitt, Aaron Kosminski and Michael Ostrog. Since then, more than eighty names have been put forward, including royals, artists, Americans, doctors and lawyers. Even Oscar Wilde and Dr Barnardo, the founder of the children's homes, have been mentioned in connection with the case. Now we were being given a new name. The twist was that this suspect was himself a murder victim.

If the diary was to be believed, Maybrick had travelled to London at weekends to murder and mutilate prostitutes in twisted revenge for his wife's adultery.

The man who laid claim to ownership of the diary was Michael Barrett, a 41-year-old former scrap metal dealer and now would-be journalist who was now reduced to living on £68-a-week invalidity benefit as a kidney patient. The day after our meeting with Smith, I flew up north to meet him.

With his bushy hair and Liverpudlian accent, Barrett did not have the glibness you usually associate with conmen. But he was suspicious of my motives and I soon got used to a pet phrase he used to justify his claims. 'If you tell the truth you cannot get into trouble for telling the truth,' he would say.

Together we went to the Saddle, a pub stranded on a street corner between the Liverpool and Everton football grounds that still looked much as it must have done in Victorian times.

Here he and Tony Devereux, a sixty-year-old retired printer from the *Liverpool Echo*, would sit drinking in the afternoon before Barrett left to meet his daughter from school. Two summers earlier, Devereux, then a sick man, had handed him a brown paper parcel in the pub and told him to go away and do something with it.

Barrett told me he took the parcel back to his Victorian terraced home in Anfield and opened it up. Inside was a 9,000-word journal.

'On the last page was the signature of Jack the Ripper,' said Barrett. 'I telephoned Tony and asked what the hell he was playing at. He said he wasn't playing. It was impossible for him to write this diary; he didn't have the capability. I asked him who else knew about it. "No bugger alive today," he said.'

I found it interesting that Barrett was so keen to raise and then discount the idea that the document was a recent concoction at such an early stage in our discussions.

The diary mentioned the author's return to Battlecrease. The supposition was that it had been found at Battlecrease House, the Maybricks' home near the banks of the Mersey in the suburb of Aigburth. I went there next to meet Paul Dodd, the deputy head of a primary school and the house's present-day owner. He knew nothing of the diary, but, shortly before it appeared, workmen had carried out rewiring work at the house.

We were supposed to assume that, raising a floorboard in Maybrick's old bedroom, workmen had discovered the journal. But why would they give it to Devereux? And why would the printer entrust it to Barrett, a man whose journalistic endeavours so far consisted of devising word puzzles and writing about Kylie Minogue for *Look-in*, a children's magazine?

It all smelled fishy and I flew back to London determined to prove whether the journal was the publishing coup of the decade or a hoax.

I found it curious that the first twenty four pages of the journal were missing. Indeed, the diary started in mid-sentence: 'what they have in store for them they would stop this instant.' The pages had obviously been cut out, probably with a knife.

At his office in Islington, north London, Smith, the publisher planning a 250,000-copy print run of the book, suggested that Maybrick ripped the pages out because there was material he did not want people to see.

It was clearly essential to submit the paper and ink to forensic tests. This is what finally nailed the Hitler diaries as forgeries: they were written on pages containing synthetic fibres not used in the manufacture of paper before the mid-1950s.

Smith presented us with a forensic report by Dr Nicholas Eastaugh, which said there were no modern fibres in the paper and that the ink contained significant amounts of iron not found in modern inks.

Unconvinced, I returned to the office and decided that Chris Lloyd and I would assemble our own panel of experts. My first recruit was Melvin Harris, himself a Ripperologist but a man well versed in scientific research from his work with Arthur C. Clarke on his *Mysterious World* series.

'One of the hallmarks of forgeries of that period is missing pages,' he told me. Victorian travel logs and scrapbooks were frequently to be found on sale at boot fairs and street markets. He counted seven such books on a visit to his local market in Hitchin. And if old paper could be bought, so could old ink.

We discovered that Smith had an earlier forensic report he had not shown us. It had been carried out by David Baxendale, a director of Document Evidence, a Birmingham-based forensic science team that helped detect fraud for half of Britain's police forces.

Baxendale had found glue stains in the book and what appeared to be a fragment from a photograph stuck in the binding. He concluded that the book had previously been used as a photograph album. Which was curious. Maybrick was a wealthy man. He had no need to remove photographs and pages from a book to write a journal. He could just go out and buy a new diary.

We found Maybrick's will with his signature and asked Dr Audrey Giles, former head of the Questioned Document

Section at the Metropolitan Police Forensic Science Laboratory, to compare the handwriting. One of the biggest differences was in the capital letters 'J' and 'M'. Considering these were his initials, this was significant. She also found the many ink blots and smudges in the diary suspicious. 'These are features which in other forged documents appear to have been introduced in order to give an appearance of a soiled, well-used manuscript,' she added.

Dr Kate Flint, lecturer in Victorian and modern English literature, read the diary at her faculty at Oxford University. She found a couple of linguistic instances in the text that made it extremely unlikely that the manuscript was written in the Victorian period. The writer referred to a 'one-off instance', but the Oxford English Dictionary records the first usage of this phrase as 1934. Later, the diarist says, 'perhaps I should top myself', a phrase not used until 1958.

'Even allowing for these phrases to have been in spoken circulation for a year or so before they find their way into print, it seems highly improbable that either, let alone both, could have been found in the 1880s,' said Flint.

The final member of our panel was even more forthright. Tom Cullen, author of *Autumn of Terror* and the first writer to identify Montague Druitt, whose body was found floating in the Thames in December 1888, as the likeliest candidate for the Ripper, said:

My impression of the so-called Ripper/Maybrick diaries is that they are forgeries of a not particularly clever character.

There appears to be a good deal of stage management involved in the repentance scene at the end, which smacks of
good old Victorian melodrama. For the rest, they seem to me
to be a farrago of nonsense.

Nineteen days after my first trip to see Michael Barrett, I flew
back to Liverpool in an effort to get him to confess.

By now the Devereux family were baffled. The dead man's
daughters said he never mentioned any diary to them. A son-in-
law said he was so mean he would never give anything away that
might be worth something. Meanwhile, the boss of the building
firm that did the rewiring at Battlecrease, Maybrick's former
home, had had the time to quiz his workforce. To a man they
denied finding anything under the floorboards, but two said they
went drinking in the Saddle, where they might have talked about
their work in a house famous for its murderous history.

Barrett said he was 'sticking to my story'. Standing with me at
Maybrick's grave, he said: 'I did not write the diary. I don't know
who wrote it. It's the gospel truth, and if you tell the truth you
can't get into trouble.'

Returning to London, I wrote up my story of the hoax in
4,795 words, the longest single piece I had yet written for any
newspaper. The problem was I had signed the confidentiality
agreement. Yet we wanted to warn the public that there was
a danger the Ripper's confessions could become the biggest
international fraud in the book world since the Hitler diaries.
The huge print run and the worldwide sale of newspaper and
television rights meant it was worth at least £4 million.

Such confidentiality agreements are common in the publishing world. They allow newspapers and magazines to read forthcoming books with a view to serialisation. But Robert Smith was now using the agreement to gag the newspaper, threatening to sue us if we printed the findings of our investigation.

I met with our lawyers and it was we who issued a writ in the High Court, seeking to be released from any obligation of confidence on the grounds of fraud, fraudulent misrepresentation or negligent misrepresentation. We also sent a dossier of our findings to Scotland Yard.

Smith took out a four-page supplement to *The Bookseller* proclaiming that the world's greatest murder mystery would be solved with the publication of the diary on 7 October 1993. The *Sunday Times* applied for a speedy trial on the grounds that it was in the public interest that the book be exposed before going on sale.

Mr Justice Lindsay ruled that there was 'a real possibility that for a period in October, if nothing is done, the public or some of its members, may be deceived'.

Smith's company agreed to release us from the agreement, repay the £5,000 'deposit' and make a contribution towards our legal costs.

On 19 September, we published our story on the front page under the headline 'Jack the Ripper Diary is a Fake' with a two-page spread inside detailing our investigation.

A year later, I had to return to the diary when William Friedkin, the director of *The Exorcist*, was preparing to shoot a film based on the diary's findings.

There had been a change of story: Barrett's wife Anne now claimed that her father had given her the diary in 1950. The *Sunday Times* co-funded a new test on the ink used to write it. The results showed traces of chloroacetamide, a product first used in ink manufacture in 1974.

Barrett confessed all. At first he told me in a taped interview: 'The diary is a forgery, but I didn't forge it. I emphasise that. I can prove beyond all doubt that there's one person in the world that forged that diary.'

But then, in a signed affidavit, his story changed again and he said he was the author of the diary. His wife wrote it from his typed notes and on occasions from his dictation. He told her: 'Anne, I'll write a bestseller here, we can't fail.' He had bought the book, which contained photographs from World War One, at an auction in Liverpool for £50. He cut out the photographs and some of the pages with a Stanley knife. The writing itself took eleven days. The ink blots and smudges had been done to hide mistakes. But then, for some reason, perhaps linked to an offer of money, he then withdrew his confession.

Not that any of this mattered to the public. Despite all the warnings, 50,000 hardback copies of *The Diary of Jack the Ripper* had been sold in the UK and the same amount abroad. In a concession to our revelations, the front cover now said: 'Is it genuine? Read the evidence, then judge for yourself.'

Michael Barrett had got his bestseller. Not that it did him much good. He lost his wife, his reputation and his home. A perusal of his royalty statements for the book showed that up to September 1994 he had earned £26,609 in royalties. But legal expenses, researchers, his agent's commission and VAT had left him with precisely nothing.

• • •

Ray Santilli is a far smarter operator than Michael Barrett could ever hope to be. In 1995, he tried to fool the world with his film of an alien autopsy that purported to prove that creatures from outer space had landed on Earth.

Despite a front-page story by me in the *Sunday Times* revealing it as a hoax, he is still earning a rich living from the grainy movie by selling the video rights every time someone wants to run footage to expose him again!

Santilli and his business partner Gary Shoefield were the producers of a 2006 film *Alien Autopsy*, in which they were played by Ant and Dec. Even last year he was still claiming the footage was an historic document in a new documentary shot for a series called *History's Greatest Hoaxes*.

Ray started out as a music promoter and producer before branching out into TV specials and video distribution. Indeed, he claimed to have stumbled across the alien film while in Cleveland, Ohio, tracking down early footage of Elvis Presley on stage.

He said he bought some footage that had been shot for Universal News in 1955 by a local freelance cameraman, now in his eighties. The filmmaker then asked if he would be interested in any other type of film and explained he used to be a cameraman for the United States Army Air Force. In July 1947, he was sent to film the post-mortem examination of two aliens from a UFO crash site in Roswell, New Mexico.

Hurtle forward to 1995 and Santilli was about to unleash the film on an unsuspecting world. He showed it to various TV companies at a screening in the Museum of London. Fox and Channel 4 both took the bait and were due to screen the film in a month's time when I went to see Santilli at his Merlin Communications offices in Marylebone.

You can never quite tell what is going to give a journalist a gut reaction that something is wrong. With Barrett, it was probably his repetition of 'If you tell the truth you cannot get into trouble for telling the truth.'

With Santilli, it was probably the posters on his office walls. As a huge fan of Tintin, the boy reporter, I immediately recognised a poster of his adventure *Explorers on the Moon*. Ray explained that he was handling the British rights to a video version. There were pictures, too, of Sgt. Bilko and the Starship *Enterprise*. What had come first, I asked myself? The film or Ray's seeming fascination with post-war America and outer space.

He played me the film in his office. It was grey, grainy footage shot on a hand-held camera. I had to stifle a laugh when I saw the first alien. It was very humanoid despite having a bigger head and an extra finger on each hand. It reminded me of images of The Mekon, Dan Dare's Martian foe, that I had seen in my brother Malcolm's *Eagle* comics while growing up. The sci-fi information I had gleaned as a child (admittedly from picture cards given away with bubble gum) suggested that an extra-terrestrial was more likely to be gaseous in form.

The film showed 'doctors' in head-to-toe white suits with hoods and plastic visors cutting into one body on a dissecting table. They lifted black lenses from the almond-shaped eyes in a matter of seconds as if they knew exactly what to expect and what to do. Certainly, the injuries visible on the rubbery-looking bodies did not look consistent with a UFO crash.

Santilli told me he had paid $100,000 for the film. He claimed that Harry Truman, the US President, was visible in the footage. He even handed me a 'letter of authentication' from Kodak, supposedly proving that the film used for the Roswell footage was manufactured in 1927, 1947 or 1967.

However, he refused to name the cameraman, to produce a receipt for his purchase, or to say where the 16mm film was transferred onto video. The original film was said to be in a Swiss bank vault.

My suspicions were aroused and, as I headed back to the office to start my investigation, I scribbled three words in my notebook: 'Clearly a fake'. Nevertheless, the images on screen certainly played to the public psyche of the time. Similar aliens had been seen for a decade or more in films like *E.T. the Extra-Terrestrial* and the Fox network already had a big hit on its hands with *The X-Files*, the series about FBI special agents Fox Mulder and Dana Scully that had introduced us to the notion of alien abductions and experimental aircraft.

I telephoned Kodak's head office in Hollywood and spoke to

Laurence Cate, the man who had signed the so-called letter of authentication dating the film to one of three years. He turned out to be a sales representative rather than a film historian. He told me that Shoefield, Santilli's partner and an American film producer, had walked into the office a month earlier. He had typed a letter for them containing the three dates.

'I didn't think we were looking at a scientific inquiry,' he added. 'There is no way I could authenticate this. I saw an image on the print. Sure, it could be old film, but it doesn't mean it is what the aliens were filmed on.'

My next call was to the Harry S. Truman Library in Missouri. I asked them to check his schedule for June to October 1947. They did and reported that he had never been in New Mexico during that period.

I then learned that when footage of one autopsy was shown at a private screening in America, it was codemarked with the words 'Restricted access, AOI classification'. However, while 'restricted access' was familiar to us in Britain, it was not a recognised US military code. When film of the same autopsy was shown to Channel 4, the coding had disappeared.

I now came to the appearance of the alien. I consulted Paul O'Higgins, a medical anatomist at University College London. He dismissed the 'alien body' shown on the autopsy table as 'basically humanoid'. He added: 'The chances of life evolving to be that similar, even on two identical planets, is the same as the odds of buying a lottery ticket every week for a year and winning the jackpot every Saturday night.'

Convinced, I started my story. 'Film That "Proves" Aliens Visited Earth Is a Hoax' ran the headline on the front page. 'Relax,' I wrote. 'The little green men have not landed. A much-hyped film purporting to prove that aliens had arrived on earth is a hoax.'

I added that Channel 4 and others were demanding new tests on the film. 'There may not be little green men out there, but millions of big green dollars are resting on the outcome.'

Santilli later back-pedalled, saying the film was a 'recreation' of what he had seen in the original footage because very little of it had survived. He insisted it still contained a few frames of the original.

It emerged that the 'alien' had been created by John Humphreys, a sculptor and special effects artist. Sheep innards, chicken guts and raspberry jam had been used for the 'internal organs' removed by the 'doctors'.

The autopsy had been filmed in the living room of an empty house in Camden, north London, mocked up to resemble a 1940s hospital room.

'All we did was enhance the film, restore the film and re-market it,' Santilli told *History's Greatest Hoaxes* in 2016. 'The film deserved to be released, although there wasn't enough of it any more. There were only a few frames left.'

By then he had already had his revenge on me. One of the characters in the 2006 Ant and Dec film is an annoying old man. For some reason, he is called Maurice.

● ● ●

I now had a reputation at the *Sunday Times* as a hoax-buster. Which is why, nine days after we published my findings on the Roswell film, I found myself aboard a plane to Cornwall on the trail of the Beast of Bodmin.

There have been sightings of a supposed big cat on Bodmin Moor and evidence of savaged sheep since the early 1980s. Like Nessie in Scotland, they have come around regularly with the first signs of summer.

What triggered our interest now was that a schoolboy on holiday with his parents had found the skull of a big cat with large fangs in a stream next to the car park at Golitha Falls, a well-known tourist attraction on the moor. The skull had been sent to the National History Museum for analysis.

The discovery came less than a week after an official report from the Ministry of Agriculture, Fisheries and Food saying there was 'no verifiable evidence' of exotic cats loose in the UK.

I booked into Jamaica Inn, the haunted smugglers' hostelry, and next morning I drove my hire car to the falls. A park ranger showed me where the skull was found, in shallow water near a footbridge over the stream. If you wanted to plant something and be certain that it was found, there would be few better places than this spot, I thought.

It did not take the Natural History Museum long to deduce that the skull probably came from a leopard skin rug. There were cut marks on the skull suggesting the flesh had been scraped off with a knife. Inside the skull was an egg case laid by a tropical cockroach that could not be found in Britain.

I hit the phones and began to ring all the antique shops from Exeter to Bristol. Eventually I found one that had sold a leopard skin rug for about £100 in recent weeks. Did they have the name of the purchaser? Yes, they did. I recognised the name. It was a well-known freelance journalist.

Did we run the story about the journalist who was behind the Beast of Bodmin hoax? No. As if the press would make things up!

CHAPTER ELEVEN

BRINGING DOWN THE GOVERNMENT

I was drinking the *Sunday Times* Wine Club champagne at the Labour Party conference at Brighton in 1997. It was five months after Tony Blair's landslide, and he had just given his victory speech. It was not exactly that I shared his sentiments. It was just good champagne.

That night I was mixing with guests at *The Times* and the *Sunday Times* party in the Victorian grandeur of the Metropole Hotel. The guests included Peter Mandelson and Jack Straw.

Glass in hand, I found myself alongside Paul Wilenius, political editor of *Today*, and Clive Soley, MP for Ealing, Acton and Shepherd's Bush and newly appointed chairman of the Parliamentary Labour Party.

'This is the man you have to thank,' Wilenius said to the future Lord Soley. 'The cash for questions scandal destroyed John Major's government.'

The Insight story three years earlier had exposed Tory MPs who were willing to abuse parliamentary privilege by agreeing to accept payments from businessmen seeking information about sensitive commercial matters inside government.

Whether what Paul said was hyperbole or not, opinion polls conducted in the wake of the story suggested it had left the Conservative Party tainted in sleaze.

Our Insight story was published on 10 July 1994. A Gallup poll conducted between 27 July and 1 August in 100 districts across Great Britain showed a 5.5 per cent swing to Labour since the start of July. The opposition had established a record 33.5 per cent lead over the government. It was the largest any party had had in the fifty-seven years since Gallup surveys began.

Of course, Tony Blair's honeymoon as Labour leader following the death of John Smith was a huge factor, but the boost that the cash for questions scandal gave Labour can hardly be denied. At the general election in May 1997, it translated into a 10.2 per cent swing from the Conservatives to Labour, ending eighteen years of Tory rule and condemning them to their longest continuous spell in opposition in the party's history.

It all began in early 1994, when Andrew Neil called me into his office at the end of the old rum warehouse in Wapping, built during the Napoleonic Wars, that served as our offices.

A week earlier he had taken me in his chauffeur-driven Jaguar for lunch at the Cantina del Ponte trattoria across the river in Shad Thames. The last time we had had lunch was a champagne affair at Quaglino's four years before, after he had won the libel case against Peregrine Worsthorne, the editor of the *Sunday Telegraph*.

At the Cantina we had a lunch of scallops and spaghetti

with chilli but no alcohol, and I presented him with a list of ten potential stories for the new investigative team I had been asked to form. He was agreeable but a little lukewarm. What he wanted most was the head of a Cabinet minister, even though that usually took the sort of sexual scandal I was more used to from my days on the tabloids than the higher ground of the *Sunday Times*.

I had been persuaded to take the poisoned chalice of the Insight job by the 'two Tones': Tony Bambridge, then the avuncular managing editor of news, and Tony Rennell, the urbane news editor. It was Bambridge who had recruited me to the staff of the paper eight years earlier. They promised to take me to lunch at Le Caprice if I accepted. Needless to say, the lunch was never forthcoming. However, Bambridge did help enhance my reputation by telling the *Press Gazette*, journalism's trade paper, that I had 'the biggest contacts book in Fleet Street'.

Now I was standing in Andrew Neil's office. He had just been to lunch and was rather pleased with having come back with a story much better than any of those on my list. His host had been a prominent businessman who told him he had paid MPs to table written questions in Parliament. The going rate was £1,000 and the money was handed over as cash in brown envelopes to avoid any record of the payment.

The businessman asked for anonymity. If someone comes to you with a story on that basis, it is the unwritten rule that you respect it. We did not reveal his identity – neither when we published the story nor later when we faced an inquiry by the House of Commons privileges committee. Even though

Mohamed Al Fayed, the owner of Harrods, had by then come forward to disclose payments to MPs.

One of the businessman's stipulations at his meeting with Neil was that we could not approach any of the four MPs he said he had paid. This may have come as a relief to Andrew Neil. One of them, Neil Hamilton, was an old rival of his from their days in the Federation of Conservative Students.

And perhaps a relief to me too. One of my first big projects after joining the staff at the *Sunday Times* was to 'ghost' Hamilton's story for a News Review front after he and another Tory MP were awarded £20,000 each when they sued the BBC over absurd claims in a *Panorama* documentary called *Maggie's Militant Tendency*.

I went back to my office in the far corner of the newsroom. I had deliberately labelled the team Insight '94 in the hope of being out by the end of the year. I had asked for Mark Skipworth, the paper's consumer affairs correspondent, to join as my deputy and together we recruited Jonathan Calvert, a keen Yorkshire-born reporter from the *Western Mail* in Cardiff and the former Welsh reporter of the year. Randeep Ramesh, then a junior but who years later would become chief leader writer at *The Guardian*, joined us from the paper's Glasgow office.

We discovered from talking to the paper's political team that rumours about cash for questions had been circulating around Westminster for several months. They had even been mentioned a decade earlier in a scholarly book on Commons procedure, when the going rate was supposed to be £150 a question. However, there was no proof.

Our hands tied by the businessman's repeated insistence that we did not investigate the four MPs he had paid, we had to start from scratch.

I began to sift through the records of thousands of questions from MPs gathered from Hansard, dating back eleven years. There were more than 50,000 written questions each year, costing the taxpayer an average of £97 for ministers and civil servants to answer. The computer printouts piled two feet high and when we spread them across the office floor to read them we discovered that some MPs had developed sudden, hitherto-unknown interests in everything from sewage treatment to ship repairs. A pattern began to emerge: MPs with links to some of the fifty consultancy firms that hovered around Westminster were asking questions of direct interest to the companies that those consultancies lobbied for.

It was circumstantial evidence at best, and we could hardly approach an MP as journalists and offer them money to ask a question. Instead, we had to turn to subterfuge.

It was not something the *Sunday Times* did lightly, but the code of practice of the then Press Complaints Commission said that 'subterfuge can be justified only in the public interest and only when material cannot be obtained by any other means'.

We decided to approach ten Tory MPs and ten Labour MPs. We would say we were looking for someone involved in public affairs' consultancy work with access to Parliament and ask if they would table a written Commons question. If they sounded interested, we would send them £1,000.

Both Mark Skipworth and I had been frequent visitors to

Westminster and there was too much risk of us being spotted by an MP or rival journalist if we posed as businessmen seeking to buy questions in Parliament.

Instead, we tasked Jonathan Calvert to approach Tory MPs and Randeep Ramesh to do the same to the Labour ones. There was a suggestion afterwards that we deliberately targeted some because they were Lloyd's 'names', private individuals who had agreed to take on liabilities associated with insurance risks in return for any profits made from premiums, but who had lost money in the venture. This was not the case. The names of the MPs were chosen more or less at random. Indeed, one of those caught in our 'sting' was only approached after he was recommended by another Tory MP.

I wanted to put our individual stamp on the investigation. The MPs were to table questions about a company called Githins doing work for the government and a drug called Sigthin being prescribed on the NHS. Both were anagrams of Insight. Later, in a different sting operation on an MP conducted away from Westminster, I adopted the name of Tim Heatings (another 'Insight Team' production, if you will pardon the bad grammar).

At first our attempts were unsuccessful. It was later suggested that the going rate was now more like £200, and some MPs had become suspicious because we had put 'too big a grub on the hook'.

The breakthrough came on Tuesday 5 July, when Calvert met Graham Riddick, Tory MP for Colne Valley, on the terrace at the Commons. Riddick, a former Coca-Cola sales manager, agreed to accept £1,000 for asking a parliamentary question about Githins.

I knew it was my lucky week when the following night I went to Covent Garden to see *Aida*. I was queueing at the foyer ticket counter to buy a £30 seat in the gods when a woman came up to me. She was selling a spare £110 ticket in the stalls for £30.

It then emerged that Michael Sylvester, the American tenor, had hurt his back and they had had to fly in an Icelander from the Verona Opera Festival to play Radames. I flogged the story to my mate Andrew Yates on the *Times* Diary for £40. So I had a great night out at the opera listening to Aida singing the great aria 'Ritorna Vincitor' (Return Victorious!) from one of the best seats in the house and went home £10 up.

On Thursday 7 July, a second Tory, David Tredinnick, MP for Bosworth, met Calvert on the terrace and agreed on tape to accept £1,000 for asking a question about Sigthin. That same day another Tory, Bill Walker, accepted £1,000 – but for a charity – to ask about Thising, an illness we had invented using another anagram. Fortunately for Labour, none of their MPs approached by Ramesh fell for agreeing to ask questions about a roadway contractor called I. T. Singh.

We had the story in the bag, but it had come too late to save Andrew Neil. I had been in his Tuesday morning editorial conference nine weeks earlier, when he had read from a News Corporation press release saying he had been seconded to New York for seven months to run a new *Sixty Minutes*-style news programme for Fox TV. He then went out to address the troops in the newsroom. It soon became clear that he would not be back.

Later I was asked to write a story for a spoof front page to mark his departure. My effort took precedence over one by A.

A. Gill and was still hanging beside his pool in the south of France when I telephoned him in 2015 to congratulate him on his wedding.

With Neil on his way out, John Witherow, the paper's former foreign editor who had only succeeded Bambridge as managing editor of news a few months earlier, was made the acting editor.

Up to this point, Witherow, an Old Bedfordian, and I, a product of Chipping Norton comprehensive school, had rarely seen eye to eye. He hardly spoke to me when I worked for the paper as a Saturday night casual. Perhaps with good reason. He had a distinguished past, sent to the South Atlantic aboard the aircraft carrier HMS *Invincible* to cover the Falklands War for *The Times*. I had helped cover the same war for *The Sun* by standing outside the Ministry of Defence waiting for the next casualty report.

In September 1984, I was the Saturday night reporter when the news came through on the Press Association wire that the Princess of Wales had given birth to a second son. I whipped up a rapid 800 words and it went out as the splash under my byline with the headline: 'Diana: A Brother for William'.

Only later did I learn that John had spent all day outside St Mary's Hospital, Paddington, waiting for the birth to happen. I had only come into the office at 6 p.m. and had no idea. It was such incidents that were to earn me the unenviable nickname of 'The Byline Bandit', which I carried for the next thirty years.

Friend or not, Witherow needed a big hit to cement his position in the best job in Fleet Street, and we were about to give it to him.

I spent the Friday writing a draft story of 2,500 words for pages one and two. On Saturday morning, it was my job to front up the MPs involved. As I telephoned each of them to reveal they had been caught, you could practically hear the desperate realisation of the mess they were in down the other end of the phone.

On Sunday, we published the story across the top of the front page under the headline: 'Revealed: MPs Who Accept £1,000 to Ask a Parliamentary Question'.

The story caused an unprecedented political storm. Prime Minister John Major, who was in Naples for a G7 summit when the news broke, was forced to suspend Riddick and Tredinnick from their government jobs as parliamentary private secretaries to ministers. But several Tory MPs accused us of illegal entrapment. There were claims we had broken the law ourselves by offering bribes to MPs and engaging in clandestine recording in the precincts of Westminster. One, Rupert Allason (aka spy writer Nigel West), suggested my background as a *News of the World* reporter meant my role in the affair had to be examined.

Riddick, who insisted he had had second thoughts and tried to return the cheque, and other MPs tried to raise it in Parliament, but Speaker Betty Boothroyd wisely shut them down. The only MP to have success in the chamber was Dennis Skinner, the maverick Labour MP for Bolsover, who slipped it into Prime Minister's Questions, which were mainly about the G7 summit.

'Why should big business have to carry this on-cost of lining the pockets of Tory MPs who have to put down questions?' he said.

John Major: 'The particular matters mentioned by the honourable gentleman with his usual delicacy were not discussed at the summit.'

We found an unlikely ally in George Galloway, the rebel Labour MP who had once tried to sue me over a story about what happened to the money spent in fruit machines in Labour clubs in his native Dundee, and with whom I had once shared a lion statue as a sanctuary during the poll tax riot in Trafalgar Square in 1990.

He said: 'There cannot be criminal intent in offering money to expose malfeasance or to expose an abuse in public life; that cannot be true. It is simply a contradiction in terms.' Even Clare Short, certainly no friend of Murdoch newspapers, said the newspaper had done British democracy a favour.

I spent the next forty-eight hours doing TV interviews and sorting out transcripts and tapes of the conversations with Riddick and Tredinnick for release to the media.

There were plenty of plaudits to counter the brickbats. Kelvin MacKenzie, my old editor at *The Sun*, found time in his busy schedule getting the paper out to ring me at home to congratulate me on the story. There were congratulations, too, from Witherow when I went to Tuesday morning conference. The next day, he sent a handwritten note to the Insight office saying: 'Well done. A terrific story. All you have to do now is supply the encores. John.'

On Wednesday, I appeared opposite Roger Gale, a Tory MP and chairman of the Conservative backbench committee, on a BBC afternoon programme called *Westminster Live*. Gale ranted at the 'Gestapo of Wapping' and made the rather silly claim that we had set up the MPs 'not in the interests of the public but because interesting the public sold newspapers'. I stayed cool and, when he said that Walker had no recollection of money being mentioned, I reached for the transcripts and read out Walker's response to our reporter: 'I mean I'm not going to bill you for £3,000. I wouldn't bill you for more than £1,000.' I discovered on my return to work that the whole newsroom had been watching and applauded my performance.

The *Press Gazette* came out with a supportive editorial that said the arrogant reaction of some Tory MPs was potentially more damaging to their party's image than the original allegations. 'The *Sunday Times* has reminded them of the importance of the Fourth Estate,' it read. 'It has shown the public that the press reports without fear or favour.'

We duly gave Witherow his encore. I stayed in the office until 2.20 a.m. on Friday writing a 4,500-word feature on 'Dishonourable Members' and on Saturday confected a story for the top of the front page headlined: 'Dinners for Cash: MPs Profit From Commons Hospitality'.

It had been inspired by a throwaway line from Simon Hughes, the Liberal Democrat MP, during a two-and-a-half-hour Commons debate four days earlier sparked by our original story. He mentioned a £10,000 offer to Sir David Steel, his former party leader, to host dinners at the Palace of Westminster. Luckily, none of the political hacks had picked up on it.

In the same edition, Lynn Barber wrote: 'All week I've longed to wear a badge saying, "Yes, I work for the *Sunday Times*."'

Over the next few months, the Insight team won what I dubbed 'The Grand Slam of Journalism' by picking up the London Press Club's Scoop of the Year trophy, the Investigation of the Year award from Granada TV's *What The Papers Say* (for some reason screened on BBC2), and two prizes in the British Press Awards for Exclusive of the Year and Team Journalism of the Year. Bob Edwards, the former editor of the *Sunday Mirror*, *The People* and the *Daily Express* and chairman of the Press Club's judging panel, said:

The judges decided unanimously that one exclusive, above all the others, deserved the title Scoop of the Year. It has all the Good God factor, especially in high places. It was vastly interesting. It was something entirely new. And it had a therapeutic, you might say sluicing, effect on public life. Incidentally, it also involved subterfuge by the bucketful...

Russell Davies, presenting the *What The Papers Say* awards, said the use of anagrams of Insight was 'one of the most enduring parts of the story'.

Tory Party grandees John Wakeham and Stephen Dorrell must have been seething inside when they had to present me with plaudits, at the British Press Awards and the *What The Papers Say* awards respectively, for helping to bring down John Major's government. In November, Witherow was appointed full-time editor.

We still had unfinished business at the Commons. Nick Brown, the Labour MP for Newcastle-upon-Tyne East, had lodged a complaint about the contents of the story and it was ordered that it be referred to the privileges committee. Of course, Brown wanted to highlight the abuse by MPs. The Tory-heavy privileges committee wanted to use it to rebuke the *Sunday Times*.

Witherow, Skipworth, Calvert and I were led into Committee Room No. 5. The committee sat in front of us in that horseshoe shape familiar to anyone who has watched such proceedings on television.

Tony Newton, Tory MP for Braintree and Leader of the House of Commons, was in the chair. He and his colleagues were tough on us – especially so when compared to the fawning approach they had used with those we had caught willing to breach parliamentary privilege. Take Newton's opening words to David Tredinnick at the very start of the inquiry: 'We are grateful to you for coming … I think all of us, whatever our perspective on the arguments that have led to the delay, are extremely sorry that it has been so long since this inquiry was first indicated before we got to this stage.'

Witherow was worried that Andrew Neil would wake up to the fact that it was his story and might try to jump on the bandwagon. We had agreed beforehand not to name the original source and to try to minimise his involvement, although both Witherow and I had spoken to him subsequently about his lunch with Neil. But, almost as soon as the questioning began, Witherow started talking about the 'prominent businessman'. Outside in the corridor afterwards, he admitted he had been 'Blabber' Witherow.

One of the MPs tried to get me to reveal my salary, while Dame Jill Knight accused us of 'conning people into thinking that they are to be parliamentary consultants'. Sir Marcus Fox, chairman of the Tories' backbench 1922 Committee, was either rubbing his forehead, shaking his head or tutting all the way through our evidence.

There was one lighter moment, when Sir Nicholas Lyell, the Attorney General, started to question me about the trawl we had done of parliamentary questions going back to 1983.

Lyell: 'Did you feel able to draw any worthwhile deduction in relation to any MP?'

Me: 'As I say, sir, only circumstantial evidence.'

Lyell: 'You keep saying "only circumstantial". Sometimes one convicts someone who murders on circumstantial evidence.'

Me: 'Well, you are the Attorney General!'

My quip had everyone laughing. Then David Alton, the Liberal Democrat MP, said that Mohamed Al Fayed had confirmed he would welcome an opportunity to appear before a Commons inquiry and asked whether 'your source' would be prepared to follow suit. We agreed to ask him…

One MP on the committee told the *New Statesman* that we 'came across as being as dodgy as a pair of boxing promoters'.

At the end of it all there was a slap on the wrist for the two MPs – both were suspended from the Commons: Riddick for ten days; Tredinnick for twenty – but the committee saved its most stinging rebuke for the messenger. 'We conclude that, taken as a whole, the *Sunday Times*'s conduct of its enquiries fell substantially below the standards to be expected of legitimate investigative journalism.'

Of course, by then the damage to Parliament had been done. The same Gallup poll conducted just after our story was published found that 60 per cent of people agreed with the statement: 'The Conservatives these days give the impression of being very sleazy and disreputable.'

Of course, the cash-for-questions story had a profound effect on Parliament as a whole, not just the Tory Party. It led to the creation of a news standards and privileges committee, the appointment of a Parliamentary Commissioner for Standards and to the setting up of Lord Nolan's committee, which recommended full disclosure of MPs' outside interests.

I spent another six months as Insight editor. We did one story about Labour 'buying' votes in Birmingham but, as the cold weather came, I found myself increasingly drawn to the south of France. I went there so often in pursuit of stories about an alleged insider share scandal involving Jeffrey Archer and a woman purported to have paid for Jonathan Aitken's stay at the Ritz in Paris that I found a favourite vineyard and brought back cases of wine.

The inevitable happened. After a lunch of *poêlée d'escargots*, entrecote and Beaujolais at Les Deux Garçons, Cezanne's old haunt, in Cours Mirabeau, Aix-en-Provence, I was woken from a postprandial nap on my hotel bed to be told I was to be replaced as Insight editor and made chief reporter instead. *C'est la vie!*

CHAPTER TWELVE

THE FIRST LADY AND
THE MOTHER LODE

'Your train. Where did you get it?'

It seemed a strange question to ask in the back of an ambulance as I was being rushed to hospital after collapsing from accidental ibuprofen poisoning. I had been taking the pills for man flu and not read the small print that you were not supposed to take them on an empty stomach.

But Chloe, a young Australian paramedic who had arrived in Britain to work the same week as the Brexit vote, had seen the cast-iron locomotive, tender and three carriages of the St Louis and Ohio River Railroad on a bookshelf on my landing. Minutes earlier she and two other paramedics had worked fast to save my life as I lay on the bathroom floor.

I owed her, so I told her. I bought it at an antiques centre in Arkansas in 1994 while on a 'foreign' – journalist speak for a story-getting mission overseas – to try to dig up dirt on Bill and Hillary Clinton.

We had got a lead from within the diamond industry about a Mauritius-born British citizen named Jean-Raymond Boulle who had somehow got permission to mine for diamonds at a state park in Arkansas while Bill was state governor. Hillary was descended from mining stock. Her great grandfather, Jonathan Rodham, a colliery overseer, had made his way from County Durham to the coalfields of Scranton, Pennsylvania.

The Crater of Diamonds State Park at Murfreesboro is the only place in the US where you can find diamonds and probably the only diamond-bearing site in the world accessible to the public. People pay a few dollars to go into a ploughed area and are allowed to take away any diamonds they can find.

The tip was that Clinton had somehow got a woman called Karen Lackey, then his director of parks and tourism, to overturn every environmental objection to allow industrial mining in the park. It would be a bit like Leslie Knope, the character played by Amy Poehler in the American office sitcom *Parks and Recreation*, agreeing to allow fracking on her children's playground in fictional Pawnee, Indiana.

I spoke to John Witherow and he agreed I should go to Arkansas. He had been appointed acting editor of the *Sunday Times* by Murdoch six weeks earlier following the sudden departure of Andrew Neil and he was desperate for a big hit to confirm his position. Then I telephoned Geordie Greig, our New York correspondent. It is journalistic etiquette to tell a colleague if you are trespassing on their patch. Besides, Geordie was a lovely bloke.

We had met about eight years earlier while on a Saturday 'doorstep' for our respective newspapers, he for the long-forgotten *Sunday Today* and me for the *Sunday Times*. His photographer opened his car door and Geordie rolled out, with his shirt-tail flapping loose, from where he had been sleeping.

A year later, we were both covering Mark Thatcher's wedding to Diane Burgdorf from Dallas, Texas, at the Savoy Chapel in central London. Like most reporters present, I was trying to get the attention of guests to talk to. Not Geordie. The guests, including Mark's twin sister Carol, came over to talk to *him*.

I suppose it came from being descended from a long line of royal courtiers. Indeed, during a career trajectory that has taken him from editing *Tatler* to the *London Evening Standard* to the *Mail on Sunday*'s editorship, *The Observer*, never a paper to doff its cap lightly, named him 'Britain's most-connected man'. By strange coincidence, he would also marry a Texas girl.

We have always got on well. I would call him 'Gordon', as if I had mistaken him for Gordon Greig, the political editor of the *Daily Mail*, and he would call me 'Mo', a nickname that I carried thereafter at the *Sunday Times*, varied to 'Big Mo' as I gained a few pounds and 'Uncle Mo' as I got older.

Geordie shared my appetite for life and my conviction that journalists should have lots of outside interests to keep them sane. With Geordie it was the arts, whether the books of Anthony Trollope, the music of the Grateful Dead or the works of

David Hockney and Lucian Freud. For me, it's more the Rolling Stones, Leicester City and spaghetti Westerns.

He had been to Arkansas the previous year in the wake of the so-called Whitewater Affair, perhaps the key financial scandal while Bill Clinton was President. It all revolved around the purchase of land in the Ozarks to build holiday homes for sale. Three inquiries failed to find damning evidence against Bill or Hillary, but two of their associates and a partner in her law firm were jailed.

Geordie and Mark Skipworth, then my deputy in the Insight team, had produced a good story about how Hillary, now America's First Lady, and two senior members of the Clinton administration had been involved in a shady multi-million-dollar deal to profit from the sale of old people's homes. Back in London, I had put it together for the front of our News Review section under the headline: 'Big Trouble at Little Rock'.

My telephone conversation with Geordie that day was less about Arkansas politics and more about which restaurants and bars to go to, both to find the best food and drink and the best receipts. I always held the view, to misquote John F. Kennedy, that one should 'ask not what you can do for the *Sunday Times*, but what the *Sunday Times* can do for you'.

So, my trip to see Karen Lackey turned into a week-long vacation in which I drove 1,500 miles in a hire car while seeing the sights of Texas and Arkansas.

In those days we flew business class, paid for hotels and meals as we went and charged the company expenses on return. Of course, in the new age of the 'suits', the accountants who run newspapers, everything has to be permitted in advance and then booked through the company. Back then, however, I sipped J&B on ice and lunched on filet mignon as I flew across the Atlantic.

On arrival in Dallas my first priority was to visit the Texas School Book Depository, now the Dallas County Administrative Building, and go to the sixth-floor window on the south-east corner of the building, from where Lee Harvey Oswald had shot John F. Kennedy. I remember thinking it was hardly great marksmanship – the distance between the window and Kennedy's car was less than 100 yards. Even someone like I, with limited clay pigeon shooting experience, could have made that shot.

It was always important to me that journalists made the most of 'foreigns' by visiting tourist sites while they were away. I once rounded on Andrew Alderson, a pal who replaced me as chief reporter at the *Sunday Times* when I became night news editor, for going to Egypt on a trip originally assigned to me and not visiting the Pyramids. I felt like I had missed out too. 'But, Andrew,' I said, 'you could have taken a taxi. It would only have taken half an hour!'

The next morning in Dallas I was busy on the phone and arranged to meet a contact in Murfreesboro at 2 p.m. I left Dallas at 9.20 a.m. Ever the trencherman, I stopped at a Denny's for a grand slam breakfast of waffles, eggs, bacon, sausages and maple syrup, arriving in Murfreesboro with two minutes to spare to find him sitting on the porch of the Jiff-Ee corner store and restaurant.

For peace and quiet, we moved into the back of a restaurant. I ordered two coffees and we talked for two hours, during which our cups were refilled at least four times. The bill when I came to pay it was just fifty-three cents. It would definitely have been a time for creative accounting when it came to calculating my expenses.

According to my contact, it was the old story of alleged cash for access, the intimate connection between political donations and official favours. He told me that the Crater of Diamonds, one of the few volcanic sites outside South Africa where diamonds can be found close to the surface, had become a state park in 1972 after the Arkansas Department of Parks and Tourism purchased the site from a private company that had operated it as a tourist attraction.

All was well until Boulle arrived from Dallas with the idea that the park contained $5 billion worth of diamonds. He set up headquarters in Hope, Bill Clinton's home town and a depressed place still hanging on to the title of 'watermelon capital of the world' when I visited it.

Boulle had lunch with Clinton, then governor of Arkansas, and convinced him of the fortune lying in the ground. Despite the protests of environmentalists, Clinton asked his friend Karen Lackey to work on a task force to study the project. A White House aide did the legal work.

In 1987, Clinton signed a bill authorising exploratory drilling as soon as the task force gave the inevitable green light. Six years later, Boulle and his wife were guests at his White House inauguration. Hillary wore a ring with a stone from the Crater of Diamonds.

My contact suggested that there had been skulduggery. We went to the Crater of Diamonds together and paid $4 each to go in. Once inside, we met James Archer, a 69-year-old who had been digging and panning for diamonds there with a pickaxe, shovel and fork for eighteen years. Since retiring, he had been coming 'every day but Sunday' for seven years. He told me he had found 5,000 diamonds. The biggest find was a diamond he sold to a dealer for $4,000.

'They should leave it to folks like us to have fun,' he told me. I bought a 10pt white diamond from him for my wife for $20. To this day she still complains that it is so small she cannot find a jeweller willing to incorporate it into a piece of jewellery. Oh well, it's the thought that counts…

I drove to Little Rock for iced tea in the bar at the Capitol Hotel and then took time out to drive another 150 miles to visit 'Hanging Judge', Isaac Parker's courthouse at Fort Smith. By the time I was back in Little Rock it was 11 p.m. but still 87 degrees Fahrenheit.

Next day I telephoned Lackey and spoke to her for half an hour, but she insisted everything had been above board. I determined to visit her. I drove to the town of Mountain View, where she was then living, for a catfish dinner and some old-time country music, first from 86-year-old Jimmy Driftwood in a barn where he gave concerts and passed the hat and then on to the Ozark Folk Center to see the even older Patsy Montana perform her 1951 country and western hit 'I Want to be a Cowboy's Sweetheart' with her great-granddaughter.

In the morning, I bought the cast-iron train from an antiques shop. It was so heavy that today it would take up the whole of my luggage allowance.

Lackey was known locally as 'The woman of 100 hats'. On my way to her house I was pulled up by an Arkansas state trooper for allegedly crossing a 'stop' sign at a T-junction without stopping. Clearly I had been expected and he gave me the third degree before letting me go.

Lackey was an ash blonde with bright blue eyes. She welcomed me into her home, which boasted half a tree polished to perfection as a feature in the spacious living room. Again, she insisted she did not know what I was talking about.

It was 91 degrees when I left and the state trooper was waiting to escort me to the county line.

Driving back towards Dallas Airport and the flight home, I decided to indulge myself with a night in Paris, Texas, the title of a cult film favourite from a few years earlier starring Harry Dean Stanton and Nastassja Kinski.

Once back in the UK, I found there were still great expectations for the story. A reporter was despatched to Antwerp to confront an alleged middleman and then to Lisbon to try to speak to Boulle. We hired an attorney in Dallas to go through court records and spent thousands of dollars to get a deposition.

But when we read it nothing shone out. I wrote a 2,000-word story on 'Diamondgate', but there was no evidence. My mission had failed but, as I told Chloe in the back of the ambulance twenty-two years later, you only have to have a 51 per cent success rate to survive.

Two weeks after my trip to Arkansas, we had a major breakthrough in our cash for questions investigation and the story of the First Lady and the Mother Lode was soon consigned to history. However, it had helped me refine the habit of taking time out while on a story to do my own thing.

I guess it had started during the 1990 World Cup in Italy, when I took in an open-air performance of *Aida* at the Roman amphitheatre in Cagliari and drove into the mountains to visit the bandit village of Orgosolo before telling the news desk I had picked up a 'tip' that England and German fans were planning a pitched battle in front of the Colosseum in Rome. That entitled a pal and I to stay in a £350-a-night Mafia-owned hotel overlooking the lions in Rome zoo.

I bit off more than I could chew during the 1992 Barcelona Olympics by imagining I could visit Salvador Dali's home in Cadaqués for lunch, cross into France for tea in the medieval city of Carcassonne and stop for dinner in Andorra on my way back to my hotel.

In the end I ran out of petrol in dense fog high in the Pyrenees and was lucky to freewheel down to the last open filling station before arriving back at my hotel well-fed but utterly exhausted at 4 a.m.

During the Summer Games in Atlanta in 1996, I managed to come up with an excuse to fly to Chicago to visit the blues clubs and do a bus tour of various gangster sites.

The 1998 World Cup in France saw me write the splash on

rioting English soccer fans on the Saturday night and then disappear until the middle of the next week visiting the white horses and pink flamingos of the Camargue and following the trail of the Holy Grail while the news desk was frantically trying to get hold of me to dig into the background of some of the arrested thugs.

Of course, my wife and young children expected family holidays too and sometimes we managed three or four foreign holidays a year. Where did I get all the time off? Well, I invented a scam I called 'Snopake holidays', after the white correction fluid we had kept in the office to cover up typewriting errors in the days before computers and delete buttons arrived. (They could just as easily have been called Tipp-Ex holidays.)

This is how it worked. The newsroom's holiday planner was in the back of a large office diary kept in the news desk secretary's drawer. Only three people were allowed off in any one week so it was common for reporters to put down dates far in the future for fear of losing them and then change their minds and delete the entry with Snopake fluid. There were always people being fired or leaving so I would take a holiday then, three months later, delete the entry in the planner with Snopake and write in the name of someone who had left. It was a simple but effective way of giving me one or two extra weeks' holiday a year. I shot myself in the foot by passing on the tip to Rosemary Collins, a reporter who sat in front of me. A few weeks later she was suddenly elevated to news editor and the holiday book disappeared for ever into the managing editor's office.

Another wheeze was to do an interview on the phone and

– confident I had enough material to write the story – claim I had to fly somewhere to speak to the person face to face.

One such trip was to see Elisabeth Schwarzkopf, the opera singer, at her home in Switzerland in January 1996, to ask her about her wartime role in the Nazi party for a news story. My interest was linked to a new biography of the soprano I was reviewing for the paper's Books section.

I caught a Swissair flight from London's City Airport. A banker was the only other passenger and, outnumbered by stewardesses, we were fed champagne and chocolate all the way to Zurich in business class.

A £100 taxi ride in a top-of-the range Mercedes took me to the Schwarzkopf residence. 'She doesn't see anybody without an appointment,' said her snooty secretary. Undeterred, I called the news desk: 'The interview's in the bag.' So were my duty frees.

CHAPTER THIRTEEN

MY ESCAPE FROM A BORNEO JAIL

The lyrics of Ian Dury's song 'Hit Me With Your Rhythm Stick' played in my mind as I flew over the shark-infested South China Sea to the rescue of five British soldiers lost on a mountain.

'In the wilds of Borneo and the vineyards of Bordeaux,' goes the song, 'Eskimo, Arapaho, move their body to and fro.'

Years later, reading a biography of the much-missed Dury, I discovered that he had once worked at the *Sunday Times* as a graphic artist. One of life's little coincidences.

I had originally been sent to Kuala Lumpur, the capital of Malaysia, to 'dig for dirt' (journalistic shorthand for looking for the skeleton in the closet) on Mahathir Mohamad, the country's autocratic Prime Minister.

To Rupert Murdoch's chagrin, Andrew Neil, my editor, had become rather dogged in his search for evidence that Britain had given £234 million of aid to Malaysia to build a hydroelectric dam in return for a £1.3 billion order from Kuala Lumpur to buy British arms.

Murdoch was worried that the furore would damage the chances of him getting his Asian satellite television system into Malaysia. According to Neil, in his own autobiography *Full Disclosure*, Murdoch yelled down the phone at him: 'I'm getting lots of letters from people asking, "Who does Mr Neil think he is, taking on a Prime Minister?" And you're boring people.' Indeed, their differences of opinion on this story would eventually lead to Neil's departure from the newspaper he had reshaped so brilliantly in the aftermath of the Battle of Wapping.

Of course, I was just a small pawn in this game. I had spent more than a week in Kuala Lumpur researching the notion that shares in the electricity company were being given to friends of Mahathir and his ruling party. This involved lengthy meetings with leaders of opposition parties and university professors together with hours spent poring over share information at the Kuala Lumpur Stock Exchange. In truth, I found little that looked incriminating. Many of the shares seemed to be going to pension funds and old comrade associations set up to help former soldiers.

To cheer myself up, I resorted to a familiar tactic of mine: sightseeing at the newspaper's expense. On a Saturday when all was busy at the office in London, I went to admire the British Indian colonial architecture of the city's railway station, the Jami Mosque and the High Court with its clock tower, a building I remembered from a boyhood stamp album.

On the Sunday, I caught the 11.15 a.m. shuttle to Singapore, claiming I had arranged to meet a contact. Instead, I took a cable car over the harbour, a rickshaw ride to Chinatown and a taxi to Raffles Hotel, where I spent an hour and a half in the Writers' Bar, once frequented by Joseph Conrad, Rudyard Kipling and Somerset Maugham, daydreaming that I might one day be mentioned in their company, listening to the pianist play 'My Way' and downing three strong Singapore Slings. I hijacked a $120 receipt from the Empress Room restaurant before grabbing another taxi to take me back to Singapore Airport for the 11.45 p.m. flight back to 'KL' as I was now calling it.

Eleven days into my trip, I was getting increasingly desperate when help came from an unexpected quarter. I was having tea with the British Deputy High Commissioner when news broke that five British soldiers, including their commander, were missing on Mount Kinabalu in Sabah, a Malaysian state on the north-east corner of the island of Borneo. It was Thursday afternoon, perfect timing for a Sunday newspaper to clean up.

Next morning, I caught a two-and-a-half-hour flight to Sabah, flying over turquoise blue water wrapped around south sea atolls.

The missing soldiers were part of an ill-fated expedition by Lieutenant Colonel Robert Neill to descend Low's Gully, an 8,000ft-deep ravine, on Mount Kinabalu. The 13,438ft mountain is the biggest in Malaysia and regarded as one of the most important sites for flora and fauna in the world. Locally, however, it is known as 'The Place of the Dead'. Sir Hugh Low, a Victorian explorer who made the first recorded ascent, said its highest peak was 'inaccessible to any but winged animals'.

Neill, his second-in-command, five experienced NCOs and

three novice soldiers from Hong Kong with British citizenship had set out on the adventure-training mission but had become separated.

The NCOs formed an advance party and abseiled a rope's length at a time down part of the gully. They then set off on their own through the jungle after, they said, waiting twelve hours for Neill and the others to descend.

In its infinite wisdom, the Malaysian government had banned the army from using radios in the rainforest, so no one knew the other five were still stranded until the NCOs emerged, dehydrated and half-starved. It was feared they were trapped in the gully, unable to move, and would slowly starve to death.

On landing, I knew I had two tasks. Try to find the missing men and get the first interview with the five who we knew had survived.

I took a taxi into Kota Kinabalu, the capital, to beg, steal or borrow a vehicle suited to the terrain. I ended up with a Mitsubishi Pajero 4x4 at an exorbitant $350 a day. Setting out on the 100km drive to Mount Kinabalu, it was obvious I needed such a vehicle when the road would suddenly drop a foot into rough rock.

Arriving at the base of the mountain, I booked into a resort hotel and found the Kinabalu Park information office, where I grabbed enough maps and leaflets to help produce a graphic of the area later.

Driving up the summit trail, it suddenly got dark very quickly. The sound of the animals and insects was so loud from the rainforest that it drowned out the engine noise of the Pajero.

In my head I had some vague notion that I would stumble across the missing men as they hacked their way out of the undergrowth, but it was soon pitch dark so I decided to return to my hotel. I started to sketch a graphic over dinner, tracing a butterfly from my placemat to decorate it. This I then sent by fax to London, knowing one of our graphic artists would turn it into something far more legible. My butterfly got lost in translation.

I went to listen and watch the locals enjoying themselves in a karaoke bar before heading back to my room and ringing around hotels in the hope of finding the survivors. I found one in his hotel room and we spoke briefly, but he was not giving much away.

Next morning, I was up at 7.30 a.m. It was Saturday, press day, but I was eight hours ahead of London so I told myself I had plenty of time. I just needed some luck.

I left the hotel at 8.50 a.m. to drive back to Kota Kinabalu in time for an expected 10.30 a.m. press conference at the Hyatt Hotel. I arrived ten minutes late but there was no one there. The receptionist said the army chiefs had left for Mount Kinabalu. We had probably passed each other on the highway. The thought flashed through my mind that the British soldiers had been found and that I was in the wrong place.

Resisting the urge to drive back to the mountain, I booked into the Hyatt and rang the Ministry of Defence in London. No, the soldiers had not been found.

I then phoned the British Embassy in Hong Kong, who told me there was a press conference being held at Malaysian military headquarters. Luckily, the firm I had rented the Pajero from had for some reason pointed out where this was on a map. I arrived there at 11.30 a.m., half an hour late but in time to dictate the press conference with questions about delays in finding the missing men.

I returned to the Hyatt to file a holding story about the delays that had dogged the rescue operation. At 4 p.m., a helicopter flew overhead. In my paranoid state, I now thought it was the newly rescued soldiers being brought to hospital.

Rousing Andy Gilbert of the *South China Morning Post*, with whom I was now cooperating to cover all the angles, we drove to the city hospital in the Pajero. There was no one there but expectant mums in the maternity ward.

We then chanced our arm and drove to the Sabah Medical Centre, a private hospital. Once there, I announced who we were. Perhaps they misunderstood 'Her Majesty's press' and thought we were with 'Her Majesty's Government', but, in any case, we were shown to a room occupied not by a newly rescued soldier but one of the NCOs who had emerged days earlier.

He, too, was reluctant to say very much about his ordeal for reasons that were to become apparent later. I asked him instead to describe what he had seen in the gully.

Returning to the hotel, I let my imagination flow and coupled it with memories from old movies about dinosaurs, carnivorous plants and giant spiders I had watched as a child at Saturday matinees.

'The Lost World of Mount Kinabalu surrendered some of its dark secrets last night, but not the fate of the five British soldiers still missing at the bottom of its innermost valley,' I wrote.

As tribal elders prepared to slaughter a chicken as a sacrifice to the spirit of a mountain they call 'The Place of the Dead', the soldiers who staggered dehydrated and malnourished from the Borneo rainforest to raise the alarm spoke for the first time about the wonders they had seen.

The five survivors were the first men to conquer Low's Gully, a glacial scar that runs across the north face of southeast Asia's highest peak, and live to tell the tale. They saw huge exotic plants, beautiful rare orchids, strange snakes and large rock formations straight from the pages of Sir Arthur Conan Doyle's novel, *The Lost World*, as they descended 6,000ft along the gully into dense jungle.

The story ran all across the top of the front page under the masthead – a spot known as the 'hamper' in Fleet Street, except it is never a picnic to write it – and turned to take up most of page two with my heavily improved graphic. 'Time Runs Out in Lost Valley Known as Place of the Dead' read the headline above my byline.

Unfortunately, it was almost joined by another story containing my name and mention of Mount Kinabalu.

Happy with my work, I joined up with Andy Gilbert and Philip Sherwell from the *Sunday Telegraph* and we retired to the 100 Per Cent Seafood Market Restaurant, where we were joined by a few others, including an ex-US Navy Seal working for Sky as a cameraman, for some much needed R&R.

The food was all live and swimming around in tanks. We ordered lobster, Indonesian red snapper, beer and ice cream for each of the waitresses.

A bill arrived for $423. The headhunters of Borneo had turned into scalpers. They were trying to charge the equivalent of £40 for one lobster. We handed over $360 and, refusing to pay any more, left the restaurant to hail a taxi back to our hotel.

We had only gone a few hundred yards when we heard the phut-phut of a scooter pulling alongside and saw two police officers on the back ordering us to pull over.

We were escorted to the police station where I went into full 'Her Majesty's press' mode. It probably did not help matters when I picked up a telephone from one of the desks and dialled the office in London.

By this time it was a busy Saturday, approaching deadline, in London. Parin Janmohamed, our letters editor, answered.

'Parin, it's Maurice. I am being held in jail in Borneo. Could you get one of our lawyers on the phone? I want some legal advice...'

I never got the chance to say I wanted advice about a disputed restaurant bill. A policeman had slammed his hand down on the cradle to cut me off.

London went into meltdown. The assumption was that I had been detained because of the *Sunday Times*'s pursuit of Mahathir.

The three of us were put into a cell to cool our heels. After about twenty minutes, a tubby, middle-aged man arrived wearing a blue padded waistcoat and clutching what I took to be the restaurant's accounts book. The policemen seemed deferential towards him.

'Thief, gangster,' I started to shout, determined not to let him hold sway in the police station.

Philip, who obviously had a better grasp of the language, finally got a word in.

'Maurice, he's not the restaurant owner, he's the police chief!'

He ordered our release and we were led to his separate office. I watched a lizard disappear into the ceiling as he started to apologise. The man had the wisdom of Solomon. He agreed with us and the restaurant owner, who had now arrived, decided to accept the original $360.

The three of us walked free and, determined to enjoy the rest of the night, went to a disco at the Rocky Fun pub. There we met a hotel worker who offered to drive us back to the Hyatt.

Alas, all hell was now brewing back home. My mistake was not calling in after our release. The *Sunday Times* had gone thermonuclear. The Foreign and Commonwealth Office had been alerted, the story of my detention had run on the Press Association wires and all three of our papers were about to run the story. The *South China Morning Post* believed we had been arrested because we had had the audacity to interview one of the soldiers in hospital.

Greg Hadfield, my news editor, had got space cleared on the front page for a report about my detention. 'Please spike it,' I begged when I eventually decided to call in. It was pulled and a contents column put in its place.

I had hardly learned my lesson. At 4 a.m. I was chatting to four girls in the hotel dining room when Clifford Williams,

Britain's naval attaché to Malaysia, suddenly interrupted and started to berate me for getting him out of bed to 'rescue' me.

He grabbed me by the arm. I pushed him away and told him to fuck off. 'This is not a British colony any more,' I told him.

'You haven't heard the last of this,' he said.

Luckily, when I telephoned London and talked to Andrew Neil, he thought it was all a great hoot. My colleagues in the newsroom were not so forgiving and instantly labelled the affair 'Lobstergate'.

Jan, my wife, rang at 5.20 a.m. my time having just returned home from a show in our village hall.

'I think I'll just claim the basic dinner allowance on this one,' I told her.

There was a postscript when I flew back to KL and waited in my hotel room for a flight home. I received a call from my credit card company. Had I bought £2,000 worth of karaoke equipment in Singapore? My mind immediately went to the karaoke bar at Mount Kinabalu. No, but someone had – on my cloned card. Another of life's little coincidences.

A few days later, the missing five were found after a search by 1,000 soldiers and civilians. They had not eaten for six days. I felt guilty about that lobster.

CHAPTER FOURTEEN

SOLVING A MURDER

The murder of thirteen-year-old Caroline Dickinson on a school trip to France in the summer of 1996 shocked the nation and had every parent questioning whether such holidays would ever be safe again. Thanks to a bizarre chain of events, spanning two continents, I was able to help put her killer behind bars.

Caroline, a pupil at Launceston Community College in Cornwall, had saved up her own pocket money to go on the trip with forty other pupils. But, after a day out to Mont St Michel, she was raped and suffocated in the middle of the night in the hostel dormitory in Brittany she shared with four other girls.

Five years later, and the trail had gone cold. The story was still in the news, largely because of the blunders by the French police and the relentless campaign by John Dickinson, Caroline's father, to keep the case in the public eye.

He had been to France eighteen times since her death and

was so critical of the way it had been handled that it led to the sacking of the investigating judge and to a mass DNA screening of the 3,700 males in the village of Pleine-Fougères, where the murder occurred.

So bad had the police investigation been that, at first, cotton wool found at the scene that had been stuffed into Caroline's mouth was dismissed as a dressing and discarded by paramedics called to attend her. In fact, it had been stolen in an attempted attack on a fourteen-year-old girl from Salford twenty-five miles away on the same night.

An alcoholic vagrant had been arrested within two days, was denied access to a lawyer and beaten until he confessed. He was in custody for seventeen days until DNA analysis proved that he was not at the murder scene. Two more men were arrested and released in the ensuing months.

My daughter was a year younger than Caroline and my sons had been on school trips to Europe so, like many a parent, I followed the case with a close interest.

At some point or another every journalist will see him or herself as an amateur detective and I am no exception. Once, after attending a regular morning press conference at St Albans police station, I spotted a stolen car which had been listed on the daily crime bulletin and called it in. Sometimes detectives use us, willingly or unwillingly, by giving us enough clues to find and interview suspects so that they can see if the story they had given to the police had changed.

I had helped a colleague who had interviewed John Dickinson by filling in the background for a page lead. It reignited my interest in the case and, with both the fifth anniversary of the murder and the delayed inquest into Caroline's death coming up, I decided to dig deeper.

The *Sunday Times* has never liked 'anniversary journalism' and I knew that the French police had virtually given up, so I needed a new, strong angle to get a piece into the paper.

Using an interpreter to reinforce my schoolboy French, I contacted Francis Debons, the investigating judge now leading the murder inquiry. He was due to travel to Britain in a week's time to give evidence at the delayed inquest into Caroline's death.

He sounded both defensive and defeatist. 'I understand Mr Dickinson's concerns that the investigation should not fall into oblivion and I am confident that the methods we are now using are correct,' he said.

'The investigation has its own dynamic, but it is also clear that the bulk of the investigation is done. We cannot demand of the gendarmerie that it maintains a large investigative team.'

So how many officers were working on the case? I asked him. 'Three gendarmes full time and a fourth on stand-by,' he answered.

How many suspects were they looking at? 'We are still seeking up to fifty people to eliminate them from our enquiries. A request has gone to Scotland Yard to help locate a man who it is known had been living in Britain before the murder.'

It was still not enough. We phoned Debons back and asked him to give us the name of the man who had been in the UK. We told him we needed it to make the story work.

Reluctantly he gave us the name of fifty-year-old Francisco

Arce Montes, a Spanish restaurant worker. He had been work-ing in London shortly before the murder and there had been previous complaints about him allegedly harassing girls at youth hostels in the Loire Valley.

It was enough to go on. I spoke to NCIS, the national crime intelligence unit, and they said that if we published the name there was a danger that this man might abscond. But I took the view that he was in Britain in the 1990s, nobody seemed to know where he had gone and there might be a restaurant owner who remembered employing him and could give the police a lead to his present whereabouts. I had discussions with the newspaper's lawyers on naming him and I persuaded them it was worth the risk.

That Sunday – 1 April 2001 – we published the story under the headline: 'Hunt for Schoolgirl's Killer Moves to Britain', and named Montes. Together with a picture of Caroline, we used an illustration of a gendarmerie captain holding up an artist's drawing of the man seen at the scene of the earlier attack. With his thick eyebrows, he looked like a caveman. It was one of five bylines I had in the paper that day.

John Dickinson had been made aware of the interest in Montes, amongst others, more than two years earlier. I do not know if it was French privacy laws or the timid French press, but this was the first time his name had been published.

I hoped that the story might kickstart something in the UK. Perhaps a hotelier would realise Montes was working for them now, I thought.

As it turned out, copies of the *Sunday Times* were amongst a bundle put aboard that day's 12.35 p.m. BA203 flight from Heathrow to Detroit Metro Airport to be read by passengers on the plane and in the British Airways lounge in Detroit. It was the custom of the BA staff to put the crumpled papers on their ticket counter when they were two days old for anyone to read.

Tommy Ontko was a Vietnam veteran who worked as an intelligence officer for the immigration and border protection service at Detroit International Airport. On Tuesday 3 April, he was walking past the British Airways desk when he saw a copy of the *Sunday Times* put out for general readership.

He picked it up and took it back to his office with a coffee and a packet of doughnuts to have for his lunch. He saw my story, vaguely remembered reading about the murder a few years earlier and wondered why it had not been solved.

Out of idle curiosity, he ran Montes' name through his computer and came up with an approximate match. He wanted to be certain and so he spent two hours trying his best to talk to the French authorities before he got Montes' date of birth. It was the same as that of the man on his computer screen.

Tommy's immediate thought was that he had to protect American girls from this man. He went back onto his computer and discovered that Montes had been arrested and jailed in Miami Beach twenty days earlier for what had been described as 'lewd and lascivious conduct'.

He telephoned Debons and two of his gendarmerie officers

just as they were about to board a ferry to Portsmouth for the inquest into Caroline's death. It looked like they had finally got their man.

The Spaniard had been living in Miami Beach for the past two years and had been lurking around a backpackers' hotel called the Banana Bungalow. One night, he broke into a room where six female students from Northern Ireland were sleeping, pulled back the covers from one, cut off her underwear with a knife and masturbated over her before sneaking out again. Luckily for her, she slept through the whole incident.

The next day, he was brazen enough to return to the hotel, and some of the students, on alert from what had happened the night before and having seen him prowling around the hostel previously, spotted him by the pool and called the police. He tried to claim he had been drunk and had entered the girls' room by accident.

He had been arrested and put in jail. When Ontko's call came through alerting the Dade County police as to who they had in custody, detectives realised they needed a DNA match to prove he was Caroline's killer.

Montes refused to supply a blood or saliva sample. Instead, a barcode-style copy of the DNA profile found in the dormitory in Brittany was faxed to Miami Beach and compared with the semen stains recovered from the bedclothes at the Banana Bungalow. It was a perfect match.

A public announcement by the assistant public prosecutor on the steps of the Palace of Justice in Rennes on Saturday

14 April gave me enough for a page-one story the next day, just a fortnight after my original 'fishing exercise'.

John Dickinson was waiting at Launceston police station to hear the result. When it came through as a positive, he said: 'We would like to thank the media for their help in ensuring that Caroline's case has never been forgotten. Nothing can bring back our dear Caroline, but everything should be done to prevent such a nightmare being visited on another innocent family.'

The press often gets stick for the sometimes intrusive way it handles murder investigations. Milly Dowler was a case in point. But here was an example of a newspaper helping to arrest the killer.

I flew to Detroit to interview Tommy Ontko in his office at the airport. He had a picture of Caroline on the wall. 'I'm glad we put our hands on him,' he told me. 'But it had nothing to do with civic duty. It is our job to keep the bad guys out of the United States.'

Of course, you would not expect me to fly all that way without a little downtime on expenses. I took a $40 cab ride to Hitsville, the Motown museum for a tour of the studios where so much fabulous music was recorded in the 1960s. As I was leaving who should be arriving but Martha Reeves. We posed together for a picture outside, each kicking a leg up. Dancing in the Streets indeed!

Flying back to London, I spent the next week delving into Montes's stay in the capital. I had another big break when I interviewed Gordon Butler, a chauffeur who still lived in the flat above Montes's former bedsit. He told me that Montes had once caused a scare at the Wimbledon tennis tournament by breaching security to harass the current women's champion.

In June 1995, a year before Caroline's death, Montes, who had gone to the tournament with his friend, had brushed past security guards to confront Conchita Martínez, a fellow Spaniard.

Martínez, then twenty-three, who was off court at the time, was there defending the women's title she had won the previous year by beating Martina Navratilova in the final. She was startled by the approach as he shouted at her in Spanish. She reluctantly agreed to autograph his ticket to get rid of him before he was ushered away by security guards, worried, no doubt, about a repeat of the 1993 attack on Monica Seles, when she was stabbed in the back by a spectator at a tournament in Hamburg. Martínez went on to lose in the semi-final.

'Francisco had taken a liking to Conchita,' said Butler. 'He was giving her the evil eye and she was quite disturbed by it. It always makes me think of Monica and the way she was attacked.'

It was enough to give me a page lead on 6 June 2004, headlined 'Murder Suspect Had Menaced Tennis Star'.

Eight days later, Montes was sentenced to thirty years in prison by the court in Rennes for Caroline's murder.

In 2015, he was convicted by a Spanish court of attempting to rape an eighteen-year-old Spanish girl in a knifepoint attack a year after the Dickinson crime. He had tricked the girl into letting him into the apartment block where she was on holiday with her parents by claiming he had lost his keys. Described as an 'extremely dangerous criminal', he was jailed for another eleven years, which he must serve after the French sentence. Hopefully he will stay in prison until he is eighty-eight.

CHAPTER FIFTEEN

AT THE MERCY OF THE LESBIAN AVENGERS

I t was all I needed. I had been at my chief reporter's desk at the *Sunday Times* until 2 a.m. that Saturday morning writing a Focus, a page-length news feature, on former Cabinet ministers who had taken well-paid City jobs in companies they had helped privatise. I had interviewed Lord Tebbit, the former Trade and Industry Secretary who had privatised BT and later joined it as a non-executive director ('What's the problem? I waited more than two and a half years,' he said) and still needed to speak to Gordon Brown, then shadow Chancellor, for a counter-view.

I got to bed at home in Kent at 3.40 a.m. and was up at 7.40 a.m. for my hour-long car journey back to work. My wife hardly noticed my presence.

Our office was then in an old one-storey rum warehouse which once formed part of London docklands and now housed both *The Times* and the *Sunday Times* alongside the cobbled Pennington Street at the front of the Wapping plant.

Once settled at my desk, I knocked out a story about a Labour punch-up on South Tyneside Council and spoke to Brown. 'The Cabinet room to the boardroom has become one gigantic revolving door,' he said.

Little did I realise that, as we spoke, someone had designs on our own revolving 'door' – a turnstile gate at the side of the Wapping plant which staff used to go to and from a nearby supermarket and which was guarded by a lone security officer.

I added Brown's quotes to the article, which was to be published the next day under the headline 'I'm All Right, John' and around a huge graphic showing Margaret Thatcher's Cabinet in 1988–89 and the plum jobs thirteen of them had landed since then. I still had a few calls into some of them and was awaiting a reply.

It was noon when I suddenly became aware that a large number of women had invaded the newsroom. At first, I saw a woman in a smart PVC coat and others with cameras and thought it was a film crew on a tour of the offices. We were used to that.

Then they started chanting. 'Print the news, not your views' and 'The *Sunday Times* prints lies. We demand the right to reply.'

I looked again. The women had pins in their ears, shaved hair and black T-shirts with the design of an anarchist's bomb, its fuse lit, and the words 'The Lesbian Avengers'. Some were 'armed', although the guns turned out to be pump-action water pistols.

It all came rushing back to me. Four weeks earlier, I had penned a page lead headlined: 'Lesbian Militants Target Gay Men'.

It told how women protesters had stormed into more than thirty homosexual bars in central London, confiscated every copy of a gay magazine called *MX* they could find and took them to a recycling plant to be pulped.

Its 'crime' was to publish an article with the headline: 'Dicks and Dykes Divided?', which questioned whether gays and lesbians really had anything in common.

'Britain's lesbians are on the warpath,' I had written, 'and their unlikeliest target is Britain's gay men.'

'For twenty-five years, the two have been thrown together in the campaign for homosexual reforms. But lesbians have found themselves increasingly marginalised while predominantly male concerns, such as Aids and the age of consent, have become dominant issues, and gay organisations have taken much of the available funding.'

Sir Ian McKellen, the actor and a leading member of the Stonewall lobbying group, said he agreed with the Avengers when I spoke to him. 'Once you have a cause, it can be extremely frustrating if your voice is not heard,' he told me.

The Lesbian Avengers had begun in New York as a direct action group. I had tracked down one of the founders of the British campaign, Lynn Sutcliffe, a thirty-year-old drama teacher from Lewisham, south London, who had written a book on coming out, entitled *50 Ways to Tell Your Mother*.

I interviewed her on the telephone. She said that pulping the gay magazine was intended to give gay 'disco bunnies' a shock.

It was one of her first actions. She had helped organise twenty other 'zaps' in recent weeks, including bursting into a Save The Children meeting attended by Princess Anne in protest at the charity's decision to drop the comedian Sandi Toksvig as the compère of its seventy-fifth anniversary celebrations after she had come out in the *Sunday Times*.

Now Sutcliffe was sitting across my desk in the newsroom. Andrew Alderson, the paper's night news editor who had joined us on my recommendation from the *Sunday Express*, usually sat opposite me but was temporarily away from his desk.

Behind, with his back to me, sat 22-year-old Simon Reeve, the future star presenter of BBC travel documentaries who had started on the paper as post boy but had shown so much initiative and charm that he had joined the newsroom as a junior reporter. He was also very good at getting coffees.

'Where is Maurice Chittenden?' asked Sutcliffe.

She and her seven companions had rushed the solitary security guard minding our side entrance and run across a car park straight into our building. It was obvious to me that they had had inside help, probably from what we called the 'soft end' of the newspaper, where they wrote about the arts, books, fashion and travel, but they were off target by one desk.

Nicholas Hellen, a colleague, chipped in: 'Maurice? He's not here. I don't think he's in.'

I joined in. 'Maurice Chittenden? No, he's out,' I said, standing up.

At that moment, Simon tapped me on the shoulder. As I turned to speak to him, his eyes motioned down towards my desk. Sitting there was a letter from the British Film Institute addressed to me. Lynn's head had turned to survey the room. I quickly flipped the letter over so the address was face down.

Addressing the room, Sutcliffe said, 'He rang me five times to get the quote he wanted, then promised he wouldn't use my name and did.'

In my defence, I had a simple code when it came to identifying sources. If they came to me as a whistle-blower and asked not to be identified, I would go to heaven and earth to protect their identity. Just four days earlier I had defied the Attorney General before the parliamentary privileges committee when he demanded to know who had been our source on the vexed question of MPs taking cash for questions. However, if I identified an interviewee, tracked them down, got them talking and they then said they did not want to be identified, I used a ruse where I told them repeatedly, 'I understand'. It may have given them the impression they would stay anonymous, but all I was really doing was saying that I realised that was what they wanted.

'The story was five months old,' Sutcliffe went on, trying to assert that the swoop on the gay bars to seize the MX magazines was ancient history.

Alderson, ever quick with a retort, said, 'That's more recent than most of Maurice's stories.'

The Avengers, however, were in no mood for jocularity. They started to blow whistles. I saw one take out a padlock. What was she doing? I thought. Why padlock that desk? There's nothing in it.

In fact, she had taken out a pair of handcuffs, and she and others were now handcuffing themselves to drawers.

There were eight of them in all; some had stayed outside, 'armed' with expensive toy machine guns that fired ping pong balls. Our security staff, fearing the worst, had dialled 999 and police vans were on their way.

I offered to help. 'I'll go and see if I can find Maurice...'

Walking out of the building, I crossed the road to the new tower block that housed our tabloid titles, the canteen and the library. Seeking refuge in the latter, I rang in for progress reports and began receiving visitors.

Down below the library, Piers Morgan, then the mischievous editor of the *News of the World*, was sitting in his office and noticed the kerfuffle unfolding outside. I had met him six years earlier when we had both been sent to cover the opening night of the Rolling Stones' Steel Wheels tour in Philadelphia. He was only twenty-four then but already showing the ability and the arrogance that was to propel him to such dizzy heights years later.

Morgan despatched reporter Sarah Courtenay and a photographer to cover the fracas.

The Avengers were still blowing their whistles and shouting 'Media lies, no surprise' when she arrived. One yelled: 'If we're still here at 5 p.m., can we watch *Brookside*?'

Another protestor told Courtenay: 'We've been misrepresented. We want a retraction.' It wasn't true. They were just using my article for another 'zap' to draw attention to themselves.

Police officers began to arrive in the office. By this time, acting editor John Witherow came out of his office to plead with the Avengers to leave. 'Inspector,' he told the lead policeman, 'I have asked them to leave. They won't.'

When I was told the *News of the World* was in our office, taking pictures and talking to the protesters, I decided to leave the plant. I telephoned Simon Reeve, who brought me my coat and car keys, but, as I tried to drive out the main gates, I found they were locked and had police officers standing in front of them – for the first time since the Battle of Wapping nearly a decade earlier.

I turned around and drove slowly through the plant to Gate 6, a rear exit in Pennington Street that was really only for use by the lorries carrying our newsprint. As I was leaving, four 'pigs' – police vans each full of seven or eight policemen and women – drove into the plant and parked outside the *Sunday Times*. Four more vans were parked outside: sixty officers in all.

Outside the plant there were twenty demonstrators from the Avengers and the Outrage gay rights' group. They had telephoned every Sunday newspaper from the Texaco garage on The Highway opposite the turning to the plant to tell them the Avengers had occupied the *Sunday Times*.

I drove around the corner to the Sir Sydney Smith, a Truman's pub in Dock Street that had been a sole refuge for reporters during the Wapping dispute when other pubs were full of striking pickets. Graham Harling, the landlord, whose family had had the pub for almost half a century, and I had become close friends. Unfortunately, it was too early and the pub was closed.

When I rang in, Charles Hymas on the news desk said the Avengers had gone. As I drove back to the plant, however, there was a huge TNT lorry carrying newsprint stuck in the entrance, unable to move for the chanting demonstrators that had surrounded it.

I spent a couple of uncomfortable minutes seated in my car, nodding my head and smiling my silent support of the protest, before I negotiated around the lorry and re-entered the plant via Pennington Street.

The demo had caused havoc. The security guards were reluctant to remove the protestors in case they were accused of assault. But, after an hour in which no stories were being written in a crucial part of the day, the police moved in and used bolt cutters to snap the handcuffs. The lesbians then left peacefully.

Apparently there was a jolly atmosphere in a pub nearby when the Avengers gathered to celebrate. There was much laughter about the supposed disgruntlement of the male journalists in the newsroom and the 'uncanny silence' that greeted the shout: 'One in ten are gay – why don't you say who you are?'

Back at my desk, I worried that other newspapers would ring for quotes. Tony Bambridge, the managing editor, had already had the *News of the World* and the *Sunday Sport* on. 'It was very unpleasant and held up production,' he told them.

I disguised my voice when answering the phone, talking to one caller out of the side of my mouth and 'taking a message for Maurice' about alleged corruption in the tobacco industry.

Alderson sneaked into the Insight office where I had previously worked and rang me as 'Dai Davies of PA'. Ian Birrell, then the news editor, tried as 'Dave Monday of the *Sunday Express*'. I recognised both their voices and saw through their pranks.

Then I got another call. 'Mr Chittenden,' said a distinguished man's voice.

'Who's calling?' said I, adopting the voice of an East End gangster.

'Norman Fowler.'

'Oh, sorry Sir Norman...'

He was ringing me back about the story of ex-Cabinet ministers taking City jobs. I called my story back on my computer screen and added his quotes before leaving the office for a quick drink with colleagues at the Old Rose pub around the corner before driving home.

Witherow had clearly been put out by the protest. I was three minutes from home when I was telephoned on my mobile. The editor wanted a figure for cash earnings on each of the thirteen former ministers featured in the graphic with my 'I'm Alright, John' feature.

There was no way I could do it over the phone, so I did a U-turn and drove back to the office. Once there, I painstakingly sat down and, working alongside one our graphic artists, added the figures to the graphic. Some were earning as much as £290,000 a year. I finally got home at 10.10 p.m. for a meal of Chinese chicken and rice.

The next day, the *News of the World* published a story over a whole page under the headline: "The Editor, Sixty Coppers, Eight Lesbians (and Four Pairs of Handcuffs!)'. The four pictures used included one of Witherow looking very uncomfortable – 'depressed-looking', *The Guardian* later said – as he tried to talk the protestors into leaving his newsroom. Birrell and Reeve looked on. Another showed Sutcliffe being led away by officers, punching the air in triumph. She said later, 'In fact, the best and fairest coverage we got of the whole action was from the *News of the World*.'

The gay press, of course, loved the theatrics of it all. 'Did they really need riot police to remove eight dykes?' one Avenger told the *Pink Paper*. 'It was outrageous and looking back, a bit humorous – I can't believe how frightened they all got of us. But it was a very good demonstration.'

The *Sunday Times*, by contrast, chose not to inform its 1.2 million readers that its offices had been invaded. Instead, it was working on its own vengeance plot. We could not help but notice that one of the lesbians pictured in the *News of the World*, handcuffed to a desk drawer, bore an uncanny resemblance to Ciaran Byrne, a young Irishman who was another of our junior reporters.

Richard Ellis, the head of news, came up with the madcap scheme of getting Byrne to infiltrate the Avengers, posing as a lesbian. They would get him a voice coach and someone from the soft end of the paper would show him how to dress like a woman.

It was almost as crazy as another news editor's plan, five years earlier, to get Mazher Mahmood, yet to become the 'Fake Sheikh' of Fleet Street legend, to board an El Al bus at Heathrow while carrying a toy gun. Most of us – especially Mazher – realised that he was in great danger of being shot dead by the Israeli airline's security guards.

Likewise, Byrne baulked at the idea, and wiser heads like

Bambridge – who used to have a poster in his office saying: 'Old age and treachery will always overcome youth and talent' – intervened. Byrne got some no-hope assignments for the next year or so before he left the paper.

Simon Reeve did not fare much better and was eventually fired for getting the score of a rugby international wrong on the front page. Witherow is rugby mad and so this was a cardinal sin at the *Sunday Times*. Luckily, Simon had the nous to write a book about Osama bin Laden three years before 9/11 and before anybody had ever heard of him (bin Laden that is). He was still only twenty-six.

Piers Morgan and I would meet again ten years after the invasion, when he attended the leaving do of James Anslow, the *News of the World* production editor whom I had known since my days as a student journalist. 'Was it really you?' he chuckled. 'I couldn't believe they missed you.'

My colleagues at the *Sunday Times* remembered, too. They produced a mocked-up front page with stories all about me when I was finally shown the door. 'Lesbian Avengers: We Will Get You', read one of the headlines. The byline was: 'Maurice Chittenden, Sexual Politics Editor'.

It read: 'Last night the Lesbian Avengers, a radical campaigning group, issued Chittenden with a chilling warning. Jangling a set of genital cuffs (junior size), a spokeswoman vowed: "We never give up. We know where you live, Chittenden. We will get you and we will exact a terrible revenge."'

I detected the humour of Ian Houghton, the paper's chief sub-editor. It added: 'Speaking from Dungarees House, the

Avengers' London headquarters, the spokeswoman added: "Chittenden will spend the rest of his days looking over his shoulder. Remember, he has to be lucky all the time, we have to be lucky just once.'"

CHAPTER SIXTEEN

RED CARPETS AND BLACK EXITS

When Hollywood actor Eddie Murphy walked down the red-carpeted stairs in Leicester Square for the British premiere of his first *Beverly Hills Cop* film, he had unwelcome company at his side. Me.

I had been refused access to the star, so I knew it was my only chance of getting a quote. I only had about ten seconds before security guards would whisk me aside so I asked him what he thought about British cops.

'I can't understand why they don't carry guns, man,' was all I got. Not much, but enough for a page-one picture story in *The Sun* the next day.

In the days before A-list celebrities were PR-managed to within an inch of their lives, the red carpet was always a good place to snatch a quote.

When Princess Diana wore a daring off-the-shoulder dress at a charity fashion event in London's Guildhall, I 'ambushed' the late Christopher Reeve, the *Superman* star, as he left the show.

'The princess looked absolutely smashing,' he said. 'It's a fabulous dress, and I am ordering one by the same designer for my wife.'

His comment helped lift the story to the splash in *The Sun* next morning under the headline 'Our Bare Lady'.

Diving into a lift at the last minute behind a celebrity was another trick of mine. For those twenty seconds that the lift is in motion, you are an equal with the star, another passenger in the same lift. I did that with Terry Wogan when he left the BBC the first time around and he told me, with false modesty, that he was just 'a jobbing broadcaster'.

I also had the audacity to ambush Rupert Murdoch as he was going to the lift at the *Sunday Times*. For a man who employs so many journalists, Murdoch doesn't enjoy speaking to them that much. I had only exchanged pleasantries with him on the odd occasion before and on this day there was a strict 'Don't approach the chairman' edict.

These were difficult times. Two weeks earlier, we had reported on our front page the arrest of five journalists from *The Sun* by detectives investigating alleged corruption of public officials. Staff at *The Sun* were in a mutinous mood as a result of the supposed 'help' that management was giving the police. Morale there was very low.

However, Rupert had a surprise for them. He was launching the *Sun on Sunday* the next day as a replacement for the *News of the World*, which he had closed down the previous year at the height of the phone-hacking scandal. I figured he would welcome either some gratitude from an ex-*Screws* reporter or an opportunity to promote the new product. He duly obliged with an exclusive quote for the next morning. That night I took part in a Radio 5 live discussion about the future of the paper with senior journalists from *The Observer* and *Financial Times*.

Show business reporting is sometimes seen as a soft option amongst journalists, but I take my hat off to those involved. I once spent half an hour in the bedroom of a Kensington hotel with George Michael. He was pleasant enough company, but he prickled at any mention by me of the money he was earning or the homes he was buying, and although we talked about the video for his new single, 'I Want Your Sex', there were no killer quotes or angles. (It was probably a good idea that I did not mention 'Wham's Whopper', a splash I once had in *The Sun* when his singing partner Andrew Ridgeley lied about being hit in the face with a champagne bucket in a row over a girl in an attempt to cover up the fact that the bandages on his nose were the result of a nose job.) I was rather relieved when the Saturday edition of *The Independent* ran its own interview with George, thus negating the exclusivity of our own chat, and my interview was dropped.

At least his lovely PR Connie Filippello did not sit in on the interview, which is an increasing problem for journalists these days. If a PR thinks their star is in danger of going off message by saying something remotely interesting that might deflect from their reason for granting the interview in the first place – to promote a new film, book or record – they will interrupt. Indeed, I believe that this close PR management of the stars coupled with the pressure from newspaper executives above to get a story was a strong contributory factor in the phone-hacking scandal.

It used to be the case that you telephoned the stars direct and they were happy to chat. 'I understand Angela Rippon was abroad and missed seeing the Christmas special she was in with you and Ernie,' I told Eric Morecambe once on the phone. 'She was a broad in the show too,' he quipped back, giving me a fun line.

Michael Winner was another who could always be relied on to come up with a witty line. The film director, who listed 'being difficult' as one of his hobbies in his *Who's Who* entry, was offered an OBE by Downing Street to honour his 22-year campaign, prompted by the murder of WPC Yvonne Fletcher outside the Libyan Embassy, to mark the bravery of officers who had been killed on duty.

He turned it down in a fit of pre-David Beckham pique. 'An OBE is what you get if you clean the toilets well at King's Cross station,' he told me. It was a good enough quote to make a page one story in the *Sunday Times* the following day.

Once, I was at *The Sun* doing a ring-round of stars to ask what present they would buy their worst enemy. I opted to phone Tommy Cooper, a brilliant comedian on stage but virtually an alcoholic off it.

When he came to the phone, summoned by Gwen, his long-suffering wife, it was clear he was in his cups from the whisky or gin or both. 'Tommy, what gift would you get your worst enemy?' Silence. Ten seconds passed. 'Tommy?'

'A jigsaw,' he finally slurred.

'With the final piece missing,' I added. Such was the way interviews were conducted and quotes obtained.

A few months later, Tommy died on live television at the age of sixty-six. I was sitting at home with my wife Jan watching an ITV show called *Live from Her Majesty's*, being broadcast from that London theatre, when he collapsed. Sandie Lawrence, his assistant, had helped drape him in a cloak as he stood in front of the closed curtains. Suddenly he went down, sinking to his knees and falling into the curtain. Both the assistant and the audience thought it was part of the act. So did I. Indeed, they tried to carry on with the show. My wife thought differently and I phoned Alan Watkins, the night news editor at *The Sun*. Of course, it was the splash next day and a few days later I was asked to cover his funeral at Mortlake Crematorium in west London.

It was not the first time my wife had come to my aid while I was a freelance. Six months before, she had been sitting watching *Blue Peter* with our two young sons, aged four and two, at our home in St Albans on a Monday afternoon when presenter Janet Ellis reported that over the weekend the fabled *Blue Peter* garden had been vandalised. She alerted me and I quickly started ringing the nationals. The tip alone brought us £1,000. It was later suggested that the vandals included teenage footballers that would later become Premier League stars.

The spring of 1984 was a sad time for Britain's comedy fans. Six weeks after Tommy's death, Watkins telephoned me at home in the early hours of a Monday morning and got me out of bed to ask me to go to the home of Eric Morecambe in nearby Harpenden.

Morecambe had been taking part in a charity show to raise money for disabled people at a theatre in Tewkesbury,

Gloucestershire, on the Sunday night. Most of it was ad-lib chat, but at one point he had spoken about his heart bypass surgery, and the theatre hushed when he began talking about his late pal Tommy.

He said Tommy had gone on too long and done too much. He joined the musicians on the stage for the encores, larking about on various instruments including the xylophone and a bongo drum. But when he walked into the wings after a string of curtain calls, he collapsed with his third heart attack in sixteen years.

He was rushed to hospital in Cheltenham. I was the first to get to his house, where his son Gary told me he had just died. He was fifty-eight. It was very late and I don't know how many copies of *The Sun* carried my copy, but two weeks later 4 million copies carried my report of his funeral at his local church in Harpenden.

Dickie Henderson, another famous comic who was to die of cancer within sixteen months of his friend, read the address and told the star-studded congregation how Eric had 'booked' him for the occasion.

He had written to congratulate Henderson on the way he had paid tribute to the late Arthur Askey at his thanksgiving audience. In the note, Eric said, 'I would like to thank you for the tribute you gave Arthur. It reminded us of what a great comedian he was. I would like to book you for mine to remind everybody what a great comic I was. PS I will pay you when I see you down there.'

Britain's best-loved comedian had left a last gag, which

brought smiles and laughter amongst the tear-filled eyes at the service. Outside, I caught up with Ernie Wise, his stage partner for forty-three years. He summoned up an image of one of Eric's favourite routines: 'For one moment I had the feeling he was going to walk across the back of the church in that raincoat and little cap with that carrier bag.'

Just three months later, I had the splash in *The Sun* again with another death amongst Britain's funny men. People say it comes in threes. Leonard Rossiter also died from a heart attack after collapsing in a theatre.

The star of *Rising Damp* and *The Fall and Rise of Reginald Perrin* was fifty-seven, the youngest of the three and a super-fit squash player too. He was found slumped in his dressing room at the Lyric Theatre in London's Shaftesbury Avenue, where he had been taking a quick break from being on stage performing in Joe Orton's *Loot*.

A doctor in the audience answered a request for help from the stage. He left his front-row seat to give Rossiter first aid before an ambulance arrived and took him to hospital where he died.

Next day, I was working at the *News of the World* and went to the small terraced house in Fulham, west London, that Rossiter shared with his wife Gillian and their eleven-year-old daughter Camille. A male relative answered the door. He was very polite but insisted that neither he nor the family had anything to say.

I went for some lunch and then, driving around Fulham to waste time before ringing into the office with the bad news, I spotted the same man walking in the street. He was clearly on an errand to the shops. I quickly parked up and 'bumped' into him as he came out of one of the shops. Leaving my notepad and pen in my pocket, I began chatting to him.

Just like the red carpet and the lift, the pavement was a leveller. He was away from the comfort zone of the family home and we were equals: two men standing in the street. He opened up and told me how Rossiter's wife Gillian had come back from the hospital and gone to their daughter's bedroom to gently wake her and tell her, 'Daddy's dead'. I immediately felt for the girl. It was almost a repeat of how I was awoken at the age of eight by my stepbrother John and told my father had died. As I filed my copy, I was sure the nation would warm to the family's situation. The story made a page lead in the next day's *News of the World*.

However, of all my brushes with show business, there was none stranger than the story of Vera Lynn, the wartime singer, and Carlos the Jackal, the international assassin.

At the *Sunday Times*, I was in the habit of going through the piles of books sent in by publishers in the hope of a review. Sometimes I was looking for a story, other times I was looking for something to read. 'Or something to sell,' my colleagues would claim. One day, in the autumn of 1998, I picked up a book called *Jackal* by a young Rome-based journalist named John Follain.

It was a history of Ilich Ramirez Sanchez, the Caracas-born revolutionary known to the world as Carlos. I thought it would be a standard biography but, flicking through the index at the back, one name caught my eye: Vera Lynn. What could the forces' sweetheart possibly have had to do with the war on terror?

I turned to the appropriate page. There were just eighteen words about how Carlos had tracked down her married name and address to include on a list of possible targets in the early 1970s.

Now, throughout my career, I have coined a few maxims to share with my fellow hacks. One is that 'A journalist tired of doing his or her expenses is tired of life'. Another, with apologies to John Lewis, is that 'My stories are never knowingly undertold'. There's 'Don't overestimate your rivals' and, apt for this occasion, 'A story is not old until it's been told'.

I was on a bit of a roll. I had had the page-three lead the previous weekend with a story I had talked out of David Bowie's London spokesman about how the rock star and his wife Iman had been to dinner with Tony and Cherie Blair at Chequers.

For many journalists at the *Sunday Times*, it is page three, rather than the front page, that is considered the best place to land a story. The splash can be any political angle done at the last minute, whereas page three is a larger canvas. A story there can be displayed with two or three images and takes a lot longer to write (although I did manage to do one in two hours and five minutes on 21-year-old England rugby player Maro Itoje in March 2016, after being commissioned at 5 p.m. because he had just won man of the match for his role in decimating Wales in the Six Nations at Twickenham).

I thought a dastardly plot to kill Vera Lynn was a natural for a page-three lead and began persuading my editors while digging into the story. The intro wrote itself: 'The image could have sprung from Frederick Forsyth's most famous novel. The Jackal steadies the rifle and squints down the telescopic sight.

The cross hairs settle on the victim's exposed temple. Except the target is not General de Gaulle. It is Vera Lynn.'

First, I established that her name was indeed included on a list seized from Carlos's London hideout in 1975 and held in the files of Scotland Yard's anti-terrorist branch. Others on the list, along with such obvious names as Edward Heath, the then Tory Prime Minister, included actor and director Richard Attenborough, Yehudi Menuhin, the famed violinist, the playwright John Osborne, and Lord Sainsbury, the retailer.

Of course, he could have just plucked the names from the pages of *The Guardian*, a paper he claims to have read as his 'daily' since 1966. But Carlos's intentions were deadly enough. In December 1975, he burst into the home of Teddy Sieff, the president of Marks & Spencer, in St John's Wood, north-west London, and, finding him in his bath, fired one bullet from his pistol, which bounced off Sieff between his nose and upper lip, knocking him unconscious. The gun then jammed. Thinking his victim dead, Carlos fled, but Sieff survived. 'Usually, I fire three bullets in the nose, which kills immediately,' Carlos said later.

Lynn and the others were spared because Carlos's cover was blown after he shot dead two French secret service agents and a fellow terrorist-turned-informer in six seconds at his Paris flat in June 1975.

An innocent friend in London, alerted by news reports of the shooting, looked into a bag Carlos had left behind in a flat in Bayswater, west London. Inside were three guns, rubber coshes and a pack of gelignite.

In Forsyth's novel, de Gaulle is targeted by an assassin while inspecting ranks of wartime veterans on Liberation Day in Paris. Lynn, who each year until she was too frail attended the Remembrance Day service in her home village in East Sussex, could have fallen in similar circumstances before Carlos was seized from a villa in Sudan by French counter-espionage officers in 1994 after more than twenty years on the run.

'But why me?' the singer, then a spritely 81-year-old, asked me when I called at her home. 'It is incredible: Carlos and Vera Lynn. I suppose he thought if he got me it might upset a few people.'

The answer to her question may have been the Queen's birthday honours two weeks before the Paris murders, which had made Lynn a Dame of the British Empire.

The recently widowed singer told me: 'I do recall some years ago I was given a little warning. The local bobby came and said I had been included on a list. He said someone was after one or two people. I didn't hear any more and it faded from my memory.'

I don't know if it was to be a kidnapping or an assassination. I suppose I was a target because I have such a strong connection with everyone in this country. Funnily enough, I have just come back from my home in France. We have a collection of books down there, including Forsyth's *The Day of the Jackal*. I just hope the Jackal is in prison for a long time.

So do I for that matter. He did not take kindly to my page-three story published under the headline: 'Vera Lynn Was on Carlos the Jackal's Murder List'. It used to be the norm for a journalist to contact anyone they were accusing of doing something criminal or immoral to get their answer to the charge before the story was published. I felt duty-bound to pen a letter to Carlos at La Santé prison in Paris, despite knowing that the censors usually intercepted letters from journalists. I was pleasantly surprised, therefore, when I got a reply a few weeks later, giving me another page lead by listing the people he wanted to kill and crossing off the names of those he claimed were never in danger. One of the latter was Tony Benn, the veteran Labour MP, whom we had not named in our article.

Those he wanted to see dead included members of the Jordanian royal family, whom he held responsible for a crackdown on Palestinian guerrillas following their Black September uprising in 1970.

Writing in English with a black ballpoint on lined A4 paper in a childlike scrawl, the assassin said:

I recall that twenty-odd years ago was published in London a supposed 'hit list' with many names, including Yehudi Menuhin and Viscount Anthony Wedgwood Benn. I doubt there is anyone in the world who would want to harm the great violinist and humanist. Regarding the 'Peter Pan' of Labour's left, what good his elimination could possibly do the advancement of the Palestinian cause? Absurd.

Others on the hit list fared less favourably. Wasfi al-Tal, the Jordanian Prime Minister and defence minister during the uprising and blamed for its suppression, was, Carlos wrote, 'executed in Cairo in 1971'. He was attending an Arab League summit when he was shot in the lobby of the Sheraton Hotel where the meeting was being held. The new Black September terrorist group claimed responsibility, one of the three gunmen pausing long enough to kneel and lick the blood flowing across the marble floor, exclaiming, 'I drink his blood.'

Carlos added begrudgingly that Zaid al-Rifai, another Jordanian Prime Minister, 'survived an attack' while ambassador in London in December 1971. He was wounded by machine gun fire. The late Abdel Hamid Sharaf, King Hussein of Jordan's cousin, was not killed – but for a very different reason. 'He was in fact, a secret member of our organisation,' the letter claimed. He signed it: 'Yours in revolution, Carlos'.

When I contacted Tony Benn, however, he knew exactly why he had been put on the list. He was added to it when he became Energy Secretary in Harold Wilson's government in 1975. As such, he was on a par with Sheikh Ahmed Zaki Yamani, the Saudi oil minister who was one of eleven OPEC ministers kidnapped by Carlos in Vienna that year for a ransom of $50 million.

'Carlos would have gone round all the energy ministers but I have always been sympathetic to the Palestinian cause,' Benn told me. 'I was a bit cross to be put on the list … I thought I deserved better than that. Yamani gave me a detailed account of the Vienna kidnapping and said what a cool guy Carlos was and how he had given the Venezuelan oil minister a letter to post to his relations.'

So, two page leads just from looking in the index of a book. I was so grateful to John Follain, the author, that, on my recommendation, he got a job working for the *Sunday Times*, first in Rome and then Paris, for about ten years before he fell victim to the economic cuts.

As for Dame Vera and her would-be assassin, I wrote in one of the articles, 'The paths of Carlos the Jackal and Lynn are unlikely to cross again.'

Not quite. On 20 March 2017, Vera Lynn celebrated her 100th birthday. On the very same day, Carlos was before a court in Paris accused of a grenade attack forty-two years earlier on a Paris shop that killed two people. He denounced the trial as 'absurd' – just as he had my story – and said he was being tried on phoney evidence. A few days later, he was sentenced to his third life term.

CHAPTER SEVENTEEN

THE LEFTIE-BASHING UNIT

When Andrew Neil became editor of the *Sunday Times*, he was alarmed at how many left-leaning journalists were working on the paper. The situation improved, as far as he was concerned, when Rupert Murdoch moved his newspaper operations to a new plant in east London and many of those whose politics he distrusted became 'Wapping refuseniks' and declared they would not cross the print unions' picket lines.

There is a folk legend at the *Sunday Times* that at about this time one edition of the paper's diary column, either Quidnunc or its successor Atticus, was so angered that the lead letter of each item spelled out the acrostic 'I'm not a Trots'. It may have been a hidden message to the editor from a sub-editor worried about being purged; it may even have been an executive doing it on the editor's behalf. Nevertheless, word soon spread that what Neil regarded as the once-fashionable, increasingly dated left-wing views of the older journalists who had worked under Harry Evans were now old hat.

As if to prove his point, Neil set out to expose the left-wing posturing of Labour councils who were spending their ratepayers' money on political propaganda rather than much-needed services. It was decided to form the London Boroughs' Unit (LBU) to look into authorities in the metropolitan area. It was not long before an office wag converted its initials into 'Leftie Bashing Unit' and it was a name that stuck with us.

I was in charge and at various times the unit's ad hoc membership included the paper's local government correspondent, someone from our financial team to crunch the numbers, a political reporter covering Labour and our latest northern stringer. Later I was given a wider brief to help attack the trade unions crippling Britain with strikes and so-called Spanish practices. As such, I clashed with the likes of Arthur Scargill, the mineworkers' leader, and helped 'discover' such stalwarts of the left as Len McCluskey, the future Unite leader, and Bob Crow, the late rail workers' leader.

Jeremy Corbyn would have been at home at most town halls in London in the 1980s and 1990s. Labour-run councils seemed to compete for the title of the looniest local authority in the land. Some of them hoisted the red flag and declared themselves 'socialist republics'.

Streets were named after South African detainees. Meetings were held with Sinn Féin leaders. Millions were spent on advertising council districts as 'nuclear-free zones', as if they were set to levy a congestion charge on any passing Cruise missile. New units were set up to monitor the police, fight against apartheid and ensure race equality and equal opportunities. While at *The*

Sun, I had rented a grotty flat in Dalston and tapped Kelvin MacKenzie for regular payments on expenses to pay the rent while trying to get a grant from Islington Council for my bogus police monitoring group. It did not work. (Nor did my attempt to get money from the Heritage Lottery Fund for the 'Biblical Art Society' while I was at the *Sunday Times*.)

Harold Wilson had warned his party in the late 1960s that the bedsit brigade were taking over and that is exactly what happened: the middle-class bourgeoisie hijacked it.

The leaders of these councils were far more colourful characters than the grey men and women in charge today.

Haringey in north London had Bernie Grant, the first black council leader, and his wife, Sharon Lawrence, who once delighted in inviting me into what she called their 'non-sexist kitchen'.

Lambeth in south London had Edward 'Red Ted' Knight and Linda Bellos. Knight became a hero of the broad left when he and thirty other councillors were surcharged and banned from office in 1986 for failing to set a rate in time. Journalists who found Knight washing dishes in a restaurant assumed he was down on his luck but I subsequently discovered that he had been granted a lease from Lambeth Council and he briefly ran the restaurant under the name of Pebbles before selling it for £75,000.

Brent had Merle Amory, a former shorthand typist whom the popular press described as 'a young black beauty'. I came a cropper when I wrote about black sections in the Labour Party with links to Libya and Islamic extremism trying to take over control of schools in Brent (much like the 'Trojan Horse' stories of recent times) and described one headmaster as 'a former professional limbo dancer'. He wasn't, but he had once won a competition dancing the Twist. An apology duly appeared in the paper and former colleagues still like to take me to task over it today.

Most of these 'lefties' are now just footnotes in municipal history, but Knight came back from the wilderness when Corbyn became leader. In November 2016, he became branch chair – in Labour it is sexist to say chairman – in Gipsy Hill ward, where he has lived for years in a house with a brass plate reading 'Edward Knight'.

There were two ways we went around puncturing these figures inflated with their own self-importance. One was to attack their waste of public funds; the other was to ridicule them for their daft rule-making or their expenditure on some useless symbol of their authority.

Take Haringey Council (motto: extending rights – defending services). I spotted a council advertisement in the local newspaper for a new post of animal rights officer. The same paper carried a story about a local family distraught at the loss of Minnie, their pet mongoose. The animal had disappeared from their home through a cat flap. John Bernal and his children had put up posters and made leaflets to post through people's letterboxes.

I sensed a chance for mischief. I wrote a piece suggesting that if Minnie was found the Bernals could expect a visit from their council's newest unit to enquire how and why they taught her to roller skate, one of the tricks she could perform. After doing what it could to eradicate the evils of racism and sexism, I said, Haringey was all set to tackle 'speciesism', discrimination by humans against another animal because it is of a different species.

I added that the council, facing debts of £500 million and a list of 5,000 homeless people, had upset political opponents by accepting applications from members of the Animal Liberation Front. Ten of its members had been given prison sentences of up to ten years each earlier that month.

A council spokesman told me: 'The council has a policy of equal opportunity for people with criminal records. So that means someone with a conviction for a firebombing or releasing animals from captivity will be considered.'

The story made it onto the front page under the Orwellian headline of 'All Animals Are Equal – Official'.

Eighteen months later, the new policy came back to bite the burghers of Haringey on the bottom, giving me a new story in the process. The councillors were left with red faces (I even worked that old pun into the story) after inviting the Moscow State Circus to put on a show and then discovering that a troupe of Cossack horsemen would ride roughshod over their ban on performing animals. The horses performing at Alexandra Park would have as many as three men riding on their backs. The last time a circus had come to town, Haringey Council deemed it cruel that a duck named Quackers should waddle into the ring merely to quack in time to music and banned Quackers after just one night's twenty-second performance.

Of course, it was not all animal crackers. One of our investigations that gave us a splash revealed that, using creative accountancy, councils had built up financial burdens totalling as much as £5 billion. The councils manipulated their accounting procedures to raise money that they could then spend but would not have to start repaying for several years.

Their ploy was aimed at overcoming government restrictions on spending, but it often relied on a future Labour government to settle the debt. Councils 'remortgaged' their town halls, schools and art galleries, or used office furniture and library books as security. The money raised in this way totalled more than the national debt of many Third World countries; much of it was owed to banks in France and Japan.

The most notorious example of this was Camden Council in north London and its leaseback deal for its parking meters. The forest of 2,800 parking meters in Camden's streets and squares showed a distinct lack of Gallic charm but I discovered that they were now theoretically owned by a Paris bank. The council 'sold' them for £125 each in a 'lease and leaseback' deal with the Banque Paribas to raise £13 million for town hall coffers.

Despite the opprobrium we heaped on such deals, they were not much different to the PFI deals Tony Blair and Gordon Brown got into to build NHS hospitals. Between 1997 and 2008, 90 per cent of all hospital construction funding was under PFI agreements, which have left the NHS with enormous debts.

I went back to the borough when its street cleaning and refuse collection service collapsed. 'Rubbish-strewn Camden Dirtier Than Khartoum' read the headline above the story. And again when the ruling Labour group admitted that it had paid a gardener £40,000 to stay at home for five years after he pointed to a can of meatballs and made a remark about his private parts to a female colleague. He only returned to work when the woman died.

I doubt if that story would have made it into the council's own monthly news magazine. Today, local authorities spend £50 million a year on these Town Hall Bugles that peddle a diet of mayoral tea parties, celebrity library openings and the glorious achievements of outsourced dustmen. They also threaten the very existence of local newspapers, which should act as a watchdog on local authority misspending. In Haringey, the local paper carried a series of page-one stories on the death of 'Baby P', often blaming the council for the scandal. The story was relegated to a left-hand inside page inside the authority's own glossy monthly magazine. 'What's the significance of that?' said a council spokesman when I asked about where it was placed.

Soon after John Witherow – never as politically motivated but always after good stories – replaced Andrew Neil, I took the LBU on a four-month tour, parachuting myself into a different authority up and down the country almost on a weekly basis to show how the loony left was still alive under New Labour.

The stories worked best if the council had a leader with a nickname to have fun with and policies that included building some silly monument or other.

First stop was Walsall in the West Midlands, where the leader was a man called Dave Church, whom I described as 'Citizen Dave, a burly former fork-lift driver with Brezhnev eyebrows and a colourful past that includes smashing a council tenant's window in an argument'. His plans included erecting two new concrete hippopotamuses in the civic square.

Such follies always made good copy. Labour-led Charnwood District Council in Leicestershire spent £23,000 on a statue of a man putting on a sock to celebrate the local hosiery industry, while Hackney in east London paid £40,000 for a clock tower to purposely tilt like the one in Pisa. 'It will lean to the left,' said Naomi Russell, a local Labour councillor. 'Some say that Hackney has done little else for the past forty years,' read my story.

Church, I discovered, lived on his generous council allowances and expenses and a £10,000 salary from the Willenhall Lock Museum, a collection of keys and padlocks illustrating the local locksmith industry. The museum survived only because of a £40,000-a-year grant from the council. It had just two employees: Church, and a former Labour mayor. Both were paid for a 37-hour week, but the museum only opened between 11 a.m. and 5 p.m. four days a week. Church was expelled from the Labour Party a few weeks after my story appeared.

Next I was in Gloucester, where Kevin Stephen, the Labour leader, 'a tattooed ex-sailor with Marx and Trotsky on his bookshelves', had plans to spend money on an inner-city farm, which would include a pen for Gloucester Old Spot pigs on a housing estate. The headline: 'Labour Council Sells Taxpayers a Pig in a Poke'.

Then it was on to Preston, where the target was Valerie Wise, 'a mousy figure in NHS spectacles who was nicknamed Olive Oyl when she stood in Ken Livingstone's shadow at the Great

London Council where she headed the women's committee.' She had moved north, reinvented herself with contact lenses and smart two-piece suits, and become leader of the council in an old mill town more famous for its football than its political zealotry.

The daughter of Audrey Wise, the town's Labour MP, she had angered Tony Blair's emerging New Labour by announcing plans to establish a socialist republic. She had launched Zero Tolerance, a campaign against alleged abuses of power by men. 'Like the Mark of Zorro,' I wrote, 'the letter Z is omnipresent in the town.' I told readers that while parents had queued at 2.30 a.m. to enrol their children on a summer holiday play scheme, she had merely telephoned to put her two sons on the list. She was found out and forced to withdraw the boys. When the issue was discussed in the council chamber she was forced to leave after the chief executive declared she had a non-pecuniary interest. Within a few minutes of her departure, her mother was spotted in the public gallery glowering at councillors.

I was in Rotherham in time for Christmas, but there were no Yuletide logs in the grate at Lord Scarborough's estate. Despite the rural setting of Sandbeck Park and the fact that fires had burned there since the eighteenth century, they had been banned by the Labour-led council under a Brussels-inspired clean air directive.

There was plenty of cheer, however, to be found in the town hall where the deputy leader, former Communist Garvin Reed, 'known as Comrade Garvin ... an Alexei Sayle lookalike with closely-cropped hair', was the architect of an anti-poverty unit.

It had a staff of three and a budget of £250,000 to prove that Rotherham was poverty-stricken, but seemed to turn a blind eye to council officers being awarded pay rises of up to £17,000 a year.

The union leaders opened themselves up to similar ridicule with their posturing and support for outdated restrictive practices.

I had first upset Arthur Scargill while at *The Sun* during the miners' strike of the early 1980s, after discovering that he had been voted the most hated man alive – ahead of Libya's Colonel Gaddafi (who we later discovered was bankrolling him) – in a survey amongst visitors to Madame Tussauds waxworks in London. Then I coined the phrase 'the Scargill surcharge' for the extra money added to household electricity bills because power stations had to burn oil instead of coal. We also took him to task for going to Moscow to address Soviet trade union leaders – 'likely to be former KGB colonels in leather coats plotting to make political capital of their guests' – and receiving Russian money to help prolong strikes. He always refused to talk to me, saying he did not talk to the 'Murdoch press', and quotes had to be obtained through a more sympathetic third party.

I discovered Bob Crow when he was a fresh-faced 31-year-old leading 11,000 London Underground workers at the Rail, Maritime and Transport Union (RMT) against a change in working practices that dated back to the 1920s. In those days, he was quite mild-mannered and almost baby-faced. 'I may be painted as a bogeyman, but in 1983 you would have thought Arthur Scargill had two horns and a tail,' he told me.

My intro was to be the foundation stone of every profile of him for the next twenty years: 'Bob Crow wears a pin-stripe suit and commutes to work in London every day like a million others. But instead of pictures of the family he has busts of Marx and Lenin on his desk.' Until his death in 2014, he was a member of so-called awkward squad of trade union leaders.

For a year or more I campaigned for the abolition of the national dock labour scheme, originally introduced as a safety net for dockers to do away with casual labour in 1947 but which, forty years later, had become the last bastion of trade union abuses known as 'Spanish customs'.

Under the scheme, employees in sixty-three ports were forced to use 9,400 registered dockworkers that had jobs for life unless they agreed to take a handsome redundancy package. These men, all belonging to the closed shop of the Transport and General Workers' Union (TGWU), could not be dismissed, and were paid even when there was no work.

Hiring of new workers under the scheme was effectively controlled by the union, which ensured most entrants were relatives or friends. It was just like the print unions in Fleet Street we had fought to free ourselves from in the Battle of Wapping all over again.

I visited ports like Liverpool, Grimsby, Bristol and Ipswich to expose how the closed shop had led to a wide range of abuses over the years. Propping up the scheme had cost the taxpayer an estimated £770 million since the early 1970s, but billions more were lost from the British economy as shippers moved to foreign ports.

It was on Merseyside I first came across Len McCluskey – re-elected as general secretary of Unite in April 2017 – who had spent eleven years working on the docks before becoming an officer of the TGWU. He had been a supporter of Derek Hatton and his Militant Tendency group at Liverpool Council but never a member of Militant. He was, however, as he told me, a strident defendant of the dock labour scheme.

I also met Alfie Kavanagh, the son and grandson of a docker, who had cadged a lift to work and toiled for five days loading steel into the hold of a Chinese freighter moored in the docks. It was the first full week he had worked for three months. But he did not suffer unduly; he got paid £29 a day to stay at home when there was no cargo to shift.

Once upon a time, he had assumed his sons would become dockers, but the youngest dockers in Liverpool were now in their forties and still sarcastically dubbed 'day-old chicks' by the older hands. In contrast, ports outside the scheme were thriving. Felixstowe in Suffolk, just a muddy creek on the River Orwell in 1947, was handling 13 million tonnes of cargo a year and had taken on 200 new dockers who were earning up to £700 a week by adding weekend shifts to their overtime. But the dockers of Liverpool were scornful of 'the farmers' place' as they called it. 'Did you hear about the Felixstowe docker who was killed last week by a bale of hay?' quipped a docker in the Atlantic pub on the Liverpool waterfront. 'One of his mates emptied the contents of his pay packet down the hatch.'

The abuses to be found in the dock labour scheme across British ports would not have been out of place on the New

York waterfront when labour racketeer Anthony 'Tough Tony' Anastasio and the Gambino crime family controlled the long-shoremen's union for thirty years.

They included 'ghost workers', who were paid to stand and watch while a non-registered but skilled contractor such as a crane driver did the actual unloading of the cargo; 'bobbers' or 'welters', who divided a job between them, so some worked on Monday and Wednesday, the other half Tuesday and Thursday, while the others 'bobbed' off but all turned up on Friday to collect their pay; 'moonlighters', who were paid a guaranteed fallback wage if there was no work and could keep busy driving mini-cabs or running market stalls; and 'dirty jobbers', who demanded extra money for working on dirty cargoes or rusty ships.

I had a major ally in David Davis, then a Tory backbencher but now the Brexit Secretary. Like me, he had grown up on a council estate and hated to see abuses of power. He was in-strumental in persuading Margaret Thatcher that the scheme had to go. While Britain was distracted by a visit by Mikhail Gorbachev, the last leader of the Soviet Union, she chaired a specially convened breakfast-time Cabinet meeting to abolish the scheme.

Neil Kinnock, the Labour leader, had at least stood up to Mil-itant. His speech to the party conference in 1985 had denounced Liverpool City Council and led to Derek Hatton shouting 'lies' at the platform. It was to be another speech, the toe-curling 'We're all right' while puffed up with over-confidence amid rock and opera music at the presidential-style Sheffield rally, that probably cost him the 1992 general election (the British public don't like triumphalism). Before that, however, he needed to boost Labour's election war chest.

Forget miners' galas and coffee mornings. The plan was to fete 230 of the rich and famous at the party's first £500-a-head fundraising dinner in the art deco ballroom of London's Park Lane Hotel. Now, while I loathe the far left, there is nothing better than a good bit of Gucci socialist bashing.

The only problem was that the press were banned (though the party was even then promising a Freedom of Information Act). I managed to chat up a female Labour press officer and persuade her to let me in to listen to the speeches. I lasted but a minute before Colin Byrne, Peter Mandelson's deputy and the party's head of press and broadcasting, grabbed me and led me to the exit. Now I can hardly describe Byrne, a PR professional, as a bruiser (although I did call him 'the Jack Nicholson looka-like' in my subsequent piece), but his grip left fingerprints on my arm for several days.

Undeterred, I opted for a different tactic. Knowing that jour-nalists from papers like the *Sunday Times* would now be on a proscribed list at the hotel, I telephoned an in-house travel company that now handled our travel arrangements and got them to book me into the hotel as a businessman who would be arriving late from Heathrow.

Once in my room, I set my travelling alarm clock for 6.30 a.m. and, on waking, dressed and headed down to the ballroom. Everything was still there from the night before: the table plans and place settings, the menus, the wine list, the flowers, and the set list for the music by the Red Rose Ensemble.

It was me who had a triumphalist breakfast that morning. I had enough material for a full-page mickey-take published under the headline: 'It's Our Party ... And We'll Pay £500 a Head If We Want To!'

It was illustrated by an artist's impression of the Kinnocks, Melvyn Bragg, Stephen Fry, John and Penny Mortimer and Barbara Castle seated together on the podium. The incongruity of it all was captured by a Hector Breeze cartoon on the menu: it showed egg and chips followed by baked jam roll and custard alongside a Labour Party official saying: 'We wanted to achieve a balance between middle-class affluence and proletarian authenticity.' The real menu was a starter of fresh salmon with lemon, cucumber, capsicums and herbs served with a lemon and chive cream followed by roast lamb.

There was the inevitable auction, details about which I obtained from guests as they were leaving. John Prescott, more used to £3-a-head sausages and mash in the Supper Club group of Kinnock's soft-left critics, had been in such animated conversation with another guest that people thought his arm-waving was a bid for an ornamental vase.

I had waited on the pavement earlier that morning for Kinnock to emerge from the dance floor at 1 a.m. with a broad smile on his face. As he stepped towards his waiting red Rover with his wife Glenys on his arm, the nifty footwork that had steered a dozen women around the ballroom helped him to dodge a party of American tourists.

What he was even more eager to dodge was the charge that champagne socialists had been having a ball with their

Bollinger and five-course dinner while outside the working-class struggle went on regardless. The planning for it had started four months earlier. Julia Hobsbawm, fund-raising consultant to the party, held training sessions for the catering staff to make sure everything would be all right on the night. Dennis Skinner, who had voted against the dinner at Labour's national executive, spent the evening lecturing to a party meeting in Lincolnshire on the folly of 'an elitist dinner'. He even took his own sandwiches.

'Is the party over?' I asked Kinnock as he stepped towards the car.

'No, it's still going on,' he said with a grin as he skilfully smoothed every last fold of his wife's pink raw-silk ball gown into the back seat of the Rover.

'I meant the Labour Party,' I said. It was a cheap shot and one I could never use in my article, but I relish it to this day.

CHAPTER EIGHTEEN

ROLLED WITH THE STONES

'**E**ight Miles High'. 'Fly Like an Eagle'. 'Leaving on a Jet Plane'. When you are writing a story about music that starts and ends with an aeroplane, any reporter worth his salt will try to weave a song title into the intro.

Well, I have failed. The Rolling Stones may have written or covered more than 1,000 songs, but apart from a fairly obscure B-side called 'Who's Driving Your Plane?', they have more or less avoided aviation.

I have been a huge Stones fan for most of my life, ever since discussing the merits of their first single, 'Come On', with 'Beano' Calcutt in second-form carpentry lessons at school.

However, this story starts not with them, but with Princess Anne and her marriage to Captain Mark Phillips.

Roy Greenslade, who was in his last months as managing editor (news) at the *Sunday Times* before leaving to edit the *Daily Mirror*, had had a tip that the couple had split after nearly sixteen years of marriage.

He asked me to fly to Puerto Rico in the Caribbean, where Anne was attending the annual meeting of the International Olympic Committee and get alongside her to confirm the split.

It was a Thursday morning when I boarded a flight to New York to get another flight to Puerto Rico. At noon, Buckingham Palace issued a statement announcing that the couple were to separate.

Oblivious to the news (this was before the days of mobile phones and rolling news on TV screens at airports), I rang into London. Roy told me the news.

'But, Maurice,' he said. 'While you're there, would you like to go to the opening night of the Rolling Stones' Steel Wheels world tour?'

Would I. I had met an impeccably dressed Charlie Watts backstage before their show at Knebworth fourteen years earlier and, much to her annoyance to this day, had dropped my wife and our children on the doorstep after a family holiday to go and see them at Wembley Stadium.

My eager reaction was probably one of the reasons Roy described me as 'the effervescent Maurice Chittenden' in his media column in *The Guardian* some years later. (Roy was only to last a year at the *Mirror*, a period which coincided with Robert Maxwell's rigged £1 million spot-the-ball competition which no one could win, but we were to meet up again twenty years later when we were both lecturing to journalism students at City University in London.)

All I had to do was make my way to Philadelphia, where the concert was to be held the following night.

Once in Philadelphia the next day, I busied myself by visiting the Liberty Bell before making my way to the Veterans' Stadium in time to pick up the tickets for myself and a photographer who had joined me, some CDs and a set list. Because we were such late additions to the guest list, we were seated in a general area next to ordinary punters.

There were a couple of young students on my left. 'I bet I know which song they'll start with,' I announced.

'How could you possibly know?' said one of the students.

'I am willing to bet it will be "Start Me Up",' I replied.

'Ten dollars says it isn't.'

Well, when the Stones opened their first tour for six years, Mick Jagger needed nothing more than the kick-start of Keith Richards's guitar to launch into 'Start Me Up'. The student stumped up a $10 bill.

Such was the output from 2.5 million watts of power that it blew the speakers and there was a four-minute break in the performance. I took the opportunity to reach into the bag under my seat to look at the playlist to see what song was next.

Unfortunately the students saw it and started to demand their money back. 'A bet's a bet,' I said.

Halfway through the Stones' set, probably during 'You Can't Always Get What You Want', which I have always found boring, I went to the bar to get more drinks. When I got back, my photographer pal had his eyes fixed on the stage to the right. The two seats to my left were empty.

'That's strange,' I thought. I reached down into my bag. My wallet was gone, along with $1,000 I had brought from the office to cover my expected expenditure in Puerto Rico.

Knowing from previous experience that Peter Roberts, the paper's managing editor, was a stickler for receipts, I knew this would be difficult to put down on expenses. Luckily, I had the presence of mind to see out the show and then find the police post at the stadium. An officer filled out a form and issued me with a crime report number.

I was just in time to jump into a stretch limousine outside, where I bumped into Piers Morgan from *The Sun* and Baz Bamigboye from the *Daily Mail*. Baz and I had worked casual shifts together on *The Sun* a few years earlier.

The car took us to the Stones' after-show party. There was food, drink and entertainment but, needless to say, none of the band showed.

I went back to my hotel and filed my review for the Arts section (the Culture supplement had yet to be launched).

'Jumpin' Jack Flash now requests a flame-thrower to give him a light,' I wrote. 'Mick Jagger may still be the Beelzebub of rock 'n' roll but the Rolling Stones are dabbling with the added dimensions of high technology these days.'

After a few hours' sleep, I rang the office the next morning, knowing they were five hours ahead.

'Maurice, we've had another tip,' said Roy.

Nick Rufford, then the paper's transport correspondent, had been told that BA had introduced a new dress code. Club class passengers who did not conform were being 'bumped' off flights.

'Could you test it to see if it works?' asked Roy.

I had a think. I would have to make myself look as grubby

and obnoxious as possible. First I went to a clothing store and bought a pair of jeans. I took them to a nearby construction site and asked a builder to pound them into the dirt, jump on them and make them as filthy as possible. To this day he probably thinks I had some bizarre sexual fetish.

Next stop was a jewellery store, where I bought a cheap, fake gold earring in the shape of a razor blade. (I thought some of Keith Richards's chic might rub off on me.) Then I stopped at a news stand and bought the latest copy of *Playboy*. I stuffed a portable cassette player in my pocket and began to play Stones music as loud as I could through the tinny speakers as I walked up to the check-in desk. I also started sniffing as loudly as I could, as if I had just taken cocaine.

I went up to the BA desk at Philadelphia Airport to check in.

'I am sorry, sir,' said one of the ground crew. 'We have a problem'.

Here we go, I thought. At least this story is going to pan out.

'Yes,' she added. 'We are overbooked.'

'Oh dear,' I replied, playing along with my eviction from the plane.

'Yes,' she said. 'What we would like to do is give you $200 for your inconvenience, take you by stretch limousine to New York, put you up in a five-star hotel and fly you back to London by Concorde tomorrow.'

For some reason my conscience got the better of me. I was due to be the night news editor on Saturday and would not be back in time. Stupidly, rather than being off-loaded, I insisted on sticking to my original reservation. Of course, they had plenty of other takers to fly on Concorde. It is still one of the biggest regrets of my life.

Back in London, I busied myself with a story about the hunt for IRA gunmen who had shot and wounded two British soldiers in a German street, and filled out a claim form for the missing $1,000. Luckily the newspaper's insurance company paid up.

The following week I did a page lead based on my experience. It was not the one originally envisaged. 'Airline Offer Bribes to Ditch Excess Passengers', ran the headline. At least no airline had yet been reduced to using security guards to drag people off planes.

CHAPTER NINETEEN

BLASTED SPORT!

The phone call came at 2 a.m. Saturday morning. Startled awake, I leapt from the top of the bunk bed at the brand new hall of residence built for the next intake of students at Clark Atlanta University.

'Maurice, mate,' said the voice on the end of the receiver. 'It's Shek. There's been a bombing at the Olympic Park. You had better get down here quick.'

It was Shekhar Bhatia, a journalist for the *Sunday Mirror* who was then married to the actress Meera Syal.

Thank heavens for the journalists' old pals act. I don't suppose it exists much today because national newspapers are scattered to all corners of London and much of the socialising has disappeared, but back then it was considered a betrayal not to help out a colleague. Indeed, it was common courtesy to tip off a mate if you had a good exclusive. Of course, you waited until your first edition had gone to press. Your pal could then tell his news desk he had picked up the story from his own sources before the first editions of the other papers landed in each newspaper office and he got it in the neck for missing the story.

One of the few occasions I remember this code of honour being breached was when Colin Mackenzie of the *Daily Express* pulled off the scoop of his lifetime by tracking down escaped train robber Ronnie Biggs in Brazil. A reporter from *The Guardian* managed to get through to him on the phone. 'The old pals act stretches a long way,' said Colin, 'but it doesn't stretch from Rio to London.' Fair enough.

Back to my early morning phone call. Shek had spent Friday night watching a concert by the Memphis soul legend Rufus Thomas at the Centennial Olympic Park, a 21-acre green space cleared and created by the organising committee of the 1996 Summer Games. There was entertainment there every night with up to 60,000 people watching free music and enjoying themselves. I had caught one show by the Georgia Satellites, a local band who had won international recognition for songs like 'Keep Your Hands to Yourself' and 'Battleship Chains'.

So far, I had had a terrific Olympics, made better by the fact that I wasn't supposed to have been there. Andrew Malone from the foreign desk had been promised the trip, but six months earlier I had resigned to join the *Sunday Express* under Sue Douglas's new editorship. It was the second time I had pulled this trick – resigning to get a better deal back at the *Sunday Times*. It's a tricky manoeuvre and not one recommended for the faint-hearted as you have to be prepared to go if they call your bluff.

Previously I had quit to join the *News of the World*, only to be persuaded to stay when Andrew Neil offered me a substantial salary increase. It easily paid for the bottles of champagne I had biked around to Patsy Chapman, the then *News of the World* editor, Stuart Kuttner, the paper's managing editor, and Bob Warren, the news editor, as an apology for my bad manners and breach of contract.

This time I was two hours away from my farewell party when I agreed to stay. When I had wobbled, Sue had tried to persuade me to leave over drinks at the American Bar in the Savoy. 'Come on, Maurice, it'll be great fun for a couple of years,' she said, which was not the right message for a man with a mortgage, a wife and three young children. In return for staying at the *Sunday Times*, I was to be promoted to assistant editor, get the job of night news editor and I was to go to the Olympics as the paper's sports news reporter. Not a bad result. And in the end I went ahead with my leaving do at the London Press Club anyway.

So here I was in Atlanta. The previous weekend I had written a half-page Olympics diary with my picture byline and an Atlanta dateline and I had got the back-page lead with the Opening Ceremony. The fire of Muhammad Ali may have been dimmed by Parkinson's disease, but there had been gasps of delight when he appeared and the torch he had held aloft in the Olympic Stadium burned bright. Indeed, as the former world heavyweight boxing champion ignited the flame that would burn throughout the centennial games, many competitors were moved to tears.

Eight Thunderbird fighters from the United States Air Force flew overhead. Gladys Knight sang 'Georgia on My Mind' and Celine Dion performed 'Power of the Dream', but the highlight was 'Summertime', a choreographed extravaganza celebrating the South that included a mock Mississippi steamboat. As I wrote at the time, it made the opening ceremony of Euro '96 in London six weeks earlier look like a maypole dance at a primary school. (Although Quentin Letts of *The Times* was to be derisory about the inclusion of pick-up trucks, the trademark of the redneck.) President Bill Clinton formally declared the Games open as Princess Anne, a member of the International Olympic Committee, and Jimmy Carter, the former president, looked on.

Later, returning to the Olympic Stadium, I had witnessed Michael Johnson, in his custom-designed pair of golden Nike running shoes, break the Olympic record for the 400 metres, finishing almost a whole second ahead of Britain's Roger Black. (Later I was to see him win the 200 metres final too.)

I had also been to the Georgia Dome to watch the Dream Team II, including Charles Barkley and the 7ft 1in. Shaquille O'Neal, win at basketball. The only downside was the accommodation. The bean counters had taken over at the *Sunday Times* and we had to suffer the indignity of staying in student quarters. There were two murders within two blocks the first night we arrived but, on the plus side, there was a great soul food restaurant called the Busy Bee just around the corner.

I knew the security around the Games was not as hot as it was supposed to be. One day I determined to see Captain Mark

Phillips to see if I could get a news line from him about 'deserting' his country. (He was now the *chef d'equipe* of the US Equestrian team.) I drove to the equestrian centre, parked my car and walked across a green expanse until I was met by two fifteen-year-old girls. One was Zara Phillips and the other was her friend. They walked me into the stables where Zara's father was busy grooming a horse with a brush. He was perfectly friendly and continued caring for the horse but kept the same reserve about his team's chances at the Games as he always has about the royal family.

Away from the sport, I had formed a friendship with Isaac Tigrett, co-founder of the Hard Rock Café chain and the House of Blues clubs and the second husband of Maureen Starkey, Ringo Starr's ex-wife. He had opened a temporary club in an old church and granted me free VIP admission. Over a few nights I had watched concerts by the Blues Brothers (Dan Aykroyd, alias Elwood Blues, was his partner in the club chain), Jerry Lee Lewis and Little Richard, and I had used his talk of opening a House of Blues in London with Sir James Goldsmith as an excuse to fly to Chicago on expenses to examine the state of the blues for our Culture section.

The fun was about to stop. Shek had been close enough to Centennial Park to hear the explosion at about 1.20 a.m. local time. A military backpack containing the biggest pipe bomb yet seen in the United States had been left in the park.

Richard Jewell, a security guard, had spotted the package twenty minutes earlier and went to get help. Someone else, too, had seen it and moved it under a bench, perhaps in the hope of walking off with it. When Jewell returned with agents from the Bureau of Alcohol, Tobacco and Firearms (ATF) and the Georgia Bureau of Investigations, he told the man to get lost. One of the ATF agents eased open a flap on the bag and spotted the wiring on the bomb.

The agents began to clear the area. They got thousands of people to leave but then the bomb went off, shooting dozens of three-inch nails into the air.

Tom Davis, a special agent of the Georgia Bureau of Investigations, said later: 'It was a wave of heat and air at the same time, coupled with a loud explosion. It forced me to the ground. It was like everything was going off in slow motion.'

Alice Hawthorne, a 41-year-old cable television company receptionist from Albany, Georgia, was killed when one of the nails penetrated her skull as she posed for a photograph next to a statue. Some nails were embedded in the fifth storey of a building opposite. At least 111 other people were injured, including Alice's fourteen-year-old daughter, seven police officers and a 53-year-old British woman who underwent brain surgery to remove shrapnel. Melih Uzunyol, a forty-year-old cameraman working for Turkish television, collapsed and died of a heart attack while running to film the scene.

All things considered, the explosion could have been much worse. The bomb was fitted with a steel plate to deflect nails out sideways into the crowd. By moving it, Jewell or the would-be thief had turned it over so the steel plate was at the bottom, sending most of the nails upwards.

By the time I reached the park, it was sealed off as a crime scene. Atlanta was in a daze. As I went towards a hotel to try to use a phone, the staff locked the door in my face. Later I found out why. At 1 a.m., a man had used a phone box outside the hotel to ring the 911 emergency service and warn that a bomb was about to go off.

I worked through the night, mopping up eyewitness accounts and getting colour. America woke up to the horror. President Bill Clinton denounced the attack as an 'evil act of terror'. He promised: 'We will spare no effort to find out who is responsible for this murderous act. We will track them down. We will see them punished.'

'America Under Siege as Bomb Shatters Olympic Spectacle', ran the splash headline above my byline in the *Sunday Times* the next day. John Witherow, the editor, was kind enough to fax me a 'herogram' for my hard work.

The Olympic authorities and the Atlanta organising committee rightly agreed that the Games should continue as planned rather than give in to terror. On Saturday, Steve Redgrave rowed to his fourth gold in four successive Games, the first British athlete to pull off such a feat. But Linford Christie was disqualified from the men's 100m final – he was the defending champion – after two false starts and in the men's triple jump Jonathan Edwards could only manage a silver medal.

I spent Sunday, my day off, at the Atlanta-Fulton County Stadium watching Cuba, the eventual gold medal winners, rather humiliate the United States in a baseball game. Chipping Norton, where I grew up, had tried to introduce the sport to Britain in the first half of the twentieth century and I had occasionally played scratch games with an American pal and his US Army Air Force colleagues at an airbase in Cambridgeshire.

By the time I was back in work mode, poor Richard Jewell, the security guard who had spotted the suspicious package, had gone from hero to zero. I do not know if it was his 'mall cop' demeanour or if he had taken a fragment of the bomb home as a souvenir, but three days after the bombing the *Atlanta Journal-Constitution*, the local paper, came out with a front-page headline naming him as the lead suspect in the bombing.

While the FBI combed through his home, his clothes and his pick-up truck looking for clues to the bombing, the media raked over his life. America was able to read his school reports, learn that he was so desperate to become a police officer that he was once arrested for impersonating one, discover that having once made the grade he was demoted for crashing his car and then lost another job on a college campus for being over-zealous.

The revelation that he once rented a lonely cabin brought immediate comparisons with the eighteen-year hunt for anarchist Ted Kaczynski, the so-called 'Unabomber', who had been arrested at his remote cabin in Montana three months earlier.

WGST, an Atlanta radio station that revelled in its title of 'official Olympic information system', was one of Jewell's biggest accusers. Sean Hannity, its morning presenter, said, 'There is a lot of speculation that a 33-year-old man who is unmarried, who lives with his mother, has got to be a weirdo, has got to be a potential terrorist.'

It was trial by media, but I never bought into this theory. I felt sorry for Jewell as I watched him sit on the stairwell of his mother's two-bedroom apartment off Atlanta's Buford Highway with his head in his hands. An army of journalists was camped outside. When two FBI agents arrived to question him, a dozen television cameras zoomed in over their shoulders.

Nevertheless, it was a long time until the next Sunday, and I had to come up with something. It did not help that a Q&A in the same Atlanta paper that was accusing Jewell reminded me that the media outnumbered athletes in Atlanta by 4,300. There were 15,000 'media representatives' and 10,700 athletes.

Our background article on the explosion the previous weekend had rightly said that the crude pipe bomb bore all the hallmarks of America's far-right militias. Back in the 1960s and 1970s, the FBI's most-wanted lists had been populated by fugitives from the Black Panthers and the Weathermen, who had tried to overthrow the conservative governments of Lyndon Johnson and Richard Nixon. With Bill Clinton in the 1990s, it was all change. The administration became more liberal and far-right militias began isolating themselves in compounds and bombing government buildings.

Jewell had not been the first suspect for the bombing. I learned that the FBI had initially turned its attention to a militia group from the neighbouring state of Alabama known as the Gadsden Minutemen (the town they used as their home base combined with the name given to militias in the American War of Independence, who were expected to turn out, ready to fight, in sixty seconds).

Using an artist's impression from witnesses at the scene of the blast, federal agents identified Derek Underwood, one of the militia's members. However, Underwood had an alibi. He was in an Alabama bar 100 miles away at the time of the bombing. I decided to drive to Alabama to investigate the militia angle.

When I called in at the Etowah County sheriff's department in Gadsden, Sheriff James Hayes could not be more helpful. He believed in the common-sense approach to law enforcement. When he died in 2007 on a hunting trip, he was the longest-serving sheriff in Alabama history and at his funeral there was a 21-gun salute, a trumpeter sounded 'Taps' and 'Amazing Grace' was played on bagpipes.

After hearing me out, he dug out his own files on the Minutemen and assured me that they were essentially harmless. It has always amazed me how open and willing to share American lawmen are compared with the uptight way the British police now treat journalists. (This gap was best exemplified after the Manchester Arena bombing of May 2017, when Prime Minister Theresa May was furious that American intelligence had leaked photographs to the *New York Times*, even though the details of which rucksack the bomber had used was hardly likely to hamper the investigation.) The sheriff said I should go to see Mike Kemp, one of the Militiamen's leaders. Kemp had also set up a subsidiary, Copwatch, that claimed it undertook 'public and private investigations specialising in law enforcement abuses'.

Minutes later, I found myself knocking on the door of Kemp's ramshackle home. An old pick-up truck was in the front yard.

As we sat in his living room, Kemp began to take out rifles, four in all. He told me FBI agents had met him and two other members of the militia at a restaurant in Birmingham, Alabama, sixty miles to the south-west, on Sunday, the day after the bombing.

Copwatch had insisted on recording their own version of the FBI interviews. He gave me a copy of the tape. As I played it, I was alarmed to hear Kemp's voice boasting that he was an explosives expert. He was asked if he knew if any ATF officers had been injured in the blast. He said: 'I don't know. I can only hope.' However, he insisted he was at home with his son at the time of the bombing.

I was getting increasingly nervous. Kemp was sat at his dining table, stripping down and cleaning a Kalashnikov rifle. There was gunpowder and primers on the table. Then I looked out of the back window. On a washing line blowing in the breeze were eleven mauve junior football shirts all emblazoned with the Minutemen name. I didn't feel so bad then.

Kemp claimed the ATF was trying to frame him because Copwatch had exposed a 'Good Ol' Boys Roundup' picnic organised by the bureau the previous year in which signs were put up declaring 'nigger checkpoint' and agents were given mock 'nigger-hunting licences'.

Leaving Kemp to play with his arsenal, I decided to drive down to Birmingham in search of colour from the restaurant where the Minutemen and the FBI had sat. 'Colour' is very important for Sunday papers, especially on backgrounders covering events that are several days old. It helps us to try to take the reader to the scene.

I remember once, when I was working for a news agency,

being sent back to a house by the *Sunday Express* to describe whether the milk bottles delivered to the door had gold, silver or red tops. Apparently, it helped the reader sum up the social class of the person who lived there.

I settled down in Rube Burrow's Food and Spirits, named after a nineteenth-century train robber and featuring décor of his antics, including wanted posters and newspaper reports. There was not much colour to be had but I enjoyed my Rube Burger. It was an odd portent of what was to come.

Returning to Atlanta, I filed a page lead for Sunday, illustrated with a photograph of Richard Jewell which was headlined 'Atlanta Bomber – or Media Victim?', and then settled back to watch Bob Dylan at the House of Blues and the closing ceremony, in which Boyz II Men sang 'The Star Spangled Banner', Trisha Yearwood sang 'The Flame' and the Olympic flag was passed to the Mayor of Sydney.

It turned out the Sydney Games had come and gone and the Olympics committee was getting ready to host the games in Athens before the Atlanta bomber was finally brought to justice.

The trail went cold until an abortion clinic and a gay bar in Atlanta were bombed in 1997. Letters from the so-called Army of God, a Christian terrorist organisation opposed to abortion, homosexuality and racial integration, claimed responsibility. Forensic analysis of metal plates used in the bombs identified them as from the same batch of steel used in the Centennial Park bombing.

A second abortion clinic bombing, this time in Birmingham, Alabama, killed an off-duty policeman working as a security guard. An eye-witness saw a man escaping in a pick-up truck and got a partial licence plate. This led the FBI to identify Eric Rudolph as the bomber, but he was to prove an elusive quarry.

He was put on the FBI's Ten Most Wanted List in May 1998 and instantly became America's most-wanted fugitive. A hard-core survivalist, he disappeared into the Nantahala National Forest in North Carolina and became something of a folk anti-hero. At least two country songs were written about him, 'Run Rudolph Run' T-shirts were sold and a restaurant in the town of Andrews served Rudolph Burgers and FBI Curly Fries.

Rudolph certainly wasn't eating them. He was finally arrested by an alert patrolman while he was searching for food in a dumpster in Murphy, North Carolina, in July 2003 and was later given multiple life sentences.

From his prison cell, he issued a statement explaining the reason for the Olympic bombing. He claimed the Olympic movement had an agenda to promote the values of global socialism. 'The purpose of the attack was to confound, anger and embarrass the Washington government in the eyes of the world for its abdominal sanctioning of abortion on demand,' he declared.

The Atlanta bombing was not the first or last time I went to cover a sports event and found myself involved in something with a loud bang.

When Italia '90 came up, I managed to get the posting. Rupert Murdoch had won the Battle of Wapping, all his titles were selling well and News International was awash with money. So I found myself in my own private bungalow in the Forte Holiday

Village in Sardinia, where my neighbours included Michelle Lineker, the wife of England's star striker Gary; Ron Atkinson, the football manager who I had watched in my teenage years as a player at Oxford United; and Nigel Kennedy, the violinist, who was enjoying huge success with his version of Vivaldi's *Four Seasons*, and his rock singer girlfriend Brix Smith. 'I hope there won't be any trouble,' Kennedy told me. 'It ruins the game for all.'

Peacocks roamed across the gardens of the pink and white adobe-walled bungalows. Every few hours a maid called to float flower petals in the lavatory bowl of the £250-a-night room. Each evening they would be back to deposit an expensive bottle of wine.

Certainly we had it much better than most of the England fans, many of whom had endured fifteen-hour ferry trips, police searches and constant surveillance to be there. Cagliari, the Sardinian capital, had caught World Cup fever all right, but it was exhibiting symptoms of a terminal case. It was gripped by *la psicos-hooligan*, a paranoia that resulted in every English fan being seen as a soccer thug. Four paramilitary battalions of Carabinieri, 3,000 men in all, had been stationed on the island.

When my colleague John Goodbody of *The Times* went for an early morning swim in Cagliari harbour, the Carabinieri mistook him for Paul Scarrott, self-styled 'king of the yobs' – *il fanatic del Nottingham* to the Italians – trying to sneak ashore and launched a patrol boat in pursuit. Another leading hooligan, Terry Last, a leader of the Chelsea Headhunters gang, was supposed to be trying to infiltrate from Algeria.

Minor incidents were reported on the scale of opening shots in a war. The jailing of three British youths after they damaged their apartment and stole sheets meant that landlords were reluctant to let rooms. This left a growing army of fans living on the streets or pitching tents in makeshift camps.

Boredom was the biggest problem. I enjoyed an open-air performance of Verdi's *Aida* in Cagliari's Roman amphitheatre on Friday night but it was hardly ideal entertainment for the average soccer fan.

The Football Supporters Association sent in a vanload of puzzle books and handed out tour guides ('The Grotto of Vipers is a Roman tomb not a disco'). Some fans tried to hitchhike to save money, but one supporter suffered a broken arm when a speeding car failed to stop for his outstretched thumb.

It was probably an hour's drive to the stadium in Cagliari from our exclusive resort, but as *la stampa* (the press) we would get a police escort on match days, which meant we could cut the journey time by half. (I might have paid my NUJ dues if they had been able to get the same special treatment for us at Wembley.)

The England vs Holland match was on a Saturday in the Sant'Elia stadium. I was in the foyer bar of the Hotel Mediterraneo, three hours before kick-off, drinking flaming sambucas with some fellow hacks and oblivious to what was being played out in the street outside. About 500 England fans had broken away from supporters being escorted to the stadium. They began hurling rocks and rubble from wasteland at police, who crouched behind riot shields. At least when I was covering

France '98 in Marseilles eight years later, the hooligans had the decency to wait until after the match before kicking off!

Suddenly a Carabinieri in full uniform and cocked black cap crashed into the foyer, clutching his bleeding head and dropping his carbine on the marble-tiled floor. He had been hit by a rock.

It was an instant call to action for us hacks. As we rushed out into the street, the police were aiming two warning shots into the air before firing tear gas canisters into the mob of rampaging English fans, who were then beaten to the ground in police baton charges. Seven were taken to hospital. Wedding guests who had attended a service at the city cathedral fled in terror as riot police chased fans up its steps. Angry locals joined the fighting. One pulled the exhaust pipe from his car to use as a weapon and another wielded a starting handle.

The match itself ended in a dull 0–0 draw, so it was only right and natural that I had the splash the next day under the headline: 'Italian Police Baton Charge England Fans'. That was not without its own drama.

As I filed my copy from a phone booth in the Mediterraneo, the door suddenly flew open thanks to a karate kick from my pal John Chapman of the *News of the World*, who had been delayed chasing some alleged sex scandal and perceived I had not been quick enough to hand over my copy under the rules of the old pals' act.

John and I had been friends and rivals since working on the *Evening Post-Echo* at Hemel Hempstead together in the 1980s and doing casual shifts together around Fleet Street. At Hemel we would both keep ringing the Scotland Yard press line of recorded news updates to see who could be the first to sell a story to the nationals.

We had had fun in Sardinia, driving in my hire car to the bandit village of Orgosolo where we would play Ennio Morricone music, wind down the window and screech 'Prepare to die, old man' to unsuspecting Sardinians who would not have had a clue what we were on about.

The fun continued when we regrouped in Naples for England's Sunday night quarter-final against Cameroon. We spent one day visiting Pompeii and climbing Vesuvius and another driving switchback roads around the Amalfi Coast. Then we had the wheeze of telling our respective news desks that we had heard a rumour that English and German fans were planning a pitched battle in the centre of Rome. We drove there in a Mercedes E-class and had £350-a-night rooms in a hotel overlooking the animals in Rome zoo.

Bobby Robson's team were now closer to winning the World Cup on foreign soil than any England side before or since. It was not to be. We saw Gazza's tears in the semi-final against West Germany in Turin and witnessed the penalty shoot-out defeat. It was a Wednesday night so there was plenty to regret but nothing to file.

The following Saturday I was in Bari in the heel of Italy for the rather meaningless game for third place. I entertained myself by hiring a BMW 5 Series on expenses to drive around the city. England lost 2–1. After the match, I managed to corner Peter Shilton, who confirmed he was giving up his green shirt after a record 125 caps as goalkeeper. 'I've thoroughly enjoyed the past twenty years,' he told me, 'but now is the time to pack up.'

It was my turn to pack up too, return the BMW, check out of my luxury hotel and fly home. It was such a different story two years later when I flew out to cover the Olympics in Barcelona. The pound was struggling in the European Exchange Rate Mechanism (ERM) – Black Wednesday was to follow – and the accountants in grey suits had arrived at Wapping to curtail our extra spending on fun. I had to stay in a tourist hotel in the resort of Calella, an hour from Barcelona, and I was reduced to driving a Renault Twingo.

All week I parked the car in a culvert designed to carry flood water through Calella, not realising it was illegal at certain times. I strolled out of the hotel on Saturday morning to discover it was missing. It had been towed away and by the time I had recovered it from the police I almost missed the opening ceremony. I arrived in time to be knocked to the ground by an over-zealous Civil Guard on a horse for daring to cross a road before he had given permission. This time a blazing arrow fired by a Spanish archer lit the Olympic flame.

The Montjuic stadium was bathed in blue light to become a portrait of the Mediterranean sea. Inside, 55,000 spectators, some of whom had paid up to £800 on the black market for tickets, reached under their seats to find a gift box from the European Commission containing presents and two plastic 'snapsticks' containing liquid. When broken in half at a given signal they gave off a fluorescent blue or gold colour depending on where people were sitting.

For a few seconds, millions watching on television around the world saw the stadium turn into the European flag of gold stars on a blue backcloth. This fleeting gesture cost the lion's share of the €4.5 million (£3.1 million) the EC invested in publicising itself at the Games. My expenses didn't seem so extravagant after that.

CHAPTER TWENTY

LAST OF THE SILVER ARROWS

I am sometimes asked what I think my greatest achievement was as a reporter. Some suggest exposing the cash for questions scandal. It certainly won the most awards. Others cite my despatch from the Piper Alpha oil rig explosion, which was repeated word for word in the *Sunday Times* on the twenty-fifth anniversary of the explosion. I usually surprise them all, however, by saying it was flying across Romania in a propeller plane in sub-zero temperatures to trace a witness to a non-fatal accident that had happened almost half a century earlier.

My quest was part of a search for the last of Hitler's dream machines, a Mercedes racing car that had become the motoring world's holy grail. It had been wrecked or dismantled at least three times but it was still worth more than £5 million.

Built in 1938 with the personal backing of the Führer to symbolise Nazi supremacy, the car was one of only ten Mercedes W154 – the legendary Mercedes-Benz Silver Arrow racing cars.

The V12-cylinder car embodied the high watermark of racing car design prior to World War Two.

Before today's F1 teams and their cars plastered with sponsors' advertising, each country had its own traditionally coloured livery. Great Britain, of course, had British racing green, while Italy had the red of their Rosso Corsa.

Germany had leaned towards white and the giant Mercedes-Benz SSKL, with which Rudolf Caracciola won the 1931 Mille Miglia, was nicknamed the White Elephant. When Hitler came to power, he ordered a challenge to the increasing Italian domination of Grand Prix racing. However, in 1934, motor sport's governing body decreed that no Grand Prix racing car should exceed 750kg in weight. Desperate to compete to win awards for their newly elected chancellor, the Germans supposedly stripped the white lead paint from their cars, exposing the shiny silver aluminium underneath. The legend of the Silver Arrow was born.

At the 1938 French Grand Prix, German drivers in W154s finished first, second and third with Manfred von Brauchitsch, the nephew of a field marshal, the first to take the chequered flag. The cars went on to reach speeds of almost 250 mph in land speed record attempts and beat every other car on the track.

Stirling Moss was one of those who sped to victory in a later generation of Silver Arrows, but the W154 was the greatest of these cars, winning eleven Grand Prix. It was designed in 1938 when the ruling body changed the rules and moved their restrictions from the field of weight to engine size. It had a supercharged 3,000cc engine.

Little wonder that these cars have become prized by collectors and are a magnet for television documentary makers. A colleague at the *Sunday Times*, Nicholas Hellen, discovered that Prince Edward and Ardent, his TV production company, had spent eighteen months working on a documentary about the last of these cars, which had disappeared behind the Iron Curtain. My job was to fly to Romania to see if I could track it down.

During World War Two, all ten of the W154 Silver Arrows were hidden by Mercedes to protect the secrets of their V12 engines, which also powered Messerschmitt fighter planes. However, two of the cars, models W154/5 and W154/7, fell into Soviet hands towards the end of the war and were shipped east for examination.

They never got further than Romania. Discovered lying in a scrapyard near the docks of Constanza on the Black Sea, they were entrusted to Ioska Roman, a motor racing enthusiast who lived in Cluj-Napoca, the historic capital of Transylvania and the fictional home of Count Dracula. Private ownership in a Communist state was not allowed so the Ministry of Culture and Sport retained ownership but assigned the cars to Cluj Railway Sports Club, where Roman was given the right to repair and race them. He also invested a lot of his own money in the restoration.

Roman had first written to Mercedes three months before the outbreak of the war, applying unsuccessfully for a job as a racing mechanic. The next time they heard from him was in 1963, when he told them he had the two missing W154s.

What had happened to them since? I drove to Gatwick, caught a BA flight to Bucharest and then took a taxi across the city to Baneasa Airport for my internal flight to Cluj. It was nine below zero and there was thick snow on the ground. Worse was to come. My plane was an old Russian Antonov An-24, a 44-seat turboprop operated by TAROM, the national airline.

Not understanding a word of Romanian and with none of the crew able to speak English, it was to be a nightmare 200-mile flight. The cabin crew wore overcoats and scarves and poured watery coffee from a Thermos flask. The plane touched down at Sibiu but, not realising there was a stop, I thought we had arrived at Cluj and began to get off the plane with the passengers ending their journey there.

Luckily the stewardess who had checked my ticket spotted me and dragged me back onto the plane. But there was snow on the rear wings and to take off again the other passengers and I had to move to the front of the plane to help with the distribution of weight. It was all very reminiscent of a passage about a hapless foreign correspondent from Evelyn Waugh's *Scoop*:

'Why, once Jakes went out to cover a revolution in one of the Balkan capitals. He overslept in his carriage, woke up at the wrong station, didn't know any different, got out, went straight to a hotel, and cabled off a thousand-word story...'

On arrival in Cluj, I booked into the decaying Continental Hotel and ate a dinner of schnitzel, chips and green salad under the cracked plaster dome of its baroque dining room while a violinist played for me, the only guest.

The next morning, I discovered my black Oxford shoes were

unsuited to the ice and fell over twice on my way to the nearby Babeş-Bolyai University. I do not know if it was the name that attracted me but I managed to find an English teacher there who, after I had persuaded her that my intentions were honourable, agreed to loan me her best student, Simona, for the next two days.

I often found that this was the best way to get an interpreter. A student was a lot cheaper and far more dedicated than a professional translator. Of course, the few dollars I paid her would be inflated tenfold when it came to my expenses. (Covering the murder of a British couple in France once, I picked up a French-Canadian student hitchhiker who agreed to translate for me in return for being delivered safely to her relatives.)

We went to the local office of the Romanian Automobile Club. It was a surprise to me that such an elitist organisation would survive under the iron rule of Nicolae Ceauşescu, the country's late Communist dictator, but I later learned that he too had fallen under the spell of the Silver Arrows.

Ioska Roman, I discovered, had died ten years ago. I asked if there was anybody still a member of the club who would have remembered him in his prime. I was put on to Laurentiu Barbely, who, at seventy-one years of age, was still racing his thirty-year-old BMW.

Barbely told me what had happened to the missing Silver Arrows. Roman had taken them to his garage in Cluj but was determined to use one of them to break a local record.

Near his home town was a hill which had long been the scene of a fiercely contested hill climb. This was one of the oldest forms of motorsport, dating back to the French Riviera in the 1890s. Drivers compete against the clock to complete an uphill course. When I heard this, it struck a chord. One of the few mementoes I have from my late father is the silver cup he won for the freak hill climb from the Old Melton Motor Club when he was twenty-seven years old.

Hill climbing has a long tradition in Romania and the Feleac course outside Cluj once formed a stage in the European hill climb championship. The gravel course was 7.2km (4.5 miles) uphill and it was driven in two minutes fifty-six seconds by Hans Stuck, a German racing driver, in 1938 at the wheel of an Auto Union Grand Prix car. Auto Union, the predecessor of Audi, was Mercedes' great rival.

Roman was convinced he could break the record in one of the W154s. He was competing in the annual hill race in 1953 when disaster struck. Barbely could only watch in horror as his friend veered off the course and hit a large marker stone. The car rolled over and the petrol tank in the tail ignited. Fortunately, Roman had put in a minimal amount so as not to overload the rear weight of the car. However, he was badly injured and it took him two years to recover.

Roman never raced again. The car almost went for scrap but he persuaded the Ministry to sell him both vehicles for 2,000 lei, the equivalent of a party apparatchik's monthly wage, and then set about rebuilding the wreck. He sold a house to finance the repairs. Tyres from a truck were pressed into service to replace those burst in the accident. He carried the cylinder blocks on his back to Brasov and took eggs and cream with him to help pay for them to be repaired. Pieces of the chassis and bodywork were cannibalised from the second car that had been on its way to the Soviet Union.

The cars attracted attention in the town and the Securitate, the Romanian secret police, began to take an interest. Barbely told me that Roman received three brand new saloon cars, a Mercedes, a BMW and a Volkswagen Beetle in return for the sale of the undamaged car in 1971. Roman sold one car to buy a new house, another for living expenses and kept a third vehicle for his use.

Ceauşescu recouped his outlay by exacting a large cash sum from a buyer for allowing the W154 to leave the country. Although it was later sold for more than £5 million, Roman's reward was no more than £50,000. The first new owner was Dieter Holterbosch, the New York-domiciled owner of the Löwenbräu beer company. The car was later owned by a Mexican billionaire and went on show in a Californian museum.

So what had happened to the other W154? The car which had been driven to second place by Manfred von Brauchitsch at the 1939 Belgrade Grand Prix on the very day World War Two broke out?

I went to Roman's old garage. It was full of broken glass and rusty engine parts but there was not a glint of aluminium. A few old cars were hidden under tarpaulin. An elderly lady living in appalling conditions without heat or light in the house next door told us what she could remember about her former neighbour and his 'shiny car' but said she had not seen it for almost a decade.

As the expensive market in rare automobiles had grown, more and more collectors had set their hearts on owning a W154. Depressed by hardship and desperate to leave Romania, Roman offered the remaining car to Westerners in exchange for groceries. In the mid-1970s, he pledged to give it to Count Hubertus von Dönhoff, a Bavarian collector, in return for two trucks of marmalade, but the deal never went ahead.

In the mid-1980s, Ralph Lauren, the designer, started negotiations to buy the car, but was eventually deterred by the corruption of Ceaușescu's officials. He did, however, acquire the leather steering wheel to hang on the wall of his Manhattan office.

When Roman died in 1986, aged seventy-eight, the Ceaușescu regime redoubled its efforts to cash in on the remaining car. Several British dealers were offered it by a front company that secured substantial deposits which were never returned.

Terry Cohn, a wealthy Sussex collector, visited Cluj in 1987 and was convinced that he had an agreement to buy the car. He handed over a Mercedes saloon as a deposit but the Roman family said it must have gone to a corrupt official because they never received it. He embarked on a legal campaign to establish his ownership that was still going on when he died in 2001. But, by the summer of 1988, the car had vanished from Cluj.

I went back to the Romanian Automobile Club. Romus Campeanu, director of the Cluj office, was back from a visit to Bucharest and, at last, I was able to obtain the inside track of what had happened to the car.

It turned out that Roman's son, Tibor, believing the car to

be his, had smuggled the vehicle across the border to Hungary and then resettled with his wife in Budapest. Tibor had been a coach for the Romanian weightlifting team when they won eight medals at the 1984 Los Angeles Olympics, so he probably had an idea what the car was worth as well as sufficient money to get it out of Romania.

'Tibor must have bribed a lot of people to get it out of the country,' Campeanu told me. 'I have heard several stories: one that it was taken across the border on a cart, the other that it was in the back of a truck packed with clothes.'

The Ceaușescus, apparently infuriated by the deception, ordered a witch-hunt. The Securitate rounded up every motor racing enthusiast in Cluj for interrogation. But that did not stop the car being sold to Dr Andrei Bilciurescu, a German ortho-dontist, for a modest £270,000.

My colleague, Nicholas Hellen, flew to Bonn to interview him. Bilciurescu was reluctant to expand on the deal or wheth-er he had any connections with the former Communist regime. However, it was believed that Mercedes had given him extensive assistance. The car was still not roadworthy, but its restoration was nearly complete.

'I'm just a collector who bought a car,' he said at his home, an unremarkable second-floor apartment near the main rail-way station in Bonn. 'I don't want to get involved with all those crazies who are disputing it. What's in it for me?'

Meanwhile, I was catching the 6 p.m. Friday night flight from Cluj back to Bucharest. Instead of a taxi, I took the bus from the airport and got off in the city centre. It was a mistake. Trudging through the snow in wet shoes and socks, I was approached by a constant flow of begging children and spivs offering me girls, private rooms and money exchange.

A few hundred yards short of the room I had booked at the InterContinental Hotel, I was stopped by two men in fur hats and blue quilted jackets who showed me what they made out was a security police ID card. My lack of Romanian meant it could have been a bus pass for all I knew.

'We are searching for counterfeit currency,' said the portly senior officer as he brushed his moustache up at the side. 'Do you have dollars?'

'Yes,' I replied, thinking that the modern equivalent of the Securitate had caught up with me.

'Let me see.'

I opened my wallet, took out my small wad of dollars and splayed them out in my hand.

He took them from me and began looking through them, holding them up to the light.

'OK. They are good,' he said, handing back the dollars. The two men took to their heels.

I looked at my dollars. My only $100 bill was gone, replaced in the wad with a $1 bill.

'Banditti!' I screamed. 'Robbers, thieves!' Too late. The two men were moving fast across the snow, their boots rising and falling with accentuated movements. My wet feet were no match.

I was more embarrassed than anything, having been suckered like a tourist. I made a mental note to stick an extra one in front of the receipt I had got Simona to sign. There was no way

I was going to put this on expenses and be the laughing stock of the office.

The next morning, a Saturday, I was at Bucharest Airport by 8.30 a.m. to take a TAROM flight to Heathrow. I caught the Speedlink bus to Gatwick to retrieve my car, popped in at home to change, have a cup of tea and see Jan and the children before driving to the office, where I arrived in time to write a 96cm splash on the previous night's IRA bombing of the London Docklands, which had killed two people and injured thirty-nine.

As I had not even been in London, it was deemed I could not have a byline. Still, Nicholas and I shared page three with 'Prince Edward Joins Hunt For £5m Nazi Supercar'. I finally got home at 3.45 a.m. on Sunday morning after a 22-hour day.

Looking back today, when newspapers have ever-tightening budgets, it seems incredulous that we once thought nothing of flying two reporters halfway across Europe to piece together such a confection. If it was happening today we would just rely on a press release and a preview tape from the television company making the documentary.

It was not the end of the car's tortuous journey, however. It was eventually restored to running order and passed through various hands to Yoshiyuki Hayashi, a Japanese collector. His right to ownership was challenged by a British dealer who claimed that the Mafia had been involved in the deal. In 2003, the Superior Court of California ruled that Hayashi was the sole legal owner. The Briton was ordered to pay him $1 million in damages plus legal costs. A few years later, the car changed hands again and now sits in the Collier Collection of classic cars in Naples, Florida.

CHAPTER TWENTY-ONE

AN ID PARADE AT THE RITZ

'I think you are an Al Fayed agent and I'm going to do you over.'

The man talking is Jonathan Aitken. He was the Tory MP for Thanet South and a former Chief Secretary to the Treasury and Minister for Defence Procurement.

All I had done was ask him if he was one of the eight MPs I had been informed was receiving artificial testosterone. Or, as I put it, 'slipping away from the seat of power at Westminster for an injection in their own seat'.

But then Aitken, once tipped as a future Prime Minister, was under a lot of pressure. He had resigned from his Cabinet job at the Treasury six months earlier after claims that he had violated ministerial rules in his previous role as Minister for Defence Procurement.

The affair revolved around who picked up the tab for his two-night stay in Room 526 at the Ritz Hotel in Paris, one of the grandest hotels in Europe and owned by Mohamed Al Fayed, who also owned Harrods department store in London. Fayed, of course, had played a key role in the cash for questions story.

The Egyptian, annoyed that his application for British citizenship had been rejected, was on a crusade to expose what he regarded as hypocrisy in public office. This time he was working with the *Guardian* newspaper. The allegation was that Aitken had been receiving hospitality from Arab arms dealers, a serious breach of the regulations laid down for ministers. Fayed, as the owner of the Ritz, should have been in a position to know. However, he was fully aware of the commercial risks involved in seeming to betray the trust of his guests. So *The Guardian* and Fayed set up an elaborate cover to enable details of Aitken's bill to be published.

In what became known in journalistic circles as the 'cod fax' (although it sounds like something from the fishing wars with Iceland), a fax on House-of-Commons-crested notepaper was sent to the Ritz asking for a copy of the bill. It was easy to get hold of the masthead (almost every reporter will have a letter from an MP somewhere on their desk) and create the fax. There was never any question of forging Aitken's signature, *The Guardian* assured me.

(We would sometimes use a similar tack to get a hotel or restaurant bill when I was at the *Sunday Times*. This was in the days when there was a print shop with a fax machine on every high street. You simply walked in and paid a small sum to use their fax and use it as a return address. You then sent a fax to the restaurant, claiming you were the diner, and requested a copy of the bill for your accounts. How many MPs, MEPs or union barons caught living it up with expensive meals must still wonder how we got their restaurant bill…)

Peter Preston, *The Guardian*'s editor, told me: 'There was no misrepresentation; nobody was misled. This was a device to protect the source who needed such protection at the time, and which *The Guardian*, like all other newspapers, was willing to provide.'

We revealed the story of the cod fax as our own splash in the *Sunday Times* under the headline: 'Secret Plot to Leak Aitken Bill Details'. The bylines were Maurice Chittenden, Mark Skipworth and Adrian Levy. We could hardly use the Insight logo on this one because we were shamefacedly covering another paper's scoop.

The article included predictable backlash from Tory MPs, who claimed Aitken was the victim of underhand tactics. It was partly there to mask our own embarrassment at missing out on this scoop. It was our job to come up with our own angle on the story. I kept making repeated trips to visit Fayed at his office at Harrods. Sometimes he would appear with a white cockatoo on his shoulder, but the bird barely concealed the chip on it he had about the British establishment. 'These fockers,' was a frequent start to any tirade. I was always offered coffee. Once Fayed kindly suggested I take a Harrods coat or umbrella to protect me from the pouring rain outside, but I politely refused, realising that I could not be seen taking a gift. So I was never an 'Al Fayed agent' as Aitken alleged, a claim we highlighted in my piece on the testosterone replacement therapy to show how absurd it was.

Fayed had one good lead for me. He said that Aitken's £1,000 bill for his stay had been paid for by a woman who said she was paying it into the account of Said Mohammed Ayas, whom Aitken confirmed booked the room. Ayas, a Lebanese businessman and friend of Aitken's, was a close associate of Prince Mohammed of Saudi Arabia. Fayed said he had spoken with the cashiers at the Ritz who had taken the payment after Aitken accused the hotel of making a clerical error. They remembered a 'brunette woman'.

For the next two weeks, the Insight team worked on trying to establish who this woman could be. Aitken maintained it was his wife Lolicia, a blonde and the daughter of a Serbian officer in the former Yugoslav national army, but we were not convinced.

The trick was trying to track down women who had worked as interpreters or fixers for the Arabs in Paris. We discovered that there were two and they worked for the Asturian Foundation, a business front for the Saudi royal family.

We traced one to Phoenix, Arizona, a city favoured by the Saudis to escape either the scorching temperatures of Riyadh or the cold winters of Paris and London. She insisted it was not her, which just left her colleague, Manon Vidal, a former model.

Did she know where Manon lived? After a few minutes, she was able to give us her address in Aix-en-Provence.

The next day, a Wednesday, I flew to Marseilles with Jeremy Young, the *Sunday Times* photographer, and Mark Franchetti, a journalist fluent in five languages who had just joined us and who was later to become the paper's award-winning Moscow correspondent.

Vidal did not want to talk and especially did not want her photograph taken.

We booked into a hotel in Aix. By now Insight had started to win its many awards for cash for questions so, despite the knockback, I knew we could enjoy ourselves a little with a jolly on this trip. We drove back to Marseilles for a dinner of bouillabaisse and a bottle of Tavel overlooking Vieux Port, the old port.

The following day saw the launch of the *Beaujolais Nouveau*, so were forced to join in the celebrations at La Maison du Porto opposite the Palais de Festival in Cannes. I had the *Moules Farcies* and *rouget grillé*. Next day it was *poêlée d'escargots*, entrecote and more Beaujolais at Les Deux Garcons, Paul Cezanne's old haunt, on Cours Mirabeau in Aix.

By now I had had a telephone call from London saying I was being axed as Insight editor. All the more reason, in my view, to make our gourmet tour of the French Riviera last as long as we could. On Saturday night, as our colleagues beavered away in London on getting the paper out, we dined in an upstairs room with Louis XIV paintings at the Café Le Grillen on Cours Mirabeau. I had pâté de foie gras and *champignons* in garlic as a starter followed by lamb chops in herbs and then raspberry tart. The Beaujolais came in 46cl bottles.

On Sunday morning, Jeremy (the fool!) got a snatch picture of Manon Vidal as she filled up her 4x4. Things suddenly escalated. She and her husband came to our hotel and started to make a fuss. The privacy laws on taking photographs are much more severe in France. I telephoned the *Sunday Times* lawyer at home and he advised we get the photograph and ourselves out of France as quickly as possible. As it was a Sunday and there were no wire facilities open to us, I sent Jeremy back to London.

Mark and I checked out of the hotel and drove to Sainte-Maxime, where we had to content ourselves with Breton crêpes. On Monday, after a visit to Montfort in a vain bid to get a case of my favourite wine, we flew back to London.

I took Tuesday off. Next day I collected the Scoop of the Year award from Bob Edwards at Stationers' Hall and went to a planning meeting with John Witherow, the editor, and Richard Ellis, the managing editor (news) at the Groucho Club in Soho that evening. Ellis had asked me if I wanted to be editor of the Focus pages or chief reporter. I had chosen the latter.

I told them my plan was to use the photograph of Vidal for an identification parade at the Ritz the next day. I had asked Ray Wells, the picture editor, to have random pictures taken of brunette women in the street so I would have a file of pictures to show the cashier and receptionist who had taken the payment for Aitken's room.

The ID parade was a disaster. Clutching the photos in a file, I met Michael Cole, the debonair former BBC journalist who was now Harrods' director of public affairs, at London City Airport, but our flight was cancelled because of a cabin crew strike. Michael drove us both to Heathrow where we caught another plane. We were collected at Orly Airport and driven to the Ritz where we were met by Frank Klein, the manager, and a French lawyer we had hired to oversee the ID parade and make it as judicial as possible.

The cashier and receptionist were shown into a room. First, I showed the cashier colour photographs of Aitken's wife. He said he was certain she had not paid the bill. He said Vidal had paid, and had complained she was exhausted after rushing around Paris to pay hotel bills.

I spread half a dozen photos on a table and asked them both if they recognised the woman who had paid Aitken's bill. The receptionist said he could not remember anything at all. The cashier picked out a different woman despite the fact that she was pictured in the street walking past an A-board advertising Ryman's, the UK stationers. The only good thing about the day was the langoustine salad and glasses of Beaujolais Michael, Frank and I enjoyed in the Ritz bar overlooking statues in the garden.

I flew back alone from Charles de Gaulle Airport. That night Aitken rounded on Michael Jones, the *Sunday Times* political editor, at a Foreign Office dinner. He claimed somebody had been ringing up the Saudis claiming they were Terry Sutton from the Treasury. There actually was someone at the Treasury by that name and they had been questioned by the security services.

For Aitken that might have been the end of the matter, but for the dogged determination of David Leigh, *The Guardian*'s investigations editor. Five months after my sojourn in the south of France, *The Guardian* carried a front-page report on Aitken's involvement with the Saudis as a precursor to 'Jonathan of Arabia', a *World in Action* documentary Leigh had been working on that was being aired that night.

Aitken, failing to stop the transmission, called a press conference at the Tory Party headquarters in Smith Square to
announce:

> If it falls to me to start a fight to cut out the cancer of bent
> and twisted journalism in our country with the simple sword
> of truth and the trusty shield of British fair play, so be it. I
> am ready for the fight. The fight against falsehood and those
> who peddle it. My fight begins today. Thank you and good
> afternoon.

He subsequently stood down from his job at the Treasury so that
he could sue over the allegations. He also walked away from a
£1 million deal to write Margaret Thatcher's biography. But the
story did not go away. In January 1996, fourteen months after
my visit to the south of France, Fayed gave verbal evidence to
the Commons privileges committee in which he described his
shock at seeing Aitken mixing with arms dealers at the hotel.
He said: 'Just imagine if you see the Attorney General sitting
with Al Capone, it will be exactly the same.'

Later he told me: 'My evidence was provided as a matter of
public duty.'

Mark Skipworth, who was by now news editor at the *Sunday
Times*, persuaded me to dust off my notebook and tell the story
of Manon Vidal. We ran it as the page-three lead (always my fa-
vourite slot in the paper) with Jeremy's picture of her in a white
Benetton fleece under the headline: 'Mystery Woman Holds
Key to Aitken Affair'.

I wrote:

At home in her native Provence she is Manon Vidal, a French housewife and mother who dresses in chic casual clothes. At work in the hallways of the grandest hotels in Paris she is the mysterious 'Madame Manon', elegant personal assistant to Arab princes and arms dealers, who carries a bag stuffed with cheques and francs to pay their bills.

She, it is alleged, is the woman who paid Jonathan Aitken's hotel bill when he stayed at the Ritz Hotel.

I had asked her on the Saturday whether she had paid the bill. 'Maybe I did and maybe I didn't,' she replied. 'Maybe if the police ask me I will answer. I will not answer to any journalist.'

Aitken lost his seat at the 1997 election and one month later the charade ended. His High Court case against *The Guardian* and Granada, which made *World in Action*, collapsed. Wendy Harris, a BA investigator, had been able to find that Lolicia Aitken had been in Switzerland, returning a hire car in Geneva and paying by American Express, two hours after she was supposed to have been paying her husband's bill at the Ritz in Paris.

World in Action busied itself preparing a new programme that it called 'The Dagger of Deceit' in a cheeky reference to Aitken's 'sword of truth' speech.

Aitken, facing a £2 million legal bill, left at once for a holiday in California with his son William, whose summer term had just ended at Eton.

Several newspapers employed detectives to try to find him.

They had discovered that private eyes were not just for finding ex-directory numbers. In those days they could also 'blag'
credit card bills. These showed where anyone was a day or two
earlier if they had used their card.

There was an entry on Aitken's bill for car hire from Hertz
at San Francisco Airport. One Sunday newspaper hired a freelance to camp out for two weeks in the terminal to await his
return. Another found the address of his holiday home and
rushed there only to find he had left for the airport just a few
minutes earlier. Suntanned and wearing a navy blazer and
jeans, Aitken said on his arrival: 'I've been on holiday with my
son. We had a great time, lots of sun. It was very enjoyable. I've
been advised not to make any comments whatsoever on legal
and family matters.'

Brendan Bourne, an old friend from our days together on
The Sun and the *News of the World*, was freelancing in California for various British newspapers. He saw that Aitken was
heading for a flight to Paris, not London. When he got to the
gate, Brendan was told the flight was closing.

'I have got to get on that plane. It's a matter of life or death,'
he said with a convincing air of desperation.

He slapped his credit card on the counter and paid $6,000 for
a seat in business class. Once aboard, as the plane was preparing
to take off, he looked around and saw no sign of Aitken. Panick-
ing for fear that he may have lost his man or, more importantly,
his $6,000 expense claim, he headed into economy and saw
Aitken sitting alone with an empty seat beside him.

Brendan plonked himself down and watched as Aitken read

from a Bible, underlining passages with a pen before turning the page. Brendan pulled out his notebook and began scrawling away.

Aitken, noticing what he was doing and thinking he might have a religious scholar as a fellow passenger, leaned over and said: 'Is that Hebrew?'

'No, Teeline,' said Brendan, a reference to the shorthand he and I had both learned at journalism college.

'You're a journalist,' accused an indignant Aitken. It was the end of the conversation. On landing in Paris, Aitken caught a connecting flight to London.

It was wise of Aitken to stay tight-lipped. He was due to be questioned on his return to London by Scotland Yard detectives investigating perjury allegations. Vidal admitted to them that she had indeed paid the bill on behalf of Ayas, a former medical coach who had built his fortune in the souk by negotiating secret commissions for Saudi royals on British arms deals. Aitken, who had lobbied for the arms deals to go through, pleaded guilty to both perjury and perverting the course of justice and was jailed for eighteen months at the Old Bailey. Once in prison he found God and a new role as a penal reformer.

I continued to have a good relationship with Fayed. I revealed the story of an imposter who had been seducing beautiful women and running up huge debts while pretending to be his son Dodi, who was to die two weeks later in the Paris crash that claimed the life of Diana, Princess of Wales. I told how he had driven to Diana's funeral service in his son's black Range Rover to feel closer to him.

Our friendship soured when I helped Marie Colvin, the *Sunday Times*'s courageous foreign correspondent who lost an eye to an army rocket-propelled grenade in Sri Lanka and was to die while covering the siege of Homs in Syria in 2012, write a story about an alleged break-in at Harrods' safety-box depository.

'Tiny' Rowland, the former Lonrho chairman who fought a bitter battle with Fayed for the ownership of Harrods in the 1980s, claimed a hoard of emeralds and Tibetan coins worth £200,000 had gone missing. It begged the question of why he would ever keep a safe box at Harrods. (Rowland once admitted to me that he too had paid MPs to ask questions in the Commons but said I would never be able to prove it.)

In March 2000, I wrote a back-page lead in the *Sunday Times* about an aerial mapping company that had spent two years 'carpet bombing' the whole of the UK with cameras and was now offering the photos at £18 a shot. The article was illustrated with an aerial view of Fayed's 226-acre Surrey estate. It showed the granite and marble mausoleum, as big as a bungalow, he had built for Dodi in the grounds.

I do not know if he thought I was being disrespectful, but a few days later he took up his pen in 'The Thoughts of Chairman Mo', a column he wrote in *Punch* magazine which he resurrected in a failed attempt to compete with *Private Eye*.

'Let battle commence,' he wrote.

The *Sunday Times* last weekend published an aerial photograph of my Surrey home. I have set myself a brief for the next issue of *Punch*. To send the Harrods helicopter over the homes of *ST* editor John Witherow and his journalist Maurice Chittenden and get some snaps of their properties. Perhaps they will be naked when the chopper hovers. Two can play at this game.

At the time there were terrible floods in Mozambique as the result of a cyclone. People were in desperate need of rescuing and 700 were to die.

I dug out a picture of my house and sent it to him with this note:

'Please find enclosed a photograph of my humble home. Please spare me the helicopter – it might scare my old Labrador – and send the cost of the aborted flight to Mozambique. Better still, send the helicopter to Mozambique.'

To his credit, he published both the photo and my letter in the next issue of *Punch*.

CHAPTER TWENTY-TWO

MY LIFE AMONGST
THE TRAIN ROBBERS

They say most people can remember where they were when they first learned about 9/11 or the death of Diana, Princess of Wales. For older generations, it is the assassination of John F. Kennedy.

For me, however, it is the Great Train Robbery of 1963. I was at my grandmother's council bungalow in Chipping Norton. As usual she had a pile of *Daily Mail*s on her dining table and I was reading through them for interesting snippets. This is how I discovered that an in-law of my late father's had been shot and wounded by bandits during a highway robbery in the Congo.

Like most boys of that age, I was into cowboys and Indians and used to read *Buffalo Bill* annuals from cover to cover. However, nothing quite prepared me for the sheer audacity of the Great Train Robbery, and how, half a century later, it was still impacting on my professional career. News must have broken on the television around lunchtime on Thursday 8 August 1963.

In the early hours of that day, a sixteen-strong gang had covered up a 'through' green signal on an overhead gantry with an old glove, attached a battery to a red signal to make it light up and stopped the Royal Mail train running from Glasgow to London at Bridego Bridge in Buckinghamshire before storming the high-value postage van and stealing mailbags. Over the next few days, with each news bulletin the amount of money stolen gradually rose. Bookmakers even offered odds on the final figure and one of the robbers, Tommy Wisbey, wanted to place a £5,000 wager on it before he was persuaded not to by his fellow robbers. The eventual tally was in excess of £2.6 million (equivalent to £50 million today). The gang had not used firearms, but Jack Mills, the train driver, was coshed with a metal bar. A year later, some of the ringleaders were jailed for thirty years, then an almost unthinkable sentence for a robbery.

It was a story that never stopped giving. The crime itself was followed by dramatic prison escapes, extravagant claims that the robbers would use atomic weapons to free their comrades, the murder of one train robber, the suicide of another and the deaths of the rest.

Young reporters like me learned the names of those convicted or on the run as they might members of the 1966 England World Cup team and wondered at the identities of the three men, plus the replacement train driver they had brought along, who had supposedly got away with their part in Britain's crime of the century.

Over the years and at various newspapers I had dealings with many of the gang, including getting the first brief interview with Gordon Goody, one of the instigators, after his release, strolling down to Waterloo station to shoot the breeze with 'Buster' Edwards at his flower stall, ringing Ronnie Biggs in Rio for a quote and trying to brush aside his demand for payment, and befriending Bruce Reynolds, the self-educated mastermind, in his later years. However, my greatest coup was opening up the Post Office documents from the time and discovering, bizarrely, that the father and uncle of one of England's most capped footballers were suspected of involvement.

My boyhood interest in the robbery was re-ignited when ex-Detective Superintendent Malcolm Fewtrell, the former head of Buckinghamshire CID, visited the training college in Hampshire where I studied journalism and I was able to interview him.

Ten years later, I was working at the *Evening Post-Echo* in Hemel Hempstead, moonlighting in Fleet Street and selling stories where I could. The Chittenden holiday to Spain in July 1981 is a memorable occasion in the family history. It was the first time my one-year-old son Scott spoke a 'sentence' (even it was only 'kick ball' in the hotel lift going down to the beach). It was also the first time I met a train robber.

My wife is used to my pursuit of criminals, dead or alive, while on holiday. On a trip to New York we had dined on scallops at Umberto's in Little Italy, the restaurant where Mafia mobster 'Crazy Joe' Gallo had been gunned down. On our previous holiday, when she was heavily pregnant with Scott, I had taken her into the hills of Sardinia to get colour for a feature I wrote on my return, 'Where the Bandit Has Fallen for the Tourist'.

Now, drinking in the hotel bar in Mojacar, I heard stories about the strange *Ingles* building a bar farther along the beach. Some locals had it that he was one of the Great Train Robbers. Who could it be? Ronnie Biggs had just survived an abduction attempt by British ex-soldiers and been sent back to Brazil from Barbados where the kidnappers' boat had broken down. Some of the others were still in jail, but most had been released and drifted back into the underworld.

'My' train robber, I discovered, was Douglas Gordon Goody, one of the ringleaders of the gang. Known to his friends as 'Checker', Goody was actually half-Irish. He had been a thief since childhood and a hardened criminal since his teens, when at the age of seventeen he was jailed for twenty-one months at the Old Bailey and received twelve strokes of the birch for the vicious robbery of a gay man, a crime known amongst his fraternity as 'rolling a queer'. He had a 'front' as a hairdresser, but I doubt if he ever cut anyone's hair. His sharp features gave him the appearance of a crook and he sometimes wore spectacles he didn't need to make himself look more respectable.

Goody was almost unique amongst the train robbers. He had been freed in 1975 after serving eleven years of his thirty-year sentence, but had not tried to sell his story to the Sunday tabloids and he had never been interviewed. I decided to have a shot and hired a car for this very purpose.

I went from bar to bar along the coast of Almeria, a province familiar to cinema-goers in Britain as the backdrop for the spaghetti Westerns of Sergio Leone. Whether they were reluctant to help publicise a rival's bar or genuinely ignorant, I will never know, but the owners all claimed they knew nothing.

I was in my last bar and about to give up. I knew I could not drink another bottle of lager and still drive. The door opened and in walked the tall, tattooed, bronzed figure of Gordon Goody. He was wearing a T-shirt and dusty jeans and was accompanied by a younger, Spanish man in similar attire. It was clear that they had been toiling away all morning and were thirsty for a beer.

I introduced myself and offered to get the drinks but Goody was not an easy drinking companion. He told me to keep my money and said he did not want to talk about his past. I tried a different tack, and spoke about his future instead. He opened up a little when I asked about the bar.

'I'm getting it ready for the height of the season,' said Goody, whose previous law-abiding enterprises since his release had included a second-hand furniture shop and selling potatoes from the back of a lorry.

He spoke fluent Spanish to the bartender and helped me with my feeble attempts to buy a gas cigarette lighter from behind the bar. But he waved away further attempts at conversation so I finished my drink and left.

It was not much of an interview but it was enough to sell to the *Sunday People* on my return home. The paper ran it under the clever title 'Goody behind bars again'. I had no hand in the headline or the new intro put on the story by the subs: 'Great Train Robber Gordon Goody is following in the footsteps of Ronnie Biggs – by becoming a beach boy.'

Roll on thirty years (the standard sentence for any heavy in the Great Train Robbery) and I discovered that the Post Office was about to release its archived documents on the crime prior to the fiftieth anniversary. The papers were to be deposited in the Post Office Museum in a similar way that Parliament releases its files to the House of Commons library.

It was February 2012. Ronnie Biggs had flown back to Britain from exile in Brazil on a private jet paid for by *The Sun*, served some of the sentence in a prison hospital and been paroled, only to suffer a series of strokes which left him unable to speak. Charlie Wilson had been shot dead in Spain, either in a drug syndicate turf war or a fallout over the gold stolen in the Brink's-Mat robbery, and 'Buster' Edwards had hanged himself in his garage, yet still the Great Train Robbery held the public imagination. That very month Charmian Biggs, Ronnie's wife, was flying to Britain from Australia to visit him as filming began on a new five-part ITV drama, *Mrs Biggs*, starring Sheridan Smith and Daniel Mays.

I had now befriended Bruce Reynolds, who had masterminded the robbery with Goody. Bruce had gone on the run for five years (some of it spent in Mexico with 'Buster') but was finally cornered in a house in Torquay and jailed for twenty-five years.

Bruce was to be featured in his own docudrama, *A Robber's Tale*, in which he was played by Luke Evans, in December 2013, but, in truth, he always wanted Michael Caine to play him. The actor is said to have based his look as Harry Palmer in *The Ipcress File* on the train robber.

He now seemed a shadow of his former self, both physically

and mentally (he died a year later). In the Swinging Sixties, he had been one of the new breed of crooks, not unlike the character Caine portrayed in *The Italian Job*. He was intelligent, charming and well-dressed, not so much a gentleman thief as a white-collar criminal who looked on crime as a business enterprise. He did not share the fondness of the 1950s villain for drinking in spielers, carrying a chiv or wearing the clothes of a B-film Chicago gangster. Instead, Reynolds drank champagne in trendy Mayfair nightclubs, cooked his own gourmet meals and wore Savile Row suits, tailored shirts and handmade shoes. He wore black-rimmed glasses (he needed his), drove sports cars and described himself as an antiques dealer.

This outward display of opulence may well have been his way of making up for an unhappy childhood. He was the son of a full-time trade union official and when his mother died when he was four he had gone to live at his grandmother's house in Battersea. His father re-married but young Bruce never saw eye to eye with his stepmother, especially when she had his pet dog put down for messing in the house.

He had left school at fourteen. Bruce had ambitions of becoming a journalist but he knew he had no qualifications. Instead he got a job in a newspaper office as a messenger at Northcliffe House, the white stone building in Carmelite Street that then housed the *Daily Mail*, hoping to work his way up.

This was not impossible in the days before career opportunities in journalism were more or less limited to young people with degrees and enough family money to live in London. Dave Morgan, one of the copy runners at the *Evening Post-Echo*, worked his way up to become chief sub at *The Sun* and another, David Connett, became an investigative reporter, while Simon Reeve started off as a post boy at the *Sunday Times*. Perhaps the greatest 'rag-outs to riches' story in journalism is that of Mike Molloy, who joined the *Sunday Pictorial* as a messenger at the age of fifteen and within twenty years was editor of the *Daily Mirror* at a time it sold 5 million copies a day. He is now a successful author of children's books. The *Mirror*'s circulation is down to 800,000.

Unluckily for young Bruce, the only advancement offered to him at the *Mail* was in the accounts department. He could see after two years that he was making no headway and left for more money as a laboratory technician in Middlesex Hospital, eventually drifting into crime (after an altercation with a policeman for riding his bicycle without lights) and becoming well known to the police. Whenever they called at his grandmother's home, where he was living, he would nip out the back, cut across a cemetery and be away.

Even in old age Bruce looked back on the Great Train Robbery, his biggest tickle, with a mixture of pride and regret. 'It has only brought unhappiness to my wife and little son,' he told police when he was arrested and it was an attitude that stayed with him for the rest of his life. Indeed, he and his wife Angela divorced while he was in prison, but they later reconciled and he had spent the past twenty years nursing her through ill health. The 'little son', Nick Reynolds, became a sculptor and a band member of Alabama 3, whose song 'Woke Up This Morning' was the opening theme of the Mafia drama *The Sopranos*.

In between writing books and acting as a consultant on films, Bruce was always civil when I talked to him at his modest housing association flat in Croydon and willing to correct any misinformation about the robbery.

He was bemused when I told him Scotland Yard was planning on introducing patrol cars fuelled by hydrogen into its fleet and bemoaned the passing of the golden days when London streets were empty enough for car chases in Jaguar Mark 2s.

'I look at these things much the same as an old soldier might look at campaigns,' he told me.

'The hydrogen cars are still being developed but obviously the police of today are highly technical and move with the times. We had the better drivers in my day as a criminal but the police have always had access to vehicles that are not strictly on the agenda.'

However, the one thing Bruce, a stickler to the old under-world codes, would never discuss was the identity of those who got away.

I hoped the Post Office files might have some clues. They were housed at the British Postal Museum and Archive in north London. On display was a wrapper addressed to Westminster Bank in Lombard Street in the City from which some of the fingerprints that convicted the gang were recovered.

I asked to see the new files, especially those of the Post Office Investigation Bureau (IB), and a few minutes later was shown to a reading desk. The first of a series of large boxes of documents was put on the desk for me to wade through. Once I had finished one box I could have another.

'Hello, Maurice.' I looked up. Standing before me were Bob Graham, a reporter, and Stuart Clarke, a photographer – both Fleet Street veterans. They had teamed up in Baghdad during the Iraq War and were now two of the smartest freelance operators around. Bob and I had once been reporters together on the *News of the World*. Stuart had been married to Margarette Driscoll, a great feature writer who became yet another casualty of spending cuts at the *Sunday Times* a few months before the axe fell on me.

It was not the first time I had bumped into a rival in such circumstances and beavered away quietly in competition with each other without anyone else present knowing. During the Fred and Rosemary West murder case, Nick Craven, then of the *Sunday Mirror*, and I had stumbled upon each other in Gloucester City Library, pulling out index files and searching for a press cutting about the couple being prosecuted years earlier for a sexual assault on a girl hitchhiker they had picked up.

Damn, I thought. Bob and Stuart will be after the same files as me. I worked diligently through them until I found what I was looking for. It was headed: 'Confidential lists of 28 suspects given to IB by Police'. It had been compiled by Detective Chief Superintendent Tommy Butler, the head of the Flying Squad, eight days after the robbery and was stamped 'In strictest confidence'.

My eye ran down the list. Goody, Wilson and Reynolds were at the top. But at numbers eight and nine were the names of Terry and George Sansom. Incredibly, I recognised the surname from my boyhood study of crime reports and from watching football matches.

Freddie Sansom had been the leader of a bunch of bank robbers known as the 'shot in the ceiling gang' from their trademark of announcing their presence in any bank branch by pep-
pering the plaster above the cashiers with a shotgun blast. He
had also been a neighbour in Dulwich, south London, of James
'Big Jim' Hussey, one of the heavies who stormed the high-value
postal van on the night of the Great Train Robbery and who is
supposed to have made a deathbed confession that it was he
who coshed the driver.

Terry and George Sansom were his brothers. The files stated
that Terry had been 'a suspect in [sic] Wimbledon bus murder
case'. Indeed, there had been wild scenes at the Old Bailey as he
was acquitted of battering to death a guard who was hit with
an iron bar when a gang of five bandits seized a £9,400 payroll from a London Transport bus. George, I was to discover
on doing background checks, was the father of Kenny Sansom,
who played eighty-six times for England and had been the
country's most-capped full-back until he was overtaken by
Ashley Cole the previous year.

Of those on the list, eleven were subsequently convicted of
involvement in the robbery. The Sansom brothers appeared
ahead of 'Buster' Edwards and Roy 'The Weasel' James, both
known members of the gang. The brothers were never charged.

Others on the list included Billy Ambrose, a former boxer
who became a successful businessman before his death, and
Freddie Robinson, a west London car dealer who was known
for his meticulous planning of robberies.

There was a Damon Runyonesque feel to some of the names

elsewhere in the boxes of files. As well as 'The Weasel', they discussed the criminal activities of crooks known as 'Freddie the Fox', 'Mickey the Fly' and 'Touchy' Lucy.

Both the Sansom brothers, who were married to two sisters, were dead – George had died of heart disease at the age of fifty-nine in 1987, Terry on the so-called Costa del Crime in Spain two years later. Kenny, George's son, had fallen from grace with the same sort of problems with alcohol that beset George Best and Paul Gascoigne. I went to his last known address, but he had moved out and was thought to be more or less living rough. Luckily I managed to trace George's daughter Maureen to a flat in Sidcup, south London.

'Dad never had a conscience,' she told me. 'He deserted Mum but came back on the scene when Kenny became famous. I don't think he was a train robber. We wouldn't have been living in a Peabody (housing association) flat in south London if that was the case.'

She also confided that Terry Sansom, the son of bank robber Freddie, had been in a car with Lorraine Wisbey, daughter of train robber Tommy, when it crashed and she and Michael Corbett, a young Charlton Athletic footballer, were killed. She was his girlfriend. 'He was later found floating in the Thames. We never knew what happened, whether he fell in or was feeling remorse.'

She offered to pass on my number to Kenny and ask him to call me. I didn't hold out much hope but at 5 p.m. on Friday, just as I was about to file my copy, he rang me.

Kenny, who played for Arsenal and Crystal Palace, said: 'The story I heard when my dad was alive was that my uncle or he was offered a driving job in the train robbery. Terry was a very quick driver. But he was too frightened and felt it was too risky.'

That made sense because, of the gang's chosen drivers, Mickey Ball had been convicted of the 1962 London Airport payroll job, leaving only Roy James as a wheelman.

When I contacted Bruce Reynolds, he was non-committal. 'No one will ever know the complete story of the train robbery because memories have faded,' he said. 'As far as the list is concerned, we put ourselves entirely in the frame. They knew exactly who they were looking for after the airport robbery.'

My story appeared in the *Sunday Times* that weekend under the headline: 'Football Star's Family Were Train Robbery Suspects'. I leafed through the *Mail on Sunday* to see what Bob and Stuart had been doing. Their story, under the byline of Chris Hastings, the paper's arts reporter of all people, was a fairly tame affair about the Post Office wrongly suspecting two postmen of being the inside men on the job because they happened to share Ronnie Biggs' surname. This just went to prove another of my favourite Fleet Street sayings: 'Don't overestimate the competition.'

Poring over the criminal records of others named on the list, I found some other familiar names. Number twelve on the list, Henry Smith, who was to be named as one of the train robbers by *The Sun*'s crime editor Mike Sullivan in 2013, had once been involved in a court case with Charlie and Eddie Richardson, later made famous in the so-called Torture Trial at the Old Bailey. Two years later, Sullivan named Danny Pembroke, number twenty-one on the list, as another of those who got away with the train robbery. It rather shows how good the police's criminal intelligence was in the 1960s. Is it possible that Terry Sansom was the third man never brought to justice?

The Krays and the Richardsons had been the two top gangs in London in the '60s. I had run-ins with both. Most of my dealings with the Krays were with the twins' older brother Charlie. I reported in *The Sun* how he had called for a 'mickey-taking' TV commercial to be banned. The advert, produced by the London Dockland Development Corporation, featured a pair of puppet crows called Wally and Wedgie. It opened with an East End pub landlord warning drinkers; 'Look out, the Crows are in.' An unfortunate bird who advised against investing in the corporation ended up in a cement mixer. Charlie claimed it blackened the family name, if that was possible.

Later, in the *Sunday Times*, I told how the Krays were using calendars, T-shirts and badges glorifying Ronnie and Reggie in an attempt to market the twins and win them early parole ('Gangster Krays Face Up to a Nice Little Earner') and a second story on a rally to press for their freedom was picked up and used by *The Australian*.

As for the Richardsons, I covered Charlie's release from prison for *The Sun* and interviewed him for the *Sunday Times*, describing him as 'the new Goldfinger' after he sold gold mining rights in Uganda for £1 million. His brother Eddie was not so fortunate. After his release from prison he visited me at the *Sunday Times* to try to persuade me to write the story of how he had learned to paint while inside. Even in his sixties he oozed menace. I ushered him into our photographers' studio so he would not alarm more delicate members of staff. But the pictures were rather garish sub-Beryl Cook caricatures of hop pickers, poachers and other East End characters. After checking he had not brought any of his torture equipment, I sent him on his way. Even I could not have got his art into our Culture section.

CHAPTER TWENTY-THREE

ONE BAD ASSIGNMENT

Newspaper executives must get bored. Sitting around in the office all day, attending endless meetings – not even their byline in the paper at the end of the day to show the world that they exist.

Which is why their feverish imaginations must work overtime to create near-impossible tasks for their journalists to complete.

Tony Rennell, the managing editor (news) at the *Sunday Times*, came up to me furtively one day and said in his silken, smoky voice: 'Maurice, Michael Medved says Michael Jackson has been doing it with Bubbles. It's not confirmed. You will have to check it out.'

Thanks, Tony. There is a saying in journalism that the unexpected always happens, but this sounded a step too far. That said, with Michael Jackson, anything was possible. Like everybody else of my generation, I had watched his progression from the sweet child star singing 'Ben' to the Wacko Jacko of crazy behaviour. Addicted to painkillers, he slept in an oxygen tent and, when he was not inviting children to sleepovers, his best friend was Bubbles, a pet chimpanzee.

Rennell said he had got his story from talking to Michael Medved, a Seattle-based American radio show host, author and political commentator. At the time, he was chief film critic of the *New York Post*, a Murdoch-owned tabloid, and the *Sunday Times* had brought him to London in the wake of his book *Hollywood vs America* to debate his argument that violence on the screen was echoed by violence in the street.

For a reporter, Michael Jackson was the story that never stopped giving. I had my first Jacko splash in *The Sun* in 1984: 'Jackson Video Fever'. It told how 'a sensational 100,000 copies' of his 'Thriller' video had been sold in Britain in three days. Some stores had to give up playing the video in their windows because it was such a traffic-stopper. I even reviewed his show for the Culture section of the *Sunday Times* when he played in Sheffield as part of the HIStory tour. I was to have one of my last splashes with him when he died in 2009 from an administered drug overdose.

I did some checking. Bubbles was about nine years old, slept in a crib in Jackson's bedroom at his Neverland ranch, used the singer's toilet and ate sweets in the ranch's movie theatre. Jackson had taken Bubbles with him to Japan on the 'Bad' world tour and they had both drunk green tea with the mayor of Osaka. Mmm...

As an assignment, it rivalled the requests of two other executives at the *Sunday Times* for its absurdity. When he was news editor Michael Williams once asked Mazher Mahmood to board an El Al coach at Heathrow and pull out a plastic pistol to test the security. (Willams, a great operator, was later deputy editor at the *Independent on Sunday*, known to all as The Sindy, where he upset his staff by asking one of them to 'do a Chittenden' on a piece about Salman Rushdie.) Richard Ellis wanted Ciaran Byrne, an angelic-faced but definitely male reporter, to infiltrate the Lesbian Avengers.

Some of these tasks were just wishful thinking brought up at conference to show that an executive is thinking out of the box. Others had a more cynical motive to push a reporter perhaps considered to be under-performing into action.

Another colleague, Charles Oulton, had the title of religious affairs correspondent, but was still asked by a news editor to check out a reportedly faulty make of parachute – by jumping out of a plane wearing it. 'When I landed,' he complained afterwards, 'I rang the news editor. What was his first question? Are you OK? No. Where's the copy?' We dubbed him 'The Flying Padre' as a result, and he left soon afterwards to become a teacher.

I had my own share of seemingly impossible tasks thrust upon me. Finding a witness to a non-fatal accident involving a racing car that had happened forty-three years earlier in Transylvania was one of them. Luckily I pulled that one off.

In May 1999, Michael Schumacher won the Monaco Grand Prix in spectacular fashion, finishing seventy-eight laps of the street circuit in his Ferrari thirty seconds ahead of Eddie Irvine, his teammate. It was Schumacher's sixteenth win with

Ferrari, breaking the record held by Niki Lauda. Word came through from the *Sunday Times* sports section that he might be using some sort of secret traction control for his fast getaways from the grid and the pit-stop. I was asked to check it out, even though my knowledge of car mechanics ended with *The Observer's Book of Automobiles*. The next race was the Spanish Grand Prix in two weeks' time.

I was not getting on too well with the news editor we had at the time, so I determined to make a weekend of it. I flew out on a Friday evening and booked into the five-star Princesa Sofia Hotel in Barcelona. I had doorstepped Juan Antonio Samaranch, Princess Anne and other members of the International Olympic Committee there when it was heavily guarded seven years earlier during the Barcelona Games, and wanted to try out the luxury myself. I spun the news desk some line about the Ferrari team probably staying there to overcome the restraint on expenses. (I always liked to stay in InterContinental or Hilton hotels when I could so that I could collect reward points, which my wife and I then used for stays at hotels like the Waldorf Astoria in New York or the Sydney Hilton.)

While my colleagues were beavering away on their stories at their desks in London, I spent a pleasant evening enjoying tapas and Rioja on La Rambla. The next day, I headed off to the Circuit de Catalunya for the practice laps and the pole positioning. I interviewed Jackie Stewart in his motorhome in the paddock and spent the day wandering around. At one stage, Bernie Ecclestone, alerted of my presence, came to give me a good looking over but neither of us spoke.

Race day was Sunday, and I managed to position myself next to a large window above the Ferrari garage so I could look into Schumacher's car as he sat at the controls. This was much to the annoyance of half a dozen Japanese photographers who wanted me to move so they could get a better shot. Of what, I have no idea, because there must be thousands of images of Schumacher behind the wheel. Anyway, I saw nothing that might look suspicious.

The race was a complete bore. There was only one overtaking manoeuvre on the track during the whole race. Mika Häkkinen, who started in pole position, finished first in his McLaren-Mercedes and Schumacher had to settle for third place. Afterwards, I got him to autograph my race programme. He was all smiles until I asked him if he had used traction control for his fast getaway at Monaco. That wiped the smile from his face. He turned on his heels and began striding off. Then he turned and signalled at me with the upraised four fingers of his right hand. I was told later that this was a German gesture meaning 'up your arse'. I had nothing to show for my trip.

A couple of years later, in the wake of the 9/11 attacks in the US in 2001, there was a suggestion that nuclear power plants had once been the original planned target for the suicide terrorist plane attacks. An idea came out of the Thursday editorial planning conference that I should check out security at one of Britain's nuclear energy sites.

What was I supposed to do? It was one of those tasks you could agonise over for days, thinking up angles and ruses. I decided to go the direct route and become White Van Man for the day. I reckoned that the easiest way to test the security was to pretend I was delivering supplies, something that must be happening on such a regular basis that it might have become a monotonous task for the guards just to wave vehicles through after a cursory search. I had previously bluffed my way into New Labour's headquarters at Millbank Tower clutching a bottle of Chiantishire wine – a bottle of Chianti with a new label we had designed on Photoshop in the office – in an unsuccessful bid to sponsor the party in return for them serving our wine at the party conference. (I introduced myself as Paul Sugget, an anagram of 'get us a plug'.)

But what could I take to a nuclear energy plant? Looking around the *Sunday Times* office I spotted two large cardboard boxes filled with plastic coffee cups. They were ideal. I concocted a delivery note in the office.

I wanted to have an absurd element to any story, just as we had used the anagrams of Insight in our stings on MPs. I found a van hire company called Big Yellow Banana, which had a picture of a huge banana on the side of their vehicles.

So off I headed to Dungeness nuclear power station, isolated on a spit of shingle on the Kent coast. Power stations have their own police force (it was then the Atomic Energy Authority Constabulary) and I knew they would want to search the van. I timed my arrival for late in the afternoon to explain why I had no other cargo in the Big Yellow Banana van.

At the gate I produced my delivery note and told the policemen that I had been instructed to deliver the cups to the kitchen in person. The guards checked out the delivery note and the back of the van, but said there was no way I was coming in. After about twenty minutes of argument and phone calls – apparently no one in the kitchen knew about the delivery! – the police decided to take the boxes in by hand and send me on my way.

I did not mention my failure the next day when I attended a ceremony to receive an Emporio Armani watch for fifteen years' service on the *Sunday Times* from Les Hinton, Murdoch's executive chairman at News International. Chris Stevens, with whom I had started out at the *Bracknell News* thirty years earlier, was there too, picking up his own award for his service at *The Sun*. However, when I got back to the newsroom I noticed a murmuring of disquiet. No one, including me, could have tea or coffee for the next two days because all the plastic cups had disappeared. I had slipped on my own big yellow banana skin.

So what of Bubbles and those sex claims? I discovered that the chimp who had once been the most powerful and pampered primate on the planet had gone the way of so many a faded star: going grey, piling on the pounds and spending his days watching television at an ape sanctuary in Florida. As I said to Tony Rennell: 'Well, I tried to buy him up but banana journalism has been outlawed by the journalism code of conduct.'

CHAPTER TWENTY-FOUR

THE LOST WORLD OF BLANKIES

Once upon a time at the *Sunday Times*'s annual newsroom Christmas lunch, my pal Andrew Alderson told this story:

It is well known in the words of Tony Bambridge in the *UK Press Gazette* that Maurice has the biggest contacts book in Fleet Street. What Maurice is equally proud of but, of course, keeps quieter is his reputation for having the biggest collection of blank receipts in the world.

Now, because there are executives here, I must stress that Maurice, of course, collects receipts when other people collect stamps and postcards, only for their aesthetic value.

How fond he is of his collection of blanks only came to notice when there was one story recently involving some hacks who had gone to the West Midlands to cover a murder. They had worked hard on the story all day and they were having a drink in the pub in the evening. One girl said: 'Has anyone got a blank meal receipt from Birmingham?'

One by one she went around the reporters and each one shook their head in turn. But then she came to Maurice. In a deft move, he flicked open the lid of his briefcase, looked momentarily inside and said: 'Chinese, Italian or Indian?'

Those days have long gone. There is no way the cut-to-the-bone newspaper managements of today would allow such behaviour. I stopped claiming expenses completely when I opted for voluntary redundancy and went freelance in 2007. By then it was all but over, anyway. The financial crisis of 2008 meant even more belt-tightening. Ironically, the MPs' expenses scandal exposed by the *Daily Telegraph* the following year which led to prosecutions for false accounting against various parliamentarians was the final death knell. The MPs were jailed for fraud against the taxpayer rather than against an employer who was almost complicit in any offence, but the message still got home.

By the time of the Leveson Inquiry and Operation Elveden, the culture of creative writing (at least when it came to your expenses) was dead. The *Sunday Times* even banned the use of taxis. Managing editors across Fleet Street put limits of £20 per diner on entertaining contacts and demanded to see a credit card receipt. The 'blankie', the blank receipt, became about as useless a piece of paper as a Zimbabwe dollar. The *Sunday Times* will not even accept a genuine lunch receipt timed after 3 p.m. Excess of any sort is now frowned upon in the new Puritan world of the press.

But, for about forty years, this sort of behaviour was not only tolerated within Fleet Street but almost expected. The fact that Andrew Alderson could tell such a story in front of executives is rather a clue to the culture that existed. There was an understanding between the newspaper and the journalist that expenses were there to be exploited so long as you did not go over the top. It was a perk that suited both sides. 'Just don't take the piss,' was the edict heard regularly in newspaper offices.

You have to remember that there has never been such a thing as overtime pay in journalism. Even reporters who log their extra hours and insist on taking days off in lieu are regarded as oddballs.

So when newspapers were making hay it was almost in their interests to overlook the exaggerated claim forms. It was a way of paying extra to staff without also having to pay National Insurance contributions. Indeed, the money went down as running costs.

It was also a way of rewarding or punishing reporters. Those who were considered to be doing a good job had their expenses claims passed. Those who were either not pulling in the stories or fighting management over some issue would find them cut or even binned.

But reporters looked on expenses as their right. As one old-timer at the Mirror Group put it: 'If the trustees of the Maxwell estate have an issue with me fiddling a few quid out of them, they can reclaim it from the thousands Old Fatso embezzled out of my pension fund.'

However, your expenses could also be a hostage to fortune. If the management wanted to get rid of you, all they had to do was dig out your expenses, find a dubious claim and threaten to report you to the police fraud unit if you did not resign.

There was a natural order to what could be claimed. For a junior it might be £50 a week, for a senior £100 a week, more for a specialist. For a good political editor, expected to wine and dine ministers, it was much more.

There would be set meal allowances for working away from the office. If you were on the go for sixteen hours non-stop in, say, the West Midlands, it was possible to claim breakfast, lunch, dinner and even late supper allowances.

Of course, these were fairly standard amounts and it was much better to 'entertain a contact', even if the contact was the photographer working with you or a reporter from a rival paper.

If you did not leave the office but managed to pull in a scoop, the news editor might well reward you by saying: 'Take your wife out to dinner and put it on exes.'

However, it was rather depressing to hear in the evidence in one of the trials that followed Operation Elveden, the police investigation into various allegations that reporters from *The Sun* had paid public officials for information, that a senior journalist was putting takeaway meals for his family on his expenses.

A far better line came in evidence from Chris Pharo, who like me had started at the *Bracknell News* and had since risen to become news editor at *The Sun*. 'There is more fantasy in journalist expenses than *Lord of the Rings*,' he said. His colleague and co-defendant Jamie Pyatt, who once accidentally claimed expenses for lunch with a murder detective before the crime was committed, said reporters routinely fiddled their expenses as compensation for working long hours in a tough environment. (Both were acquitted. Out of twenty-nine cases against journalists, only one reporter was found guilty. He was given a suspended sentence. By contrast, twenty-six public officials were convicted following the £20 million investigation into newspapers' activities.)

Of course, the expenses claim had to say something that sounded legitimate to make sure it got through the managing editor's office. It didn't have to be too sophisticated, although one reporter at the *Sunday Times* was rumbled when he tried to put his laundry bill from Greece through as a meal receipt because somebody in the office spoke Greek. Someone else did much better in putting in a receipt for an expensive pair of shoes from a shop in Germany called the Schuh-Keller as a lunch claim, theorising that the name might sound like a beer hall. Derek Jameson, once my editor at the *News of the World*, would have liked that story. One day, while northern editor of the *Daily Mirror*, he was signing his reporters' expenses when he came across a lunch receipt missing the name of a restaurant at the top. Jameson peered more closely and made out the small print at the bottom: 'These shoes cannot be exchanged.'

A pal at the *Daily Star*, Dick Durham, used to religiously put down 'FDT … £5' on each weekly claim. When someone finally had the nous to ask him what the initials on his expenses stood for, he replied: 'For doing them.' Quite right. They can take ages.

Editors, of course, had their own allowances. When Geordie Greig left his job as literary editor at the *Sunday Times* in 1999 to edit *Tatler* on his rise to the top, Richard Caseby, the managing editor, told those of us gathered for the farewell party that Geordie was well known for being cavalier with his expenses and then read out from the files about a £118 lunch with Peter Palumbo for which he had not produced a receipt.

Photographers, in particular, were so keen to get blank receipts, or 'blankies', that they would seek to get them in advance. One of their number would be chosen to fly out a month ahead of a World Cup tournament or Olympic Games to harvest what receipts he could. It was always lost on the office why I started a family holiday in Atlanta in 1996 three months before returning there for the Summer Games.

There were various ways of obtaining receipts. One colleague had an ex-husband who ran a restaurant just off Piccadilly Circus and she was able to come up with whole books of receipts that could be traded with other journalists. Often a restaurant would agree to give multiple receipts for the same meal, which could be shared around, or, in return for a generous tip, a waiter might slip you a couple of blank bills.

More hazardous was the route of 'borrowing' a book of bill receipts. I was in Dunstable with Keith Deves, an amiable if eccentric Australian colleague from *The Sun*, the night the police finally arrested an evil rapist known as The Fox after a reign of terror over several counties. After filing our copy, we adjourned to a Chinese restaurant for a celebratory dinner, during which Deves helped himself to a book of receipts from a trolley. I have this lasting memory of Deves stretched over the bonnet of his car a few minutes later with a waiter holding a meat cleaver over his head, threatening to kill him if he did not hand back the book.

During the 1990 World Cup, I was lunching with some

colleagues at a restaurant in Pompeii. By some sleight of hand, a bill from a neighbouring table landed in my pocket. Unfortunately, one of the diners saw it had gone and the waiters chased us down the street even as we sped away with me at the wheel of our hire car. The receipt was for about £600 and unusable anyway. Still, I could taste my chutzpah as much as the pasta.

I was more enterprising when we were having dinner in Zeebrugge after the *Herald of Free Enterprise* disaster. I had given the news desk in London the restaurant's number in case there were queries on our copy. The *maitre d'*, who had a *Poirot*-style moustache, seemed particularly suspicious of us. The news desk duly phoned and the *maitre d'* called me to his desk before disappearing into the kitchen.

As I was dealing with the query, I leaned over the desk and saw a book of receipts. I picked them up as London cleared at their end. Just then I spotted the beady-eyed *maitre d'* staring at me through the window in the kitchen door as he twisted up the corner of his moustache. Quick as a flash, I turned the book over as if it was a notepad and began scribbling notes while continuing an imaginary conversation with the news desk on the other end of the phone.

'Foreigns', as overseas trips were known, were always good for expenses. One pal built a conservatory on the expenses he made from the 1990 World Cup. War zones might not be compatible with fine restaurants but news desks back in London had no idea how much you might have to pay for a guide or interpreter. When I was away I always liked to use local students anyway. Much cheaper.

Once you had collected a wad of receipts from one restaurant it was advantageous to trade some of them with colleagues who had their own source from other dining places. This was done quite openly at night in the *Sun* newsroom. Others met at El Vino's wine bar on Tuesdays for a regular trading session known as the 'London Bill Exchange'.

You could also exchange stories of how you got your blankies or your near-misses with the management. One reporter at the *Express*, specialising in security stories, regularly claimed for lunches with a Colonel Popov from the Czech Embassy. After a few months some jobsworth from the accounts department decided to check, called the Czech Embassy and found there was no such person. He dared to go into the newsroom to challenge the reporter. 'Doesn't exist, eh,' said the reporter. 'I won't trust anything else he tells me.'

Bills in books were consecutively numbered, probably for VAT reasons, so you had to be careful not to put a bill in from the same restaurant two weeks running. One reporter failed to notice this and put in bills numbered twenty-one, twenty-two and twenty-three in consecutive weeks. He was confronted by an accountant who suggested that either his claims were fraudulent or the restaurant had no other customers. Quick as a flash, the hack replied: 'No, there's a simple explanation. I am such a valued customer that they keep a special receipt book just for me.'

Mileage in your own car was another big earner. This was sometimes stretched to ridiculous lengths. I remember announcing a prize at one boozy Christmas lunch to James

Dalrymple, a talented writer who had joined the *Sunday Times* from *The Independent* where he had campaigned for the release of Winston Silcott, wrongfully convicted of the murder of a policeman during the Broadwater Farm riot, and who had recently departed back to his native Scotland.

'The *Fistful of Dollars* award for the most imaginative expenses claim of the year goes to 'Spurs row. Mileage in the City 63 miles at 34p a mile,' I said. 'Now we all know why they put that ring of steel around the City of London. It wasn't because of the IRA. It was because of Jimmy D driving round and round, stopping every so often when he saw a policeman on picket duty, winding down the window and saying; "I'm telling you, Winston Silcott is innocent."'

Tony Bambridge, the managing editor at the *Sunday Times*, once asked Dalrymple how he managed to drive 200 miles in London each week. 'How do you fiddle your expenses?' he shot back.

Of course, you were expected to take taxis instead of buses or the Tube in London, even though anyone used to the capital knows the underground is quicker. 'I didn't come into journalism to travel on public transport,' was the mantra of Bruce Kemble, education correspondent at the *Sunday Times* until he was one of those made to 'disappear'.

Reporters on the *Sunday Express* were once told never to travel by bus but always take taxis. It was a question of credibility, they were told. If the public thought that *Sunday Express* reporters traversed London by bus, confidence in the paper might be shaken.

A taxi driver would always hand over a couple of blank receipts if you gave him a good tip. If you wanted more it meant a trip to the holding zone for taxis at Waterloo station. Sometimes I would look at 'Buster' Edwards, the train robber, selling flowers from his stall as I paid a cabbie £10 for a book of receipts and wonder who was the bigger villain.

There was also the wholesale route. One day, quite by chance, I saw a taxi take an unmarked exit from a roundabout under The Westway in west London and decided to follow. I found this strange oasis away from the traffic jams, a rest area for cabbies complete with their own canteen and shop. The only proviso is that you were supposed to be a licensed taxi driver to use it.

Next week I returned, posing as a cabbie with a cushion shoved under a jumper to make me look the part, and bought ten books of receipts, each with fifty bills, for £5.

Of course, new arrivals in the newsroom had to be told about this culture before they rocked the boat by submitting an expenses claim so pitiful it exposed everybody else's as ridiculously inflated. Expenses were to be tackled with imagination. 'The journalist who is tired of doing his expenses is tired of life,' is one of the most repeated adages.

As a young reporter I was put straight by the older hands at *The Sun*. There I was twice called in to see Ken Donlan, a tough former news editor who had been moved 'upstairs' as managing editor. After asking about my young family, he told me not to claim so much for going out on jobs when I was staying in the office and doing them on the phone. Jamie Pyatt told Kingston Crown Court that when he joined *The Sun* in 1987 he was taken to task because his expenses were far lower than everybody else's. 'I was sat down with an experienced reporter who redid my expenses for me, to show me roughly where to pitch them in relation to my colleagues,' he said. 'We did not get overtime, it was part of your package. That was the culture, it was what everybody in Fleet Street did across the board for the newspapers.'

It wasn't just fellow reporters who showed newcomers the way. Executives claimed expenses, too, and wanted their share of the expenses pie.

When Jancis Robinson was wine critic of the *Sunday Times*, she was sent to the Mediterranean port of Sète by the news desk to try to sniff out a story about France importing Italian wine after years of hostile opposition, which, not unlike the lamb war with Britain, had seen smashed tankers and fire bombs as militant French growers tried to protect themselves from joining the Common Market. Unsuccessful in her efforts, she filled in a modest expenses claim and then had lunch at L'Escargot with James Adams, Andrew Neil's right-hand man who had succeeded Peter Roberts as managing editor.

'Adams gave me a dressing down,' Robinson later recalled in her book *Confessions of a Wine Lover*.

Not because of the disappointingly mild nature of the story I filed but because of the shockingly modest nature of my expenses claim. It really was letting the side down to claim only for the basic hotel I stayed in and the few simple meals I ate. It would set a dangerous precedent, I was told.

Adams was replaced as managing editor by Tony Bambridge, famed for such one-liners as 'Look, I have a simple view of journalism. If the editor says do it, do it.' It was a motto I shared. When Tony died of cancer, nobody batted an eyelid when a reading from *Towards the End of the Morning*, Michael Frayn's brilliantly funny novel of a Fleet Street newspaper, was included in his memorial service at St Bride's. In it, Reg Mounce, the picture editor, bullies an older photographer named Lovebold into lending him £5:

> Lovebold fetched an expenses chit, while the matter was still fresh in Mounce's mind, and wrote down at random on it two nights' expenses in Wolverhampton, with lunches and entertainment for contacts, adding up to £6 8s.4d. He gave it to Mounce to sign.
>
> Mounce folded his hands and closed his eyes. 'For what we are about to receive,' he said, 'may the Lord make us truly thankful.'

Foul play in the West Midlands? It was clearly where Andrew Alderson got the idea for his ridiculous story about me.

CHAPTER TWENTY-FIVE

THE QUEEN SAYS THANKS

The invitation came as a complete surprise when it landed on my desk at the *Sunday Times* in March 2002. 'The Master of the Household has received Her Majesty's command to invite Mr Maurice Chittenden to Windsor Castle,' it said.

Whoops. A few weeks earlier I had written a front-page story below the masthead headlined 'Prince Harry Admits Smoking Cannabis'. It said that he had confessed to his father that he smoked joints over a two-month period during his school holiday at Highgrove the previous summer. He was sixteen at the time.

The piece had recapped some of Harry's errant behaviour while his brother William was on a gap year in Australia and his father was often away. Harry was effectively home alone with staff at Highgrove in Gloucestershire. Though accompanied by his royal protection officers, he was allowed to roam as he wanted and began to frequent a country pub called the

Rattlebone Inn in the nearby village of Sherston. It was there, I recounted, that Harry had become involved in a late-night fracas over a pool session. The prince was said to have been thrown out after insulting the French chef and calling him 'a fucking frog'.

It was in an outhouse at the rear of the pub that Harry was introduced to cannabis. One of Harry's new-found friends later brought the drug into Highgrove where staff eventually noticed the pungent odour.

Prince Charles, the excellent father that he is, confronted his youngest son after staff reported their suspicions, and then sent him to meet hard-core addicts at a rehabilitation centre run in south London by the drug charity Phoenix House.

As I clutched my invitation in my hand, I wondered if that was the first time the Queen, never one to pick up a tabloid, had read about her grandson's naughty side. I feared that I was in for the royal equivalent of Sir Alex Ferguson's famous 'hairdryer treatment', when he stood so close to his players at Manchester United as he bawled them out that they could feel the heat of his words.

But, no. I had been writing about Harry since the day he was born and my latest piece was accompanied by a page-three lead inside headlined 'Red-Blooded Rise of a Princely Chancer'. In it, I wrote: 'Harry, who once struggled to see over the dashboard of a Range Rover while driving, aged twelve, on the estate roads of Balmoral, has at last emerged from his brother's shadow to become his own man.'

A colleague piped up across the office, 'I've got one too,' and held up his invitation. So I was not alone.

The Queen had invited 800 journalists to Windsor Castle as part of her Golden Jubilee celebrations. Alcohol would be served. Was this wise? Few occupations can claim to have had a greater impact on the life of the royal family than that of news reporter. Few occupations can claim to have suffered a greater impact from alcohol than that of news reporter. Some, like me, will have suddenly recalled a story in the *Sunday Mirror* when a Crystal Palace player named Gerry Queen had been sent off in a home game against Arsenal. The ensuing headline, 'Queen in Brawl at Palace', is now part of journalistic folklore. However, this was Windsor Castle, and she wanted to show off the remarkable restoration work that had been done since it was engulfed by a devastating fire in November 1992.

My report on the fire, 'Royal Cuts That Caused Delay as Windsor Castle Burned', had taken up most of the front page of the *Sunday Times* and had described how the Queen's favourite home had been left exposed by the bean counters.

'The fire that ravaged Windsor Castle was allowed to burn for a vital seven minutes before the fire brigade arrived because of a royal cost-cutting exercise,' I had written.

'The castle's own fire brigade was powerless to fight the flames in the crucial first minutes because of a decision to scale it down and transfer direct responsibility for tackling fires to the Berkshire fire brigade. Firefighting equipment was withdrawn and officers were told not to use breathing apparatus.'

Buckingham Palace documents leaked to the paper showed that the castle was even considering abandoning its computerised alarm system because it was 'very labour intensive'.

I discovered that, months before the fire, accountants had been asked to prepare a feasibility study on the castle's own fire brigade, an elite force made up of firefighters drawn from the armed forces and the civilian fire brigade and based in stables two miles from the castle.

A former member of the castle brigade told me that the changes meant that it was powerless to fight the fire. 'They did not have a pump strong enough to reach the flames,' he said. 'They are only supposed to act as fire patrolmen and pathfinders for the Berkshire service but they broke rules to go into the blazing Brunswick Tower to see what they could do.'

Ray Wells, the picture editor of the *Sunday Times*, sent Bob Collier, one of the paper's best photographers, up in a helicopter to take pictures. The one we used across six columns showed history in ruins, with smoke pouring from the fires and extensive damage to the Chester and Brunswick Towers.

The Queen, who was at Buckingham Palace at the time, was alerted by a phone call from Prince Andrew, her second eldest son, and arrived four hours after the fire started. 'She stood on planks of timber, a headscarf wrapped around her head looking up at the skyline of the castle with the anguished look of a mother whose favourite home is in danger,' I wrote. 'Her son breached royal protocol and acted as family spokesman, popping up in front of cameras like a cub reporter to give the latest news.'

Away from the cameras, Prince Andrew led rescuers into the smoke-filled buildings and organised a human chain to salvage antique furniture and works of art hanging on the walls.

In the courtyard, polished Renaissance tables, velvet chairs and Chinese chests sat in the open air waiting to be taken to a place of refuge in a convoy of removal vans, Army trucks and even a horse box.

I do not think people have ever realised the fullness of the impact this had on the Queen. It happened on her forty-fifth wedding anniversary, a day that should have been full of laughter and happy memories. Instead, at one stage, she went into the burning castle to help supervise the salvage operation, taking pictures off the wall herself. Four days later, in a speech at the Guildhall, she would use the Latin phrase *annus horribilis* to describe the year of the fire. '1992 is not a year on which I shall look back with undiluted pleasure,' she said.

The fire had started in her own private chapel. There was major renovation work being carried out at the castle at the time and early reports suggested that the fire was started by hot bitumen being spread by workmen which had fallen onto the curtains and set them alight. My report was nearer the truth than any others: 'Investigators want to know if arc lights used to illuminate work on the castle's stonework were placed too near to curtains in an area next to a private chapel.' Which is what the official inquiry concluded had happened. The curtain had probably been pushed towards the light fitting by a large picture frame being placed upon it.

The flames burned up the thirty-foot-high curtain like a fuse.

Secret passageways and hollow walls fanned the flames. It took 220 firemen more than eight hours to gain control of the blaze. They used 7 million litres of water, even taking some from the nearby River Thames.

Hugh Pearman, our architecture correspondent, estimated on our front page that it would cost up to £60 million to repair the damage, but the actual total was £36.5 million. The Queen paid £2 million from her own money. Nevertheless, it meant the monarch had to pay income tax and led to Buckingham Palace being opened to the public to help pay the bill and, in that sense, triggered the modernisation of the royal family.

The castle was provided with a system of red telephones linked directly to the fire control room and wireless smoke alarms were introduced to detect any future fire without harming the look of the building by drilling holes.

Four weeks before my invitation went out, Princess Margaret, her sister, had died. I had written a sad piece about her last years:

> Increasingly frail, her face masked by sunglasses whenever she ventured out, Princess Margaret spent her last months in a twilight world of dependence on nurses and servants … Two previous strokes and a badly scalded foot had left her virtually housebound. Gone were the glittering balls, the weekend house parties in the country where she was the most demanding of guests, the dinner parties where she enjoyed singing around a piano and the visits to Mustique where she had gifted her villa to her son, Lord Linley, to

avoid inheritance tax, only to be saddened when he had sold
it to an American.

Of course, my piece did not mention a fiendish piece of entrapment I had designed while Insight editor. I had recruited one of
our stringers, Graham Hind, to telephone Clarence House as an
unworldly Midlands businessman, make contact and ask what
he had to do to get a royal visit from the princess. He was told
to write to Lord Napier and Ettrick, private secretary to Princess Margaret, Countess of Snowdon, at Kensington Palace.
We then devised some letterheads from Foresight Innovations
(I had run out of anagrams but Insight is still in there if you
look). The company was supposed to have invented 'electronic
sledges', which went down sewer pipes filming as they cleaned.
We invited the princess to open its new studio in Chesterfield.
The idea was that when the prospect of a royal visit was rejected we would try to tempt the princess with the promise
of a piece of jewellery as a gift. A future headline along the
lines of 'Gems for Royal Visits' was already swirling around in
my head.

It never got that far. Two days after we sent the letter, Lord
Napier telephoned Hind and said that the princess would be
delighted to come to the opening in a few weeks' time. Not only
that but he had contacted John Batler, the Lord Lieutenant of
Derbyshire, asking him to co-ordinate the visit. Three days later
I telephoned both Napier and Batler, made up some story of
a sudden crisis at the company and asked them to cancel the

visit. We destroyed all the documentation we had devised for our cover story, fearing an imminent visit from Special Branch or the Royal Protection Squad.

Then, four weeks before my scheduled visit to the castle, the Queen lost her mother. She died at 3.15 p.m. My report, filed at 7 p.m., filled the entire front page of a 'Special Memorial Issue' of the *Sunday Times*: 'The Queen Mother died peacefully in her sleep at Windsor yesterday afternoon, aged 101,' it began.

> The Queen was at her bedside as the final moment came. Her death marks the end of a grand epoch for the British monarchy. She was born while Queen Victoria was still on the throne and lived long enough to be mourned last night with a black page on the royal family's official website.

I gave the second byline to Margarette Driscoll. She was not even in the office that day but she had written an obituary for the Queen Mother about ten years before which had been kept in a file and from which I took a few lines. I had somehow acquired an unfair reputation at the *Sunday Times* as a byline bandit and it was something I wanted to dispel, especially on a story this big. (When I finally left I was presented with a mocked-up front page of the paper with the splash headline: 'Byline Bandit Rides Off Into the Sunset', next to a photograph of me on a carousel taken at a family wedding.)

It was true I liked to see my name in print. 'Maurice has to have his byline in the paper,' John Witherow said, only half-jokingly, at one of the Saturday night conferences where we discussed how the paper could be improved between editions. 'It's in his contract.' And it was also true that I hated having the second byline on a story, or, even worse, an 'additional reporting' credit at the bottom of a story. Once, Richard Palmer, now the royal correspondent on the *Daily Express*, was sent to cover an IRA bomb attack in Colchester while I made calls on the phone. When he complained I had got the byline, I said: 'But, Richard, I had the story before you had got out of our car park'. I hoped sharing a byline with Margarette on the Queen Mother story might redress the balance, but no one noticed. Still, John Witherow sent me a nice 'herogram'. 'From a standing start, we did very well, and, in the words of one reader, "creamed the opposition"', it said.

The Queen Mother had once been very kind to me, although she did not know it. When I was 'Chittenden of St Albans', the struggling freelance, I used to do an 80-mile round trip on a Friday morning to pick up the weekly papers, from the *Royston Crow* to the *Watford Observer*, and scan through them for stories. There was one in the *Luton News* that told how the Queen Mother had sent a wedding gift of silver spoons to a young girl she had last seen as a 2lb premature baby, born three months early, when she was opening a maternity ward twenty-one years earlier. The story made a *Daily Mirror* page lead and also had 'shows' in *The Sun*, *Daily Mail* and *Daily Star*, much to the chagrin of my rivals, Ron Fairley and Barry Simmonds, who ran the South Beds News Agency in Luton.

The Queen hardly had time to mourn before it was our date at the palace. I organised two Ford Galaxy people carriers to take our contingent to Windsor. Once there, David Leppard, Nick Hellen, Rupert Steiner and myself, all from the *Sunday Times*, plus Simon Walker of *The Times*, walked up the approach to the castle. We were then ushered into the Great Hall and two adjoining rooms where the Queen, Prince Philip, Princess Anne, Prince Andrew and the Duchess of Gloucester joined us.

When the Queen asked me what I did on the paper, I told her, and said I had covered the fire ten years before. She said the restorers had done a marvellous job in bringing the castle back in such fine condition.

I did not get around to meeting the Duke of Edinburgh on that occasion but in 2014 he accompanied the Queen when she attended a champagne reception at Stationers' Hall, midway between old Fleet Street and St Paul's Cathedral, to mark the 150th anniversary of the Journalists' Charity and its predecessor, the Newspaper Press Fund. Over the decades, the charity, of which I was elected a life member in 1998 and which was granted a Royal Charter by Queen Victoria, has helped thousands of journalists in need.

Lord Rothermere, the charity's president and chairman of the media group which includes the *Daily Mail* and the *Mail on Sunday*, presented the Queen with a bound copy of a speech given by her father, then the Duke of York, to what was then the Newspaper Press Fund.

The Duke's words are still relevant today. He said he knew the 'high pressures at which reporters and sub-editors, critics and leader writers work is probably greater than in any other profession.'

As he was leaving, Prince Philip took one look at my loud tie, showing a US meteorological map, extended his hand and said: 'And where are you from? *The Sun*?'

'No sir, the *Sunday Times*.' But he was half right.

CHAPTER TWENTY-SIX

GOODBYE TO FLEET STREET

The day I got whacked I was telephoned at home by a man I had never met who read from a script and told me I need never come into the office again. I did not even get a black refuse sack into which to empty the contents of my desk. Instead, someone 'borrowed' from underneath it the golf umbrella that was a gift from one of my sons.

Sadly, that's how you get the bullet in newspapers these days. Journalists like to use movie imagery to put a bit of spin on the clinical way it is done. In Andrew Neil's day, we spoke of the *disparus*, colleagues who disappeared as if overnight, so called after those who were 'disappeared' by the death squads in countries like Argentina and Chile. Nowadays, Mafia vocabulary is more in vogue.

Indeed, the departure of Charles Hymas, managing editor of the *Sunday Times* news section, in April 2017 would not have been out of place in that scene from *The Godfather*, when

Michael Corleone is having his baby baptised at the same time his enemies are being gunned down.

Hymas, nicknamed 'Mad Dog' by *Private Eye* for a reason none of us at his leaving do could remember, is a driven journalist who was always the first to arrive and the last to leave. His departure was announced, after twenty-six years at the paper, at the very moment Martin Ivens, the editor who succeeded Witherow, was at a London Press Club awards lunch lavishing praise on his colleagues for helping the *Sunday Times* to win the Sunday Newspaper of the Year award.

John Witherow once told me there is no room for sentiment in newspapers and he is right. They have to be like any other business. Getting rid of me was going to save the paper tens of thousands of pounds a year. Supposedly the trigger for my sudden departure was that I had missed a 2 a.m. deadline for Mo Farah's 10,000-metre triumph at the 2016 Olympics in Rio, but when delays on the track meant he didn't cross the finishing line until 1.57 a.m., it became a tall order. I was also told by colleagues that executives had pored over my email account to see if I was behind a series of embarrassing stories about the *Sunday Times* in *Private Eye*'s Street of Shame column. Of course, they found nothing, because I was not guilty and the stories have continued. Not least about me and this book!

I cannot complain. I have had a terrific run. When I first joined the *Sunday Times*, the news editor of the day said you were considered a success if you survived three years on the paper. Ivan Fallon, the deputy editor, said he did not think anyone over forty should be working there. Well, in all I lasted more than thirty years as a casual, a staff man and a freelance. I survived four editors, five different offices and fifteen news editors.

Today the *Sunday Times* is almost down to half the circulation it enjoyed in the headiest days of Andrew Neil and John Witherow's editorships. Looking back through the yellowing newspaper files I found one edition in which I had seven bylines, including two on the front (one of which was a genuine scoop I had obtained from an Olympic insider about Princess Anne writing to all fellow members of the organising committee telling them to clean up their act after allegations of bribery by Salt Lake City to win the 2002 Winter Games) and four page leads. Now that the News Review has been absorbed into the main section, it is sometimes hard to find seven good home new stories in the paper. At times, it has been in danger of looking formulaic, with regular stories about J. K. Rowling's wealth, Roman Abramovich's latest yacht, not forgetting the hardy annual nature study about some woodland bird facing extinction with a colourful accompanying graphic of it sitting in a tree.

The *News of the World*, of course, has gone to the typesetting room in the sky. We 'banged out' the staff (an old Fleet Street printers' tradition) by hammering on the office windows rather than bashing trays of hot metal type on metal benches when its staff left for the last time. The *Sun on Sunday* is no real replacement. One splash in May 2017 promised 'the most revealing interview in years' from George Michael's ex-lover. What it told us, in a spread inside, was that George liked to sit around at home in his pyjamas, eating Coco Pops and watching daytime

TV. Don't we all, sometimes. Even *The Sun*, once Rupert Murdoch's cash cow, struggles to entertain us like it used to. As one of my fellow villagers complained: 'The papers have become so boring. Isn't it time we went back to the good old days, by which I mean the bad old days?' Perhaps she has a point.

With some newspapers losing as much as 15 per cent of their circulation each year, it is not difficult for commentators to predict that the writing is on the wall for an industry that feels under siege. Hardly anyone under forty actually buys a newspaper. That includes my own children, who grew up in a house full of newspapers. They get their news from the internet, the TV or, increasingly so, social media.

Some titles which should have closed are kept going by proprietors who want to be part of the establishment and fear that their readers will be swallowed up by their rivals if they leave a vacuum (although experience suggests that more than half just disappear).

Fleet Street, the place, may no longer have any journalists, but it remains our spiritual home, even if the only time we go back is to honour a fallen colleague at St Bride's, 'the journalists' church'.

The street was ideally located for us, within walking distance of the City, the High Court, the Old Bailey and Westminster. The eighteenth-century French author Abbé Prévost once hailed its coffee houses, 'where you have the right to read all the papers for and against the government' as the 'seats of English liberty'. They have given way to coffee bars where people read stories for free on their phones or in giveaway newspapers.

The printed press has been sucker-punched by the quadruple

whammy of the internet, which has stolen its advertisers and questioned its very *raison d'*être; free newspapers, which have cheapened its worth; rolling news on television, with which it can never compete; and social media, which has made everybody a journalist.

When the Battle of Wapping was won and the days of hot metal ended, journalists like me looked to a rosy future. Instead of money going to the greedy printers, it could be spent on news gathering. Well, we had a honeymoon of about four years and then the proprietors realised they could make even more money by bringing in the suits to cut expenditure and reduce staff. One deputy managing editor, drunk on power, decided to cut the mileage rate for those using their cars for work by a third and stop first class rail travel. I saw that off by getting everyone in the newsroom to sign a letter of protest (one office wag claimed it was the only time I insisted names at the bottom be in alphabetical order rather than grab first byline) and then inviting them to our local pub, the Old Rose on The Highway in Wapping, for lunch on a Friday and asking everyone to stay. We made no demands but, when the news desk realised there was no copy to process, Andrew Neil knocked some heads together and the planned cut was abandoned.

It was a small victory but it didn't end the belt-tightening. I realise now that I was part of the problem. My long lunches, insistence on luxury hotels, choice of tasting menu dinners and fine wines just added to my reputation for being 'high maintenance', as one managing editor described me. It was little different to the Spanish practices I had tried to expose elsewhere.

Newspapers are struggling to stay afloat. Opinion columns, which often rely on stories from TV soundbites or drama plots and need little fact-finding, are the current vogue, rather than far more expensive investigative journalism.

Reporters today do not have the freedoms I enjoyed, deciding myself who to interview and where to go. It is one of the downsides of the mobile phone. In the good old days a reporter had to ring in to the news desk every two hours to say where they were or how a story was going. We were supposed to wear pagers but I always refused. In the back of my mind I still think they contributed to the liver cancer which killed some colleagues. The introduction of mobile phones means that the desk can contact a reporter whenever they wish, certainly while in the UK. However, this too has a downside. Reporters do not think on their feet as much as they used to or rely on the camaraderie of colleagues. Instead, they constantly ring the desk for instructions.

Today, in new buildings spread across London, newspapers struggle to balance their print and digital formats. In 2016, *The Independent* decided it was no longer up for the fight and moved online. *The Guardian*, perhaps the next to follow that route, talks internally about the 'iteration of content atom' (no, me neither). At *The Sun*, the talk is of business development rather than breaking news and there are brazen plugs for Fox films and Sky TV. The *Sunday Times* has a Going Viral barometer to measure internet trends. The *Telegraph* runs paid-for supplements from regimes in Russia, China and all points east, hopeful for an easier ride in the news pages.

The old great publishing houses have become banks and film locations. Peterborough House, the *Telegraph*'s building with its Egyptian columns, and the art deco splendour of the *Express*, nicknamed the Black Lubyanka after the KGB building in Moscow although they are nothing alike, have both been occupied at times by Goldman Sachs. *The Sun*'s Bouverie Street site became at first a Japanese bank, and now it and the old *Daily Mail* building are the headquarters of an Anglo-German law firm. *The Mirror* in New Fetter Lane was demolished and rebuilt as a Sainsbury's. The White Hart, the pub opposite, which rejoiced in the delicious nickname of The Stab (in the Back) and where I once monstered Richard Stott, the late *Daily Mirror* editor, closed due to lack of custom.

The pubs that remain, of course, are a shadow of their former selves. The Tipperary, built in 1605 with stones taken from Whitefriars Monastery and which allowed it to survive the Great Fire of London, still stands. But the King and Keys, once the *Telegraph*'s watering hole, is now a sandwich bar. The Wig and Pen is a Thai restaurant. The Witness Box is a Jamie's restaurant. The Punch Tavern has been chopped to a third of its size.

In the parlous world of newspapers, survival is momentum. Yet still young people want to work for them. In my day youngsters worked on local newspapers first, sitting in magistrates' courts and keeping local councils on their toes before shifting at night on Fleet Street. The decline of the regional press, especially the closure of most evening papers, means this avenue is no longer available. Direct entry from university is now the norm and I have contributed to that. For nine years I was a visiting lecturer in the journalism department at City University until I annoyed the academics there by labelling it 'Fleet Street's boot camp'. Students have to fork out around £10,000 for the one-year postgraduate course and live in London while they are on it. It means only those from rich families can now enter the profession. Andrew Neil's idea of a meritocracy in which anyone could succeed has gone out of the window. According to a study published by the Social Mobility Commission in June 2017, Britain's media now has a greater proportion of privately educated journalists (51 per cent) than in 1986, the year of the Battle of Wapping. It perhaps explains why some journalists seem out of touch with the effects on 'ordinary' people of government policies such as austerity and mass migration. Journalism has become part of the establishment by default.

During my time at City I helped train 350 students, many of whom have gone on to take leading jobs on national newspapers. Amongst those to whom I passed on my words of wisdom are Ollie Shah and Peter Evans at the *Sunday Times*, Fay Schlesinger and Kaya Burgess at *The Times*, Katherine Faulkner and Emily Kent-Smith at the *Daily Mail*, Emily Fairbairn at *The Sun* and Simon Murphy at the *Mail on Sunday*. In case you're wondering, I never taught them how to do their expenses. I wish them all the very best on what now passes for Fleet Street. I hope they have at least some of the fun I have had before it finally ends.

Maurice Chittenden
June 2017

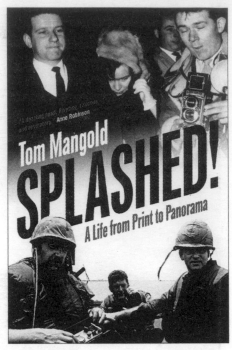